THE PUNCH BOOK OF CRICKET

THE PUNCH BOOK
OF
CRICKET

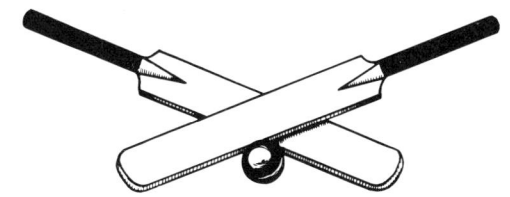

Edited by
David Rayvern Allen

Foreword by
John Arlott and Alan Coren

GRAFTON BOOKS
A Division of the Collins Publishing Group

LONDON GLASGOW
TORONTO SYDNEY AUCKLAND

To Rosemary

Grafton Books
A Division of the Collins Publishing Group
8 Grafton Street, London W1X 3LA

Published by Granada Publishing 1985
Reprinted 1985
Reissued in paper covers by Grafton Books 1986

British Library Cataloguing in Publication Data

The Punch book of cricket.
1. English wit and humor   2. Cricket—
Anecdotes, facetiae, satire, etc.
I. Allen, David Rayvern
827′.914′080355   PN6231.C7/

ISBN 0 246 13023 7

Printed in Great Britain by
William Collins Sons & Co. Ltd,
Glasgow

Contents

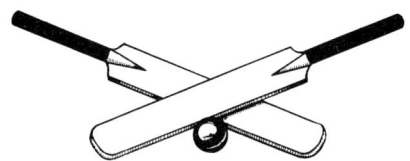

List of Contributors*

*Includes named writers only

Acknowledgements

To leave the nods of gratitude until last is a mistake. In most books the names of those who have assisted appear first, and that is as it should be. But the actual putting-down of a column of thank-yous is often attempted some time after the manuscript has set off on its lengthy and convoluted journey towards publication. The reason for wanting to write 'gramercy' is, quite simply, fear. The thought of omitting to mention some kindly helper who has lent a hand in the final stages of compilation causes considerable unease. The worry, of course, is that it is more than likely that the unacknowledged help happened at the beginning.

With that, I hope, acceptable apology in advance for an almost certainly fallible memory in the past, let me not nod but bow deeply in the direction of several saintly souls. I am indebted to *Punch*'s editor, Alan Coren, who so readily and enthusiastically said 'yes' to the initial timorous suggestion for the book; to *Punch*'s publisher Brian Knox-Peebles for so wisely lending his agreement; to John Pawsey for his steadfast optimism and advice in moments of doom and doubt; to Mary Anne Bonney, who smiled benignly and helped with research; to Caroline Parton, who also smiled benignly even in the midst of staggering feats of weight-lifting that should guarantee her a place in the next Olympics; to Sue Dunford, who retained her cool while becoming puce at the photocopier and dreamt of the marathon in the last Olympics; to David Taylor for his charity in making cups of tea; to Sheridan Morley for his charity in not making them; and to that unflappable commissionaire who reserved a weather eye for traffic wardens as ever more volumes of *Punch* went back and forth between car boot and library shelf. Grateful thanks to them all.

And three and more cheers for dear Alan Coren and John Arlott, who one dim December night and at great inconvenience to themselves took the trouble to find a restaurant in the fastnesses of Fulham to say the following, which comes in the form of a Foreword.

Foreword

by John Arlott in conversation with Alan Coren

ARLOTT: You see, the trouble about cricket is that too many people regard it as Establishment. They regard *Punch* as Establishment and that's not true about either of them. Because they both span the entire social range of Britain.

COREN: They look as though they belong to a particular class, but they don't. Because the real hag-ridden attitudes of class, which exclude the good things which happen to have been developed by the middle classes, still continue. Many people still perceive both *Punch* and cricket to be the special province of special people and say 'it's not for me'.

ARLOTT: But urchins and mill-workers play cricket and play it well . . .

COREN: And miners ride . . .

ARLOTT: Yes; and also, which is important, the Establishment get cross with *Punch*, especially nowadays, as you know.

COREN: Oh yes, they feel disloyalty because they think it belongs to them.

ARLOTT: That early *Punch* joke, 'I 'ad a h'over from Jackson', spanned the entire range of people in England who played cricket.

COREN: I think cricket's like so many other important things buried in the English personality. It actually annihilates class. OK, there were gentlemen players, but really it's a yeoman game played by gentlemen and a gentleman's game played by yeomen and it destroyed the class differences, which didn't happen in other countries. It didn't actually happen in other sports either. Rugby and soccer divided people class-wise. Every school played cricket. Every

kid played up against a wall. There was always a field.

ARLOTT: I think that *Punch*'s cricketers' jokes are jokes valid for all cricketers. The essence of *Punch* humour is that it's non-class, and *Punch*'s cricket is non-class – unlike so may other periodicals which have treated cricket like an Establishment game.

COREN: It's associated with a lot of the trappings of Empire, that's the trouble – the idea that wherever a flag was raised, or a sahib's topee flourished, or wherever a foot was put on the sand, a strip was laid and the heathen were taught to play cricket. That's an unfortunate nineteenth-century legacy. It's enshrined in other areas, not in the magazine. Cricket was an activity which drew Englishmen with their Englishness together. And colonials. I think there's nothing wrong with the feeling that the West Indians or the Indians or Pakistanis or the Australians, or whoever else, change as a result of an Englishman's view. There's nothing wrong with feeling that. It's something to share.

ARLOTT: You see, not only the Establishm͏ but much of the rest of England tends over-emphasise the importance of cricket. As Len Braund said to Fred Tate that night after he'd lost the Manchester Test of '02, 'Oh, go up the stairs and get your money, Fred, it's only a game, you know!'

COREN: Exactly. It would be nice to think that the magazine had locked in to the way cricketers looked at the way they made their living. They didn't see themselves as idols, they saw themselves as blokes taking a few bob and on a good day it would go well for them and if it rained and if it turned . . .

ARLOTT: *Punch* in any situation is nearer the pros than the amateurs.

COREN: I'll tell you a *Punch* anecdote. Bernard Hollowood, once editor of the magazine – Hollowood played for a minor county, played for Staffordshire . . .

ARLOTT: Went in first . . .

COREN: And Humphrey Ellis, who was a rugby player more than a cricketer, but I used to play cricket with him when I first joined them – the *Punch* cricket team in their salad days. And we buried Bernard five or so years ago and Humphrey Ellis bent down – it was a wettish day – and he bent down outside the crematorium at Guildford and pressed the ground and he said, 'It would turn a bit today!'

ARLOTT (*chuckling*): And I suppose most importantly of all, you see, cricket is funny. It's funnier than most sports. First of all because too many people take it too seriously and very often they're people who don't play it very well and don't know much about it and their very seriousness is funny. But somehow it seems to me contrived to make a man look silly. I'm sure it wasn't, but that's the effect it has – the man in the pads, the gloves, the bat, and the striped cap, the cravat, the tie supporting his trousers, who comes out, takes guard, marks it out with a bail, moves the sight-screen and is then bowled first ball – you see he is funny. He's also tragic, mind.

Dropped catches are funny except to the person who drops them and the bowler. So many things about the game – ridiculous, ludicrous, yet tragically so. I mean nothing's funnier than the man who, faced with a bouncer, pulls violently back from it, drops his bat and falls on his bottom, or the man who is run out by a mile and is struggling and dives flat on his face after the bails are off. All these things are funny. Alas. I suppose it's impossible to play the game at the immensely high level it is played at in Test matches and for the humbler side of the game to retain all its dignity.

Punch is an observer, and you only have to go to a very serious match indeed, not just

an ordinary Test match, but say, Yorkshire and Lancashire, you've only got to go there and still, – no, perhaps not among Yorkshiremen, certainly among Lancashiremen and people from outside who are from beyond the pale – you'll hear sniggers, laughs, as even a top-class player makes himself look a little bit ridiculous. And if they do that at the top level – oh dear, they are going to do that at the bottom. And I speak from the heart as one who must have looked damned silly many times when he was out. I've bought the googly, I've been yorked, I've been run out by yards – I've done all the wrong things and I suppose, if we tell the truth, so have most people.

The fact is, humour lies in the seriousness which ends in comic disaster, and the good observer – and *Punch* has always been a good observer – catches them at it.

COREN: That's true. I think another link is: *Punch* is about England and cricket is about England and there are accidental moments when the two coincide. Nobody else has a game quite the way in which the English have cricket. One's very uneasy about saying all these things because it gets to sound like jingoism, it gets to be 'the breathless hush in the close tonight', but there's a quality about it that, if it's played right and if it's done right, encapsulates and concentrates the idea of what a decent man is – how he works with his friends, for pleasure, but taking it seriously. For practical purposes it's a craftsman thing, isn't it?

ARLOTT: Now you're getting near it. *Punch* is about fundamental values. It's about craftsmanship, integrity, accuracy, workmanship, fundamental merit. Difficult to say righteousness, because that sounds pompous but rightness . . .

COREN: Yes, I think it's got moral values built into it.

ARLOTT: Well, what about saying rightness?

COREN: There's no divine right. Pompousness gets kicked in the shins, automatic assumptions about birth and all those things get set aside because a certain sort of achievement that's admired comes out – values embodied in the idea that somewhere there is the ideal cricket match. There's a need in people to imagine somewhere the quintessential cricket match. My kids draw up this eleven. They draw up this eleven and play it against *this* eleven, because they really want to think that somewhere there is a cricket team where the weather is absolutely perfect, the crowd is absolutely right and the pitch is absolutely right and twenty-two people who are perfect for one another come out and play this game which is only played once. Everything else is only an imitation. A real

essential – there's a game in heaven that's played by two sides – they'll program computers to do it one day.

ARLOTT: It was Robertson-Glasgow, wasn't it, who talked about the parent who went out after the little boy had been playing, belting a ball against the wall and playing it back with his bat, and heard him say, 'Hobbs, bowled me, 0; Sutcliffe, bowled me, 0; Me not out at close of play, 286.'

Introduction

by David Rayvern Allen

On the very day in 1841 that Mr Punch jocularly introduced himself to the public, the venerable members of MCC were watching their side have the last laugh in a match against the undergraduates of Oxford at Lord's. Now, it would be apposite to report that one of those young undergrads burgeoned into a responsible and respected editor of the new magazine but, unfortunately, history is not often what you would like to make it and so we are left with only a tenuous thread between the two events. In the winning side was a relative of W. M. Thackeray, the novelist, and it had been Thackeray who had taken part in many of the early discussions that led to the birth of the journal and who was later to become a major contributor to its pages.

The first reference to cricket in *Punch* that I can discover is partly in Latin, which probably accounts for the fact that it is not to be found in the body of this book. Hard on the heels of 'Stumpy – metaphora a ludo vocato "cricket" sumpta' (There! most of it is in, after all) came an ever-increasing assortment of period puns, prose and verse heightened by sketches, drawings and cartoons. These reflected happenings not only on the cricket field but in other totally unconnected avenues of activity, which when infiltrated by cricketing similes took on another life altogether. This is especially noticeable in purely pictorial form. To see, for instance, a platoon of cricketers in their 'battle-dress', wearing pads instead of gaiters and marching in step with bats at shoulder-arms, is to suspect that for a while those who were carrying the accoutrements of war had had their load lightened a great deal: conflict and concern relieved by levity in the manner of all the best squibs and caricatures.

Likewise, many other events of national political import during a century and a half when very little has seemed unimportant have tended to lose their *gravitas* in *Punch*'s cricketing arena. Figuratively, the old boy is unmatched in recounting incidents on the cricket field from the benches in the House of Commons as often as he relished the warts of politicians from the Mound at Lord's. We are just as likely to encounter Gladstone, Lloyd George and Maggie Thatcher in pads and protectors as 'W.G.', Don Bradman and Mike Brearley in pinstripes with pipe. Where else is to be found Winston Churchill in the nets at Question Time delighted by the chance of meeting a barrage of devious deliveries with a straight bat? Or Harold Macmillan casting a quizzical eye at the hapless King Baudouin as he descends the pavilion steps? Or Roy Hattersley having the nous to realise that attendance at the House is unnecessary if you can make all the political points that *are* necessary – to wit, those on cricket – within the columns of *Punch*? 'Don't blame me, I voted Conservative,' says the umpire with finger up, dismissing a disconsolate batsman in a Hollowood cartoon.

To peruse every single page of *Punch* from 1841 to today is to appreciate what a splendid history lesson is given by even the cricket-connected material alone. This particular pupil would have paid far more attention to the worthy tomes of G. M. Trevelyan and his buddies had the Land Bill of 1887, the rise of the suffragettes, Palmerston, Disraeli, Hitler,

Mussolini and all the rest been presented in the context of a first innings, follow-on, 'That's it, match over, folks!' situation. And incidentally, an index to the game in the magazine that was compiled on the way amounts to 120 foolscap pages, which shows that cricket anyway is definitely not 'all bunk'.

How then did one choose the ripest from the ripe? How do you begin to make a representative selection from such an array? Inevitably, the first forage becomes a personal choice, based wholly on the sometimes misguided principle that what appeals to one individual is bound to appeal to nearly all the others. Then questions of balance arise, overall and within categories. Is each period in the run of the magazine reflected fairly? Is there sufficient variety? Next to be put on one side are some skilfully-built verses and cartoons surrounding topical issues of a century ago that nowadays would need a tour through reference books and would be obscure to all but the specialist. Nevertheless, there is still so much that has irresistible charm: arrows laced with happy humour and not venom, as pertinent for tomorrow's reader as yesteryear's. Yet so many treasures have to be dropped back into the sea. A pattern takes shape: articles and pictures fall subjectively into chapters.

There is the Foreign View. No, nothing to do with the Yorkshire baronet who conceived the idea of getting together a Cannibal Eleven, or even Saint Geoffrey, an ecclesiastical encomium from Frank Keating – they eat their own up there, don't they? But cricket across the Channel, the bat in Batavia, Tovarich at the Test, cricket à la Grecque, Sicily versus Barcelona in the old Gillette Cup – Play! Olé! In other words, those nationalities that have longed to play the game for ages, but can't afford to buy that tea-towel containing the instructions on sale at Lord's.

And it was at the headquarters of cricket, which deserves and gets a chapter to itself, that Mr Punch first noticed the ladies' game, or rather, observed their reaction to the game gentlemen. The bright young things adorning Eton and Harrow engagements put idle and unanswerable questions to their chinless chums over the picnic baskets, while elsewhere in the ground an 'important lady' addresses the deepest of deep square-legs with some asperity: 'Would you kindly move away? It's quite impossible for my daughter to see my nephew, who is batting.'

Punch's attitude to feminine focus on cricket has remained consistently chauvinistic, acknowledging women with an amused glance as they subtly put men in their pockets. The club cricketer of every era contends with earnest ignorance, active indifference or passive antagonism towards his favourite religion from the lady wife or missus – depending on his neck in the woods. We see the growing emancipation of women surfacing in semi-ironical lines during the latter part of the nineteenth century and particularly in a picture from 1891, when at a match between young ladies and boys a 'fair batter' exclaims: 'Now, just look here, Algy Jones – none of your patronage! You *dare* to bowl to me with your left hand again, and I'll box your ears!'

Those kids knew their place, they did – the back-street cockney urchins with a lamp-post for a wicket aping their better batters: 'No, you be Len Hutton . . . Have you got Bradman?' Or, if they happened to own the ball, 'You're aht,' drawing the response, 'Call yourself Larwood.' The essence of the game is to be found in its primitive form and where the essence, there the laughter. The same applies to the average village club as well, of course; different surroundings, differing personalities, conjoined more or less harmoniously in an age-old ritual sustaining the English psyche – the blacksmith, the 'bobby', the parson and the military protagonist:

Major Podmore: 'Congratulate you, dear boy!'
Disappointed Cricketer: 'What do you mean? Bowled first ball – never got a run!'
Major Podmore: 'Quite so, dear boy. But in this hot weather – 80° in the shade – so much better, if you can, to take things coolly!'

What would dear Mr Coward have had to say about that? 'A pootlesome bat,' no doubt.

An awareness of snobbish class structure and its loosening hold in the aftermath of the First World War is evident in a cartoon of 1928. An obsequious butler has 'volunteered' to umpire a match on the green. His master, captain of the fielding side, imperiously disperses his players to this point and that. 'And where would you like me to go, sir?' fawns his servant.

Social changes are marked clearly, though the repetitive march back from civilisation through so-called progress is tramped with a soft shoe on *Punch*'s pitch. He is 'warm-hearted rather than hot-tempered . . . and takes the radical line from generosity and not from spite'. He is also inventive. During the 1890s motor-cars were proposed as a possible alternative to batsmen actually having to run their runs. Golf has beaten cricket to it with that innovation and long may it continue to do so. There was also that incredibly advanced imaginary depiction of new cricketing dress in 1854 to be worn as protection against 'round-arm bowling'. The suits and helmets are straight out of Cape Canaveral and the cartoon which was resurrected for the 'bodyline' controversy in 1933 and again more recently is as modernistic today as it was 130 years ago. For readers of the London Charivari then, such apparel would have been literally 'out of this world'.

It is no surprise to find the parade of cricket's personalities dominated by the 'Leviathan' figure of Grace: 'Good old Grace', 'The Two W.G.'s', 'A Century of Centuries', 'His New Title', 'Another Title'. These last two inclusions appear in his national testimonial year of 1895 and refer to the knighthood which *Punch* suggests 'W.G.' ought to receive. The next season it is Ranji 'the Black Prince' who is singled out for attention as champion cricketer of the year, and rewarded with a portrait from Linley Sambourne. 'Buns' Thornton ('the great slogger of sixes'), 'Bobby' Abel, George Gunn, C. B. Fry, Jack Hobbs, 'Percy' Chapman, Don Bradman, Peter May and Frank Worrell, all find a place in *Punch*'s gallery as the years progress. And as the years accumulated, so did international encounters. 'Advance Australia', the Ashes are at stake, the visit of the Philadelphians, the Triangular series, South Africa and then the widening horizons of the last fifty years, All India, the West Indies, the New Zealanders, the Pakistanis.

The tourists were usually assessed with

more straightforward factual reporting than was general in *Punch* either by E. V. Lucas, the phenomenally industrious prince of anthologists, or, in a later generation, by Bernard Hollowood, avid cricketing economist from Staffordshire. Lucas, of Quaker roots, adopted a mask for his work. He liked, as he said, to make readers think he had a long white beard – no doubt resembling Father Time at Lord's – for Lucas was delighted to introduce cricket to any of his writings without an excuse. He had a congenial habit of sitting in his office apparently day-dreaming, 'deep-set blue eyes turning their musing gaze inwardly to the themes that were determined by his idiosyncrasies'. J. M. Barrie, describing Lucas's batting after a game with the Allahakbarries, was cryptic: 'He had (unfortunately) a style'.

Hollowood, who was editor of *Punch* from 1957 to 1968 and a contributor from 1942, had played minor county cricket in the 1930s and was, as can be seen, a clever cartoonist as well as an author of humorous books on both his vocations. It is no coincidence that the cricket content in the journal multiplied many times when these two men were at their desks. In fact, in the decade from 1903 when Lucas first put his feet under the Table, until the outbreak of the First World War, the material on the game matched in volume that of the initial sixty years of *Punch*'s existence.

A contemporary of Lucas was A. A. Milne, playwright and, similarly, a light essayist. For his writing on cricket he elected to pose as a light-hearted diner-out at weekend house-parties who was accepted more for his repartee than for his athletic ability. The characters present were often 'something in the City' and the china cups complemented the flippancy of the conversation. The game is, paradoxically, at the same time integral and yet incidental to the plot.

A. P. Herbert, Oxford University MP and 'Water Gypsy', and E. V. Knox, 'Evoe', editor of the magazine from 1932 to 1949, have left their imprints on *Punch*'s cricket field, too. In fact, Knox could be said to have made his mark in incandescent fashion. He practised flicking still-lit cigarette-ends into a waste-paper basket over his shoulder until the resulting fires caused the basket to be confiscated.

More latterly Neville Cardus, John Arlott, Michael Parkinson, Robert Morley, Frank Keating and the current editor Alan Coren have been among those who have buckled up their enviable resources and produced articles on cricket of an ingenuity not found elsewhere outside an irregular offering in the sports periodicals. 'Lif' dat bail', invites Mr Coren in a sparkling piece during the summer of 1983, and he certainly has not missed a chance in commissioning contributions to *Punch*'s cricket score.

This procreation has been matched in cartoon. Bernard Partridge, who joined the paper in 1891 and overlapped the legendary Tenniel, staying until his death in 1945, would maintain that his ideal cartoon had two characters of equal size, 'whether Samurai warrior or Russian bear'. Rawle Knox, contributor to *Punch* and son of the former editor, writes that to meet Partridge 'was like lunching with W. G. Grace or a man who had been on familiar terms with the Duke of Wellington. He lent an air of timeless distinction to the proceedings.' Second cartoonist to Partridge for a time was the fiery Leonard Raven-Hill, whose refined cartoons of 'Percy' Chapman and Don Bradman in the late 1920s and early 1930s are more in line with dignified portraiture than caricature. His successor in 1935 was Ernest Shepherd, 'Kipper' to his friends and colleagues, who will be forever remembered for his children's illustrations for Milne's *Pooh* and Kenneth Grahame's *Wind in the Willows*. Then Frank Reynolds, who started drawing for *Punch* in 1906 and was art editor during the 1920s, and who continued cartooning long after, displayed an energetic freedom of line that comes to the fore on the backs of village cricketers.

The Young 'Un: 'Come on, it's an easy one! Lummy. I could run two.'
The Old 'Un: 'Could yer? Then just run back again.'

In recent years Norman Mansbridge, Kenneth Mahood and Michael ffolkes have been largely responsible for the breadth of imagination exposed in the cartoons of cricket. The names are lustrous and the lists incomplete.

But in whichever capacity the creative artist has chiselled his signature onto the Table, without losing their identity they have become *Punch* people. The name itself now conjures an aura, a feeling, an expectation. Much of the recorded history of cricket travels alongside the entire lifeline of the magazine, the glories of one cherished by an informed observer at the boundary ropes, and if it has occasionally seemed that there has been an armoured car instead of a breathless hush in the close, we have only ourselves to blame. Indeed, that's life; it should, after all, be only a game. Let us reflect that there will always be a compensatory chortle in prospect if *Punch* and cricket remain together. They must. For each in its own way is a great distinctive institution of Anglo-Saxonhood, racing towards the twenty-first century with heads full of confidence from the days when the prevailing sentiment was that 'the British Umpire rules the wide world over'.

Punch's Preface

The game of cricket, though very ancient, is not quite as old as the hills; for the hills are naturally inclined against a sport requiring a level surface. Cricket is a promoter of cheerfulness and hospitality; for it causes one player to open his gate to another, and invite him, in a double sense, to take an innings at his homely wicket. The achievements of the bat are frequently celebrated by a ball; and even enemies who have met as bowlers, have been known to forget in the bowl all their animosity. It is not important to know the precise date at which cricket was introduced, who set up the earliest wicket, or was the first to stir his stumps in this country.

In a MS, dated 1344, in the Bodleian Library at Oxford, a woman is represented in the act of giving a ball to a man; while in the background are several tall and little women trying, as so many long stops and short stops, to catch the ball; but they are all ugly, and there does not seem to be any great catch amongst them.

The game familiar to our eyes, and much too familiar with our heads, known in the streets as Cat, is believed to be the origin of cricket – which was formerly known as Cat and Dog; but as the passing stranger, or the pane of glass, forms the wicket aimed at in this case, the game is only popular with the more mischievous portion of the juvenile community.

In modern times cricket is the favourite game with the soldier, the sailor, and the

" He's still nibbling at the outswinger."

A Game At Crykette

clergyman; among each of which class there are many who learn the art of long stopping while waiting for promotion or preferment; and who, though they have often had the ball at their feet, get, somehow or other, bowled out in the long run. For these trials of life, cricket is an excellent preparative; and it is said, on the authority of Captain Gordon, that, on the eve of Waterloo, some of the officers were amusing themselves with the bat, while others were dancing at a ball.

It is a curious fact that the antiquarians have not yet tried a turn at cricket, for though they have groped among the foundations of almost everything, the brick-bat is the only bat they have hitherto taken in hand.

We, in a spirit of deeper veneration for antiquity, have explored a wider field in the hope of finding it a cricket field, and having taken a walk with old Suidas – we fancy hearing the reader asking who is Suidas? but let that pass – we have stumbled over a species of cricket being played under the classical name of Cottabos in a retired corner of Greece. In this game a piece of wood stuck in the ground enabled the Athenians to put up a stump without much expense, and being stumped up to this extent, another piece of wood placed horizontally completed a cheap and effective wicket. A dish hung down from each end, but instead of a ball, the player threw a vessel full of wine; and thus the game might be termed, to a certain extent, a game of bowls.

Cricket can only be played by men of excellent temper, who are willing, like Hampden, to fall in the field, who can submit cheerfully to the chances of battery from the bat, and of assault from the ball. The game is essentially English; and though our countrymen carry it abroad wherever they go, it is difficult to inoculate or knock it into the foreigner. The Italians are too fat for cricket, the French too thin, the Dutch too dumpty, the Belgians too bilious, the Flemish too flatulent, the East Indians too peppery, the Laplanders too bow-

legged, the Swiss too sentimental, the Greeks too lazy, the Egyptians too long in the neck, and the Germans too short in the wind.

A good cricketer must have an eye as sharp as a needle, a hand as tough as a thimble, and a leg as light as a bodkin. Russia should be able to produce no leather equal to his lungs, and India should not show a rubber half as elastic as his muscles. He should have an eye as steady as a glass, with a frame of iron, and his limbs should be a study to the limner. With these qualifications, we may hope to make him a cricketer, if he will accompany us into the field we are now entering.

1851

WICKET JOKES.
By Dumb-Crambo Junior.

Winning the Toss.

Point and Hump-ire.

Excellent Fielding.

Long Stop.

Out, and Not Out.

Following On, and opening with a Wide.

Bowling his Off Stump.

Caught at the Wicket.

CHAPTER ONE

Cricket Charivaria

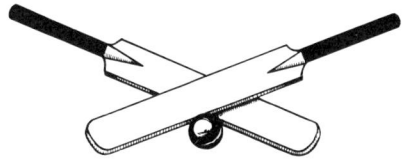

A Caudal Lecture
Or, Darwinism in the Cricket Field

When Man first arose from the primitive ape,
He first dropped his tail and took on a new shape.
But cricketing Man, born to trundle and swipe,
Reversion displays to the earlier type;
For a cricketing team, when beginning to fail,
Always loses its 'form', and 'develops a tail'!

August 1892

Baron Alderson on Cricket

The learned Baron has delighted a Suffolk grand jury, and many worthy folks besides, with certain intelligent and humanising remarks on a game of cricket which he saw played by a noble earl, tradesmen and labourers. He said he believed, if the aristocracy 'associated more with the lower classes of society, the kingdom of England

NEW CRICKETING DRESSES, TO PROTECT ALL ENGLAND AGAINST THE PRESENT SWIFT BOWLING.

would be in a far safer, and society in a far sounder, condition. I wish I could put it to the minds of all to think so, because I think it is true.' This may, or may not be true; but we put it to the Duke of Richmond, Lord Bentinck, Captain Rous, and other gentlemen of the turf, whether after all their association with the lowest of men – and only of course for the purpose of elevating them – they, the plebeians, have not remained the knaves and sharpers that they were before. Certain we are, the evidence in the Gaming Committee showed the vast condescension on the part of the wealthy and the high-born. To be sure, cricketing may have a healthier moral influence upon the vulgar than betting; and, with Baron Alderson, we wish the aristocracy would try it.

1844

–|●|●|–

Cricket – June 10th, Dublin. First meeting of the Irish Cricket Clubs, well paddy'd.
Great Cricket Match of the Season – A single wicket is to be married? Further particulars will be duly announced.
Lost Ball has been defined as missing a dance.

June 1863

The Cricketer's Gravestone

'Our Sheffield Correspondent telegraphs: An extraordinary tombstone dispute has arisen at Wadsley Bridge, near Sheffield. The widow of one Benjamin Keeton, a recently deceased cricketer of some local renown, has erected a tombstone to her husband's memory, on which is carved a set of stumps, about a foot high, with bat and ball. The vicar and churchwardens declare the stone was surreptitiously fixed, and have ordered its removal, which has caused intense local excitement.' – *Pall Mall Gazette*

O Wadsley Bridge, where Keeton bloomed,
    Thy vicar's wits what ails?
To bowl the stumps of Keeton tombed,
    Estreat his buried bails!

Could Keeton plead, to his life's fame
    He'd urge the symbols german,
More home, than to some parsons came
    Prayer-book, and bands, and sermon.

That hit, and all, he now must waive,
    Score closed, runs run, green-swarded;
Alas! he cannot guard his grave,
    As his mid-stump he guarded.

But why disturb the symbolled stone
    Above this quiet sleeper,
Who with his life's score fairly shown,
    Must face Heaven's wicket-keeper?

MR. PUNCH KEEPS HIS EYE ON CRICKET.

THEN (1841)   and   NOW (1891).

THE PLAYTHING OF CIRCUMSTANCE.

He. "HULLO, THERE'S SMITH OUT FOR A DUCK AGAIN!"
She. "DID HE EXPLAIN HOW IT WAS HE MADE NO RUNS IN HIS FIRST INNINGS?"
He. "WELL, YOU SEE, HE HAPPENED TO GO IN JUST WHEN JONES WAS IN THE MIDDLE OF HIS HAT TRICK."

Dying, perhaps, he thought, 'If he's one
  As is fit to keep wicket,
He'll know a cricketer when he sees one,
  And hand me my gate ticket.'

December 1876

-|o|o|-

Why Stir His Stumps?

What, in the name of common sense, could the vicar and churchwardens of Wadsley Bridge have meant by objecting to the bat, balls, and stumps on the tombstone of Benjamin Keeton, the cricketer, with the loving and Christian inscription, which, thanks to the kindness of a Sheffield correspondent, a cricketer too, *Punch* is glad to be able to append:

'Farewell, dear wife, my life is past:
My love was true until the last.
Then think of me, nor sorrow take,
But love my Saviour for my sake.'

Altogether we never heard of a more creditable gravestone: nor is this professional symbolism a new thing in the tombstones of those parts. The vicar and churchwardens may see in Wadsley Bridge Churchyard a musician's tombstone, with its music-bars and the notes of Handel's sublime strain, '*The trumpet shall sound and the dead shall be raised*', carved upon it; and a blacksmith's charged with the hammer and pincers flanking the horseshoe of his grimy but useful occupation.

Did not the vicar at least know – whatever the churchwardens may have known – that in

MR. PUNCH'S GUIDE TO CRICKET PHRASEOLOGY.

"Bowling 'lobs' with three short legs."

"'Hooking' it to leg."

"The Australians fielded well on the floor all day."

"Maclaren and Hayward started for England."

Captain. "Will you take 'cover,' please?"

—He takes cover.

the good old times this carving on the tombstone of the implements of the sleeper's handicraft, beginning with the soldier's sword and the dame's distaff, was an almost universal practice? And bat and balls were Keeton's tools as a professional cricketer.

Then, if we turn from the practice in the matter to the principle at the bottom of it, where can be the objection to what is a mere record of the sleeper's craft – true labour wherein was one of his life's best prayers, – *qui laborat, orat*, – but a record addressed to the eye, at once picturesque, and encouraging local art; instructive, as showing what trade implements have been; directly intelligible, and more vivid in its appeal to the memory than any description in words would be, while infinitely closer to the fact than most monumental enumerations of the virtues of the departed – your gravestone mason being the one recorder who observes the law, more charitable than honest, *de mortuis nil nisi bonum*.

The more *Punch* considers the matter, the more he feels inclined, instead of objecting to the practice of such symbolic stone-cutting, to wish it were everywhere restored in the English churchyards, till the proverb should run 'True as a tombstone', instead of 'False as an epitaph'.

We are glad to find that Wadsley Bridge vicar and churchwardens having thought of it, have naturally thought better of it, and have determined to leave Benjamin Keeton's bat, balls, and stumps where his widow has placed them.

January 1877

-|o|o|-

The Surrey ABC

A   is for Abel, who can certainly block well;
B   stands for Bowley, and Beaumont, and Brockwell;
C   is the Captain, John Shuter his name;
D   is the Devotion he gives to the game;
E   is the Eleven, deservedly great;
F   is the Funk which their bowlers create.
G   stands for George – our only George Lohmann;
H   for young Henderson, valiant young foeman.
I   is the Innings, beloved of the gapers;
J   is the Jargon they put in the papers.
K   is for Key, the accomplished Dark Blue;
L   is for Lockwood, who bowls a bit too;
M   is for Maurice, his other name Read;
N   poor old Nottingham, beaten indeed.
O   is the Oval, the home of the crowd;
P   the Pavilion, the seat of the proud.
Q   is the Question, 'Oh, umpire, how's that?'
R   is for Gentleman Read, who can bat.
S   stands for Sharpe, it will pay you to mind him;
T   is the Trouble they were put to to find him;
U   their United attempts – hard, to beat them;
V   the Vain efforts oft made to defeat them.
W   represents Wood at the wicket;
X   is the Xcellent style of their cricket.
Y   ends the county, not played out in a hurry.
Z   stands for Zero, a stranger to Surrey!

August 1891

No Ball!

Lord Harris, the most energetic of men,
Desires the enforcement of Rule Number Ten
        In cricket;
Insisting – a thing our obstructives might stare at –
That they who bowl straight and bowl swift shall bowl *fair* at
        The wicket!

Oh, pride of the emerald swards of green Kent,
Could you bring the 'fair play' of the field and the tent
        To St Stephen's,
Perhaps it might lead to a pleasant revival,
And parties might battle as fairly as rival
        Elevens!

The difference *there* betwixt 'bowling' and 'throwing'
Appears clean forgotten, the mischief is growing
        Appalling.
Of manly fair-play there is scarcely a tittle.
It's oh for a Rule Number Ten, and a little
        No-balling!

May 1883

=|●|●|=

The Useful Cricketer
(*A Candid Veteran's Confession*)

I am rather a 'pootlesome' bat –
  I seldom, indeed, make a run;
But I'm rather the gainer by that,
  For it's bad to work hard in the sun.

As a 'field' I am not worth a jot,
  And no one expects me to be;
My run is an adipose trot,
  My 'chances' I never can see.

I am never invited to bowl,
  And though, p'raps, this seems like a slight,
In the depths of my innermost soul
  I've a notion the captain is right.

In short, I may freely admit
  I am not what you'd call a great catch;
But yet my initials are writ
  In the book against every match!

For although – ay, and there is the rub –
  I am forty and running to fat,
I have made it all right with the club,
  By presenting an average bat!

June 1892

=|●|●|=

Cricket in Days to Come

(According to a contemporary, bicycle paths have been recently laid out on several American links, so that the golfers, accompanied by their caddies, can mount their bicycle and pedal after the balls. The Oakland Golf Club is about to construct a private tramway line completely encircling the links; chairs and iced drinks will be provided.)

At the England *v*. Australia match played at Lord's yesterday, a motor-car was at hand by the batting wicket so that the batsman, after making a hit, could leap into the car and score his runs without much physical exertion; all the fielders, with the exception of the bowler and the wicket-keep, were mounted on donkeys. To gallop after the ball, spring from their steeds, and gallop back was the work of a few moments, and save for the mounting and dismounting, entailed but slight trouble on the part of the fielders.

The bowling-crease was covered with a board, over which the roller-skates of the bowler moved with hardly a motion.

The wicket-keep was supported by a patent shooting-stick seat, while behind the wicket itself was an arrangement in the form of an

Wretched Deep Field (who has already dropped a few). "HERE IT COMES AGAIN!"

A REARGUARD ACTION.

Ingoing Batsman (who has been commandeered at the last moment). "ER—HAVEN'T YOU ANOTHER PAIR OF GUARDS? MY LEGS ARE QUITE EXPOSED AT THE BACK."

umbrella, by which the batsmen were protected from the sun.

The umpires were seated in easy chairs to
which the umbrella arrangement was affixed,
with iced drinks close at hand.

The batsman who was not in play rested
quietly in a swinging hammock, while an
automatic dummy did the running.

July 1899

Cricket for Angels

(A certain nonconformist divine, according to the
Glasgow Herald, was recently asked to become vice-
president of the local cricket club. He accepted the
post, subject to the fulfilment of the following
stipulations.)

Pray, cricketers, remember, if you want to play with me,
　　How you carry on your little conversations,
You must give up your wicked swear-words and abjure the big, big D,
　　And moderate your hasty exclamations.
Should a ball rise unexpectedly and take your wind away,
　　This is no excuse for making such a pother;
You must bear it like a Christian, for I certainly sha'n't play
　　If there's any stronger language than a 'Bother!'

You must all be good teetotallers. Beer savours of the pit,
　　And is of every evil thing symbolic.
It's ruin, moral, physical – I would as soon admit
　　The fiend himself as liquor alcoholic.
And as for gin and whisky – pour the filthy stuff away!
　　Who drinks these deadly, poisonous pig-washes?
Bring tea and ginger beer instead! I certainly sha'n't play
　　If there's any stronger drink than lemon-squashes.

Of course you mustn't gamble! (When we once begin to bet
　　No power on earth can ever check or turn us.)
Nor smoke, for the insidious seductive cigarette
　　Is the *facilis descensus* to Avernus.
But if you'll follow me, and fling your vices all away,
　　Observing my conditions well and duly,
Why then it is just possible I may consent to play,
　　If there is no stronger batsman than yours truly.

May 1898

'The first three balls puzzled him and he appeared a
trifle nervous. A ball from Macartney jumped over
the batsman's shoulder, hit Macartney on the head
and went for a single.' – *Birmingham Evening
Dispatch*

The boomerang ball is very deceptive, but
sometimes defeats its own end. Too much
back spin, therefore, should not be employed.

9.6.1909

From the report of a cricket match in the
Glasgow Herald:

'W. White, thrown out 93.'

It is no part of the scorer's duty to comment on
a bowler's action.

1.9.1909

The Cricketer in Winter

The days are growing short and cold;
  Approaches Autumn, ay and chill Yule;
The latest bowler now has bowled
  His latest devastating pillule.
Gone are the creases, gone the 'pegs';
  The bungling fieldsman now no more errs
By letting balls go through his legs
  And giving batsmen needless fourers.

Things of the past are drive and cut,
  With which erstwhile we would astound men;
The gay pavilion's doors are shut;
  The turf is given up to groundmen;
Gone is the beautiful length-ball,
  Gone, too, is the batsman who would snick it;
Silent his partner's cheery call.
  Football usurps the place of cricket.

Now, as incessantly it pours,
  And each succeeding day seems bleaker.
The cricketer remains indoors,
  And quaffs mayhap the warming beaker.
Without, the scrummage heaves and slips;
  Not his to play the muddied oaf. A
Well-seasoned pipe between his lips,
  He reads his *Wisden* on the sofa.

Or, if in vein for gentle toil,
  Before he seeks a well-earned pillow,
He takes a flask of linseed oil
  And tends his much-enduring willow,
Feeling the while, what time he drops
  The luscious fluid by degrees on,
Given half-volleys and long-hops,
  How nobly it will drive next season!

Then to his couch, to dream till day
  Of fifties when the pitch was sticky,
Of bowling crisply 'put away',
  Though it was manifestly tricky,
Of umpires, confident appeals,
  Hot shots at point, mid-off, and cover,
Of cricket-lunches (perfect meals!):
  Such dreams attend the cricket-lover.

And, though the streets be deep in snow,
  Though slippery pavements make him stumble,
Though rain descends, though blizzards blow,
  It matters not: he scorns to grumble.
What if it lightens, thunders, hails,
  And common men grow daily glummer,
In him contentment never fails;
  To such a man it's always Summer.

September 1903

One of the persons who object to the Rev. F. H. Gillingham playing cricket for Essex is a Mr Hen. Is he afraid that the redoubtable parson will produce a duck's egg?

June 1912

=|o|o|=

Cricket Notes

Mr P. F. Warner has received countless expressions of regret on his retirement from first-class cricket. Among these he values not least a 'round robin' from the sparrows at Lord's, all of whom he knows by name. In the score-book of Fate is this entry in letters of gold:
  'Plum' *c*. Anno *b*. Domini 47.
Long may he live to enjoy the cricket of others!

Mr Fender and Hobbs are said to be actuated by the same motto, 'For hearth and home'. Both are pledged to return covered with 'the ashes'.

Bowler. "WOULD YOU MIND STANDING SIDEWAYS, OLD CHAP?"
Umpire. "I WILL—BUT IT'S WORSE."

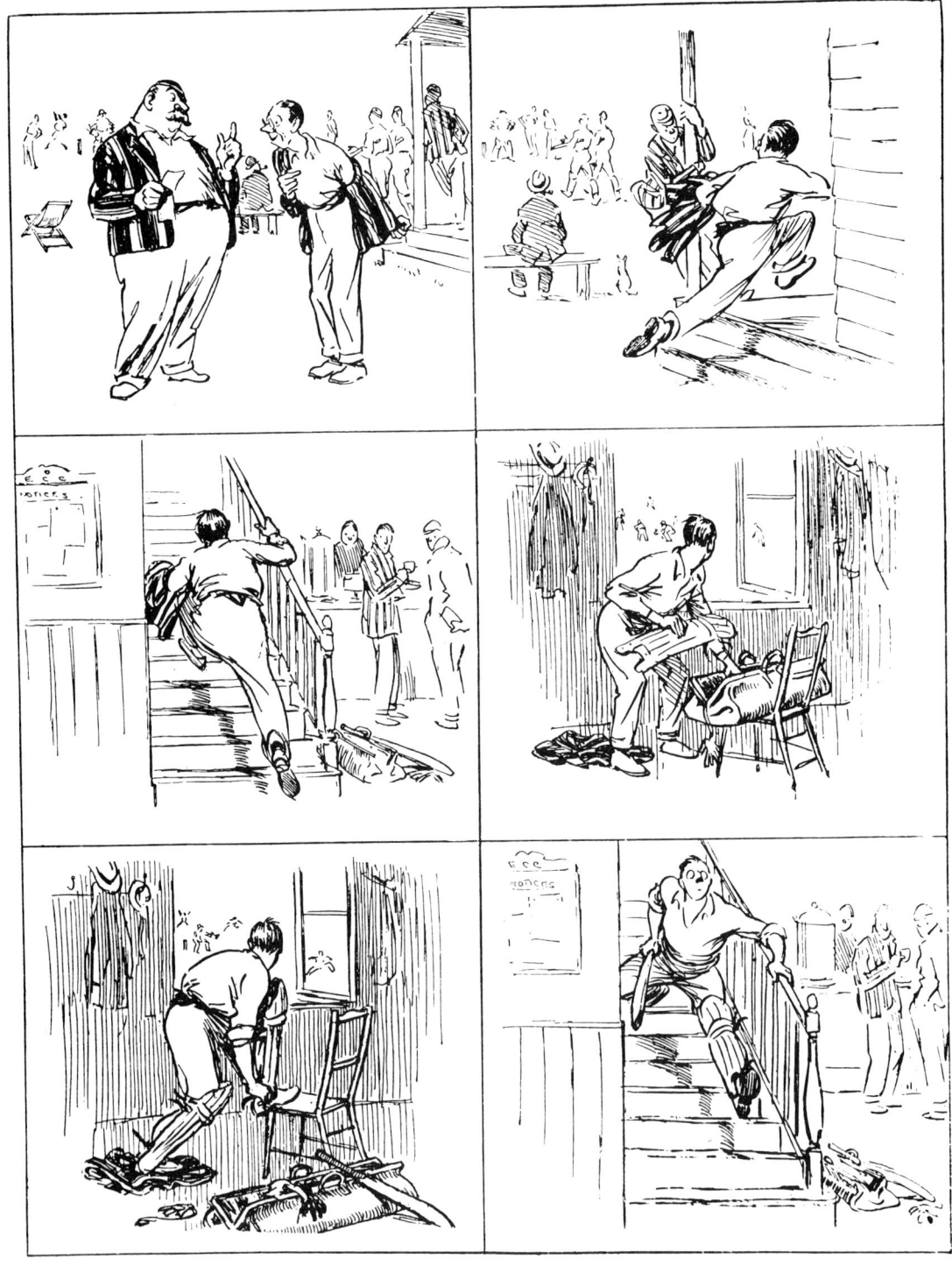

FIRST WICKET DOWN; OR, THE CHANCE OF A LIFETIME.

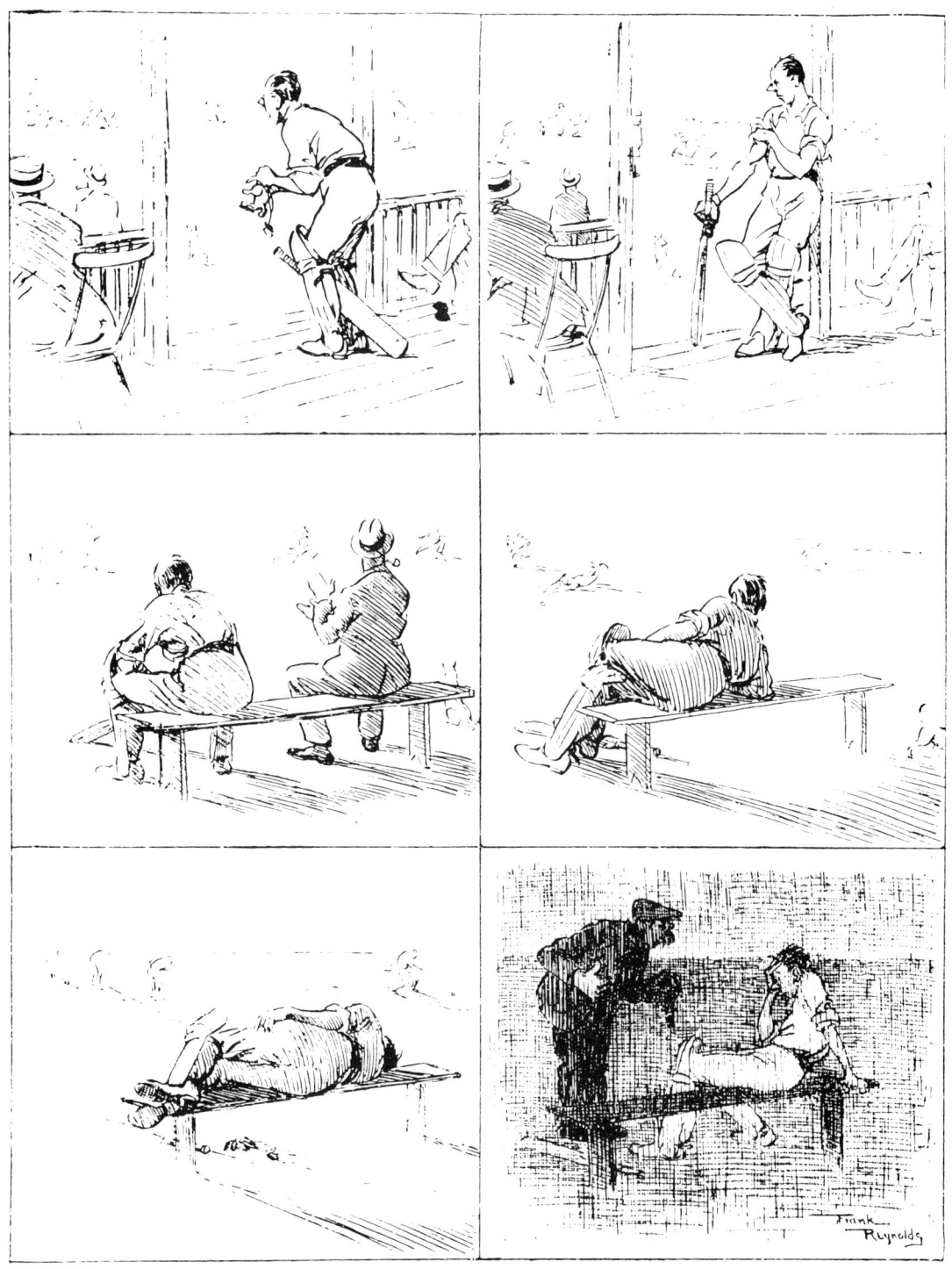

FIRST WICKET DOWN: OR THE CHANCE OF A LIFETIME.

THE EVIL THAT MEN DO.

THE LAST MAN WAS IN AND WITH ONLY ONE RUN WANTED—

SMITH, OF ALL PEOPLE, DROPPED A CATCH.

HE STOLE AWAY—

BUT HIS SIN FOLLOWED HIM.

HE DECIDED—

TO LEAVE THE COUNTRY.

AFTER MANY YEARS HE RETURNED.

"GOOD HEAVENS, SMITH, I HAVEN'T SEEN YOU SINCE YOU DROPPED THAT CATCH AT THE CIRCLE."

"YES, I ONCE SAW HIM PLAY WHEN I W QUITE A LAD. ON THAT OCCASION HE F THE MISFORTUNE TO DROP A CATCH.

In the recent Surrey and Middlesex match Mr Skeet bewildered the crowd by fielding as he liked it. Hitherto this vulgar manifestation has been confined to Hitch and Hendren.

Although so late in the season Yorkshire has great hopes of a colt named Hirst, who has just joined the side. He was seen bowling at Eton and was secured at once.

There is a strong feeling in Worcestershire that a single-wicket match between Lee of Middlesex and Mr Perrin of Essex would be a very saucy affair.

August 1920

A cricket match was played the other day between two teams of dairymen. It is whispered that both sides were suspected of watering the pitch.

August 1923

Mr A. C. MacLaren deplores the modern batsman's style of standing full-face to the bowler. We ourselves, when playing fast bowling, are more in favour of facing the wicket-keeper.

June 1924

From a Cricket Writer's Notebook

Make this season memorable for prose-beauty. Encourage musical analogies ('At the Oval a concert, a symphony, a percussion solo . . . Brahms? Tchaikovsky? Shostakovich? . . .') Cultivate antitheses. Quote Virginia Woolf. Avoid statistics.

Humour, humanity essential. (*Mem.* Rhodes joke – 'Get 'em in singles' – once *only* this season. Also ball in beard.)

Themes for season: decline and fall; no fast bowler since Kortright; Ranji; Trumper; Pooley (E.). Reserve phrase *laudator temporis acti* for mid-July at earliest.

Use colons sparingly for increased effect. No footnotes this year. Italics at sub-editor's discretion.

Now in order to call Charles Fry a sage.

ANOTHER RECORD.
The Test Match that did not produce a record.

Useful phrases:
'It was dark satanic, batsmanship/bowling/fielding/wicket-keeping/captaincy.' (*Mem.* Best used with a Mills. Is there one playing now?)

'He poured forth from the cornucopia of his glorious art.'

'. . . like the bat in the adage.' (*Mem.* No need to quote adage.)

'Those who go down to the knee in slips.'

'A bowling analysis should not, *per se*, be subjected to the counter-analysis of the psychologist.'

'The sheer hulk of Tom bowling.' (*Mem.* Goddard only playing occasionally. Dollery?)

'He drove more furiously than any Jehu.'

'My summer's babble of green fields is ended.' (*Mem.* Not until after Scarborough.)

Remember to report play.

Eric Walmsley
June 1952

Point (appealing for catch at wicket). "'OW'S THAT?"
Umpire (supporter of batting side). "MIND YER OWN BUSINESS." (*Appeal dismissed.*)

A famous wicket-keeper has given a testimonial in favour of a certain brand of chewing-gum. Some umpires, however, are prejudiced against appeals made with the mouth full.

July 1930

–|e|e|–

To a Bad Wicket-keeper

Air – 'Oh why do you walk through the fields in gloves . . .'

Oh, why do you stand on the field in gloves,
Missing so much and so much?
Oh, fat white booby whom nobody loves,
Why do you stand on the field in gloves,
When the air is loud with my 'Heavens above's!'
As you drop each ball that they touch?
Oh, why do you stand on the field in gloves,
Missing so much and so much?

June 1926

'Convicts Play Cricket', reads a headline. Presumably over the wall was 'out'.

September 1933

A correspondent says he once played cricket against Gilbert Jessop in Rutland. During Jessop's innings he fielded mostly in Lincolnshire.

July 1941

Television Cricket

My love a cricket fan is he,
 He wouldn't miss a game;
Old Trafford, Lord's or Headingley,
 He'll watch it just the same,
And from the same position, which
 Is right up in the air,
Moving at ease around the pitch
 Within the best armchair.

In shades of grey to suit his choice
 His little kingdom glows;
Booms loud or soft that kindly voice
 To tell him what he knows;
For him the scoreboard's fleeting view,
 The ash tray on the floor,
The coffee brought by people who
 Creep out, and shut the door.

And there through all the summer's day,
 A soul apart, he sits;
Now pushing back his chair, that they
 May carpet-sweep the bits,

A journalist claims that he once saw Goering playing cricket. When he came out to bat the umpire signalled a wide.

July 1943

Man from the North. "SIT DOWN!"
Man from the South. "WHAT FOR?"
Man from the North. "CAN'T SEE COVERS."

"Just a little more to leg."

Now answering the telephone,
  Now taking in the bread,
Now, till four-thirty, getting shown
  A cowboy film instead.

And now upon the quiet screen
  The shadows melt and fade;
My love is happy; he has been
  Where cricket's being played,
And in him is the deep content
  All homebound crowds can share
Who ever turned a knob and went
  Back to the best armchair.

Ande
June 1952

–|o|o|–

Dreamers on the Green

Hypnotism, already established in the maternity ward and the dental surgery, is now making its influence felt on the cricket field. Members of a Yorkshire club find that they can wake up and play with unusual skill after a

period of hypnotically induced sleep. Spectators are not yet used to the change, and after a similar experience simply wake up and go home.

May 1954

–|o|o|–

Benaud says that Griffith throws (he has to fill his column somehow), but E. W. Swanton is indignant about this (properly so) and concludes by saying he will return to the subject 'in a calmer moment'. Now there's a *real* pro – he gets *two* columns out of it. And, of course, the whole row is very, very, soothing to *Telegraph* readers.

March 1965

A Brief Guide to CRICKET

by ffolkes

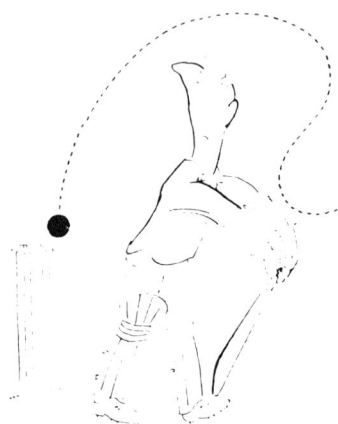

This is known as
being beaten by the flight.

This man enjoys
absolute power.

This young fellow is known as the
Twelfth Man. He can probably play
cricket but has not been asked to
on this occasion.

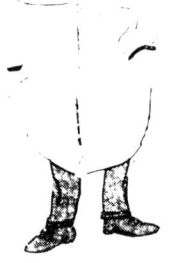

Unlike other forms of the
great national game this is
being played for pleasure.

This player will shortly
be chaffed by onlookers.

There is no useful
purpose to be served
by arguing with this man.

This was intended as no more than a
light-hearted gesture by the bowler.

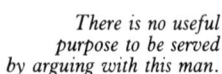

HOW FAST BOWLERS ARE MADE.

Captain (to hurricane performer). "OF COURSE I SHOULD HATE YOU TO HURT ANYBODY, CHARLIE, BUT I THOUGHT YOU MIGHT LIKE TO KNOW THAT THIS FELLA COMING IN IS SOMETHING TO DO WITH INCOME-TAX."

Gary Sobers left his team for a week before the first Test Match to go to Melbourne 'on business'. Gallant attempt to revive the tradition of the amateur captain, if nothing else.

December 1968

Grundy

Listening to Denis Compton's perceptive comments on the Test and seeing his goodly, portly body in El Vino's from time to time makes me think back to those glorious immediate post-war years when I used to watch two particular run-stealers flicker to and fro, to and fro – 'Oh my Compton and my Edrich long ago'. It also reminds me of Denis's wonderfully relaxed approach to the game.

Ken Barrington once told me of the time Denis was driving across Vauxhall Bridge on his way to the last day's play in the Oval Test. It was just 11 a.m. and Denis was on the last minute, as usual. He switched on the car radio for a time check, only to hear John Arlott saying, 'Well, now that Bill Edrich is out, we'll be seeing Denis Compton next.' He was wrong. In his light-hearted way, our Denis had forgotten that on the last day, play starts half an hour earlier.

A final note about cricket. Watching Tony Greig's long legs eating up the pitch on the first day of the Test, and David Steele's short ones scampering after, I was reminded of Harry Pilling of Lancashire, the shortest cricketer in the first class game. Asked if he didn't feel at a disadvantage when batting with the giant Clive Lloyd, Harry replied, 'Naw. Not so long as 'e doesn't tread on mi.'

August 1975

Grundy

I bumped into my old friend Mr Frederick Sewards Trueman last week, on the very day Lance Gibbs equalled Freddie's world record bag of Test wickets. I got the impression Fred thought each of his wickets was worth about ten of Lance's because of the effort he put into them, whereas Gibbs glides up like a cross between a snake and a panther and barely breaks sweat however many overs he bowls.

"Marvellous, Rodney, it's the best field placing you've designed yet!"

How Green is your Cricket Cover?

Cricket may not have survived without sponsorship—but will the game remain the same once it falls into the hands of the ad-men and MAHOOD?

"My God, Tubby! It's the new MCC tie!"

"Now the West Indies are objecting to the English batsmen flicking the ash from their Players No. 3 on the wicket . . ."

"Hold it, they're moving the sight-screen . . . Bells must have come up with a better offer."

Another reason for my impression, of course, could be that Lance Gibbs is black. Frederick has never been all that diplomatic about colour: there's the story that, sitting next to a member of the Indian Government at a tour dinner, he nudged him with his elbow and said, 'Hey up, Gunga Din, pass t'salt, wilta?'

But on this occasion Freddie was doing a wonderful job looking after some disabled people appearing on a TV programme. His only concession to his usual self came after I'd introduced him to the woman I was with. I'd warned her that, outside talking cricket, Freddie's only conversation was cracking jokes.

"Of course, for maximum exposure we had to lengthen his run."

"Test score . . . but first a few words on behalf of Walls Sausages . . ."

"I let him have that beamer because his advertising exceeded the bounds of decency."

"The sooner Brooke Bond find a new ad agency the better I'll like it!"

Sure enough, as soon as he'd shaken hands with her, he put his arms around our shoulders and straightway said ''Ere, 'ave you 'eard this one?', and then proceeded to tell us a joke about Arthur Scargill so outrageous that I cannot repeat it here, although, since I told it the next day to the Tory Party Director of Information, it stands every chance of turning up, in necessarily modified form, in Maggie Thatcher's next speech.

February 1976

MANNERS AND CVSTOMS. OF Yᵉ ENGLYSHE IN 1849.   Nᵒ 17

A VIEW OF Mᵣ LORDE hys CRYKET GROVNDE.

CHAPTER TWO

Lord's

Mr Pips his Diary

Monday June 18, 1849. This day a great cricket match, Surrey against England, at Lord's, and I thither, all the way to St John's Wood, to see the place, having oft heard talk of it, and the playing which Mr Longstoppe did tell me was a pretty sight. Paid 6*d* to be let in, and 2*d* for a card of the innings, and bought a little book of the laws of the game, cost me 1*s* 6*d* more, though when I had got it, could hardly understand a word of it; but to think how much money I spend out of curiosity, and how inquisitive I am, so as to be vexed to the heart if I cannot thoroughly make out everything I see! The cricketing I believe very fine; but could not judge of it; for I think I did never before see any cricket since I was a little varlet boy at school. But what a difference between the manner of bowling in those days, and that players now use! for then they did moderately trundle the ball under-hand; but now they fling it over-handed from the elbow, as though viciously, and it flies like a shot, being at least five ounces and a half in weight, and hard as a block. I saw it strike one of the bat-men on the knuckles, who danced and shook his fist, as methought well he might. But to see how handy some did catch it, though knocked off the bat by a strong man with all his force; albeit now and then they missing it, and struck by it on the head, or in the mouth, and how anyone can learn to play cricket without losing his front teeth is a wonder. The spectators sitting on benches in a circle, at a distance, and out of the way of the ball, which was wise; but some on a raised stand, and others aside at tables, under a row of trees near a tavern within the grounds, with pipes and beer; and many in the circle also smoking and drinking, and the drawers continually going the round of them to serve them liquor and tobacco. But all as quiet as a Quakers' meeting, except when a good hit made, or a player bowled out, and strange to see how grave and solemn they looked, as if the sight of men in white clothes, knocking a ball about, were something serious to think on. Did hear that many had wagers on the game, but doubt it, for methinks there had been more liveliness if much betting, and chance of winning or losing money. The company very numerous, and among them some in carriages, and was glad to see so many people diverted, although at what I could not tell. But they enjoyed themselves in their way, whatever that was, and I in mine, thinking how droll they looked, so earnestly attending to a mere show of dexterity. I, for my part, soon out of patience with the length of the innings, and the stopping and interruption after each run, and so away, more tired, I am sure, than any of the cricketers. Yet I do take pride, as an Englishman, in our country sport of cricket, albeit I do not care to watch it playing; and certainly it is a manly game, throwing open the chest, and strengthening the limbs, and the player so often in danger of being hit by the ball.

Vol. 17, 1849

Heard at Lord's

'Were you at Eton, or Harrow?'

'No, my education wasn't neglected to *that* extent. Why do you ask? Any bad English in the note I sent you?'

(*Counter-check quarrelsome to an epigram on which our dear boys seem to plume themselves.*)

23.7.1870

–|●|●|–

Reflection at Lord's

The Duke of Wellington did or did not say that the Battle of Waterloo had been won in the Eton cricket-field. That was in the old time; but if the cricket of those days was a pastime equivalent to military training in skill, courage, coolness, and endurance, how much more so is it now in this improved age of swift and over-hand bowling, which really amounts to a cannonade?

(*Our correspondent says he was proceeding into some further improving meditations, when a ball flew at him viciously and laid him on the turf.*)

12.7.1873

–|●|●|–

At Lord's

WHAT A YOUNG LADY SAYS: I do *so* like cricket matches, they are *so* pretty, and I am quite *learned* about them. But *do* tell me, why are they running after that ball; and is it *really* necessary to put three bits of stick near the bowlers with their bats? You didn't think I knew so much about it, now, *did* you? Thank you *so* much. I will take a little more champagne cup. No raised pie, thanks – I have got some lobster salad. Oh, *do* smoke. I am awfully fond of the smoke of a cigar in the open air! And now, you must tell me *all* the news.

WHAT A DOWAGER SAYS: I shall certainly keep my umbrella up, in spite of shutting out the view from a carriage-load behind me. I really *must* think of myself in this hot weather a little!

WHAT A YOUNG MAN SAYS: Really too bad of that old woman to put up an umbrella, eh? Can't be any good to her, don't you know. Nonsense to think she wants to keep her complexion. Got no complexion at all, don't you know? Hasn't had one, I should think, for the last twenty years, eh, don't you know?

WHAT AN OLD SCHOOL-FELLOW SAYS: Hallo, my boy, why it's you! Haven't seen you for twenty years! How fat you've got! Why, what used we to call you? Oh, 'Nosey', to be sure!

WHAT ANGELINA SAYS: My dear Edwin, you don't mean to say you were ever called 'Nosey'! How you have deceived me!

WHAT EDWIN SAYS: Hang that fellow!

WHAT A GOOD BOY SAYS: My dear father, this is a very painful sight! It grieves me to see two-and-twenty young men spending in recreation time that might be so usefully employed in study!

WHAT A BAD BOY SAYS: Look here, old man, let's give the guv'nor the slip, and have some more grub!

WHAT EVERYBODY SAYS: Capital way to spend a summer's day pleasantly.

AND WHAT THE UMPIRE SAYS (ESPECIALLY AT 7 PM): Over!

8.7.1876

–|●|●|–

New Regulations for Lord's
(*Hourly expected*)

1. Members of cricketing county elevens will be charged a guinea a head gate money daily.
2. Umpires will pay a fee of five guineas a match of three days.
3. Balloons passing over the ground will be expected to pay a shilling a second during the passage.
4. Residents of houses surrounding the ground by paying five guineas per annum can avoid the erection of view-impeding hoardings, and thus secure a splendid view of the matches.
5. A small charge (*2s 6d* per person) will be made for the use of the ground during the luncheon interval.
6. Competing county elevens requiring the pitch to be rolled will pay five shillings a time between the wickets or three times for twelve and sixpence.
7. After rain sawdust can be secured at four shillings an ounce.

AIDS TO THE POPULARITY OF CRICKET.

8. Should the crease require re-marking, pipe-clay can be obtained at ten shillings a brush full.
9. The scoring boards will be erected in a tent, and the public will be permitted to examine them at a shilling a peep.
10. Tickets for gentlemen of the press will be issued at a guinea a day, and accommodation will be found for the ticket-holders behind the chimneys of the grand stand.

18.7.1900

—|o|o|—

The Man about Town
Lord's – and Ladies

I love Lord's. I love Eton and Harrow. I love the sunny green, the happy crowds, the coaches, the frocks, the pretty ladies, the grey top-hats, the cultured talk, the little walking-sticks of the boys, the ribbons on the walking-sticks, the flowers in their coats; I love to feel that this is England, this is the national game, a manly dangerous game; and I think with pity of the effeminate Dagoes who can only play pelota, basket-ball and lawn-tennis. Fops!

Joan is as keen on cricket as I am, and she was the best-dressed woman there. We sat on a very hard seat for the greater part of a hot day and saw hundreds of frocks. The wicket was 'plumb', the batting orthodox, and if there is anything more boring than orthodox batting on a plumb wicket I suppose it is professional billiards. But no doubt the blame lay with me. I find that my presence casts a blight on cricket. As soon as I leave the ground a batsman comes in and smites the ball with great violence to all parts of the field in a charming unorthodox fashion, scoring sixes in every over and constantly hitting the ball in the air. But as soon as I arrive a perfect plague of orthodoxy sets in; the batsmen settle down to a sound defensive game, hitting the ball mildly to mid-off and mid-on alternately, with an occasional four through the slips, and that along the ground. I have never seen a genuine British slog, and I suppose I never shall.

As for this absurd modern fetish of keeping the ball low, I cannot understand it. There is none of that nonsense when I play village-cricket, for we play in a rich pasture, and if you don't hit the ball in the air you don't hit it anywhere. A little village-cricket would do these schoolboys a world of good. After all, if I am only to hit the ball along the ground, I might as well play golf.

The only real relief in this match was the delicious badness of the bowling. Indeed, had not the bowling been so bad I don't know what we should all have found to talk about. It was so bad that I knew it was bad. There are moments, I confess, when I find it difficult to distinguish between a half-volley and a good-length ball; but when a ball bounces three times I know at once that there is something wrong with it; and when the wicket-keeper just manages to reach it by bounding into the air I know that it is a full-pitch, and a bad one.

But, personally, I go to Lord's for the conversation; and as soon as I had pointed out some of the badder balls to Joan, I settled down to enjoy some of that charming idiocy which only flourishes at Lord's. This year there was prevalent a sort of pose of being interested in the cricket; and everybody I sat in front of was commenting bitterly on the conversation of the people behind them. And the sum-total of these comments was like the sound of a Cairo bazaar in the American season. The following dialogue would not go well on the stage, I daresay; but that's because it's true.

'How that fellow jaws!' said a male voice, bitterly. 'My hat, that's a bad ball!'

'Tommy said they were bowling rather well.'

'They're bowling muck. *Muck*. I never saw such muck. Look at that!'

'Oh, I missed it,' said the lady, waking from a stupor. 'What is it?'

'A long-hop. Ought to have gone for four.'

'Why do those boys stand so close to him?'

'That's the short-leg trap. Plucky fellows! Did you hear what that fellow said just now?'

'No.'

'He said he hoped they'd get hurt. Nice sort of thing to say.'

'Will they?' said the lady nervously.

'Not they. The bowler's too frightened to bowl on the leg stump, and the batsman's too frightened to hit it anywhere near them if he did.'

'Then why is it plucky?'

'Well, you know what I mean. There's always a chance.'

'They don't seem to do much.'

'No, it's all eye-wash really. Silly rot. O Lord, they're going to have another lemonade.'

'Poor boys; they've been fielding for an hour and a half. I expect they *want* something.'

'Well, in *my* day – I say, did you hear that?'

'Hear what?'

'This fellow behind me –'

'The one with the moustache?'

'No, the one with the nose –'

'Yes?'

'Well, he's been telling a story about some girl or other. It was after a dance and – damn it, how was he out?'

'Afraid I didn't see. "Bowled", somebody said.'

'Always the way. As soon as you say a word, a wicket falls. Well, this girl's terribly proper, it seems – been kept very close by her mother and all that. That lad wasn't bowled, he was caught – caught Number 4. Who's that?'

'Crossman.'

'No, Crossman's Eton. It's Stewart-Brown. And one night, in the country, or somewhere after a dance or something, they played hide-and-seek. Only this girl was supposed to be in bed. And she was found in a cupboard with Major Somebody or other. Rather funny!'

'Do you mean she was found by her mother?'

'I don't know. I didn't catch that. This fellow's been telling the story for the last quarter of an hour. That's all they come here for, most of these people.'

'I know. I like that black frock in front.'

'Jolly. I never *saw* such bowling. It's about time they had another lemonade.'

'It's funny they don't bowl better, isn't it?'

'Yes. I don't know what's the matter with

FORM AT LORD'S.

Small Etonian (to his sister). "I say, Joan, *must* you look so beastly keen?
I enjoy an ice as much as anybody, but, dash it all, I don't *show* it."

them. They can't bowl a bit.'

'You'd think they'd *teach* them bowling, wouldn't you? After all, it isn't like *batting*. And it's a big school.'

'Yes, it's a fine school. But they can't bowl. Good Lord, he's out! How was he out?'

'I didn't see. Bowled somebody said.'

'Yes. Clean bowled apparently. It's a most extraordinary thing but, whenever I look away for an instant, a wicket falls.'

'Yes. I've noticed that. Isn't it funny? It was just the same at the Varsity match.'

'Sort of fatality, I suppose.'

'I suppose it is.'

'They're talking about racing now. Have you been to *RUR*?'

'No.'

'These batsmen are little better than robots.'

'What d'you mean?'

'Perfect mechanism but no soul. Have you been to *Stop Flirting*?'

'No. Have you been to *Robert E. Lee*?'

'Yes, we have no banannas.'

'What do you mean?'

'Haven't you heard that? It's the new American password. The universal answer. Coming over here, they say. You'd better learn it.'

'Yes, we have no bananas.'

'No, not *bananas*. *Banannas*. You ought to hear an American girl saying it. I say, what dull cricket this is!'

'I wish somebody would get out.'

'Let's start talking. Then somebody's sure to. I say, did you hear that?'

'No.'

'This fellow behind us – the one that told that story about the girl in the cupboard – he's complaining about the people behind him talking so much. Pretty good, that. He's never stopped talking since the moment he sat down.'

'Awful, isn't it? Somebody's out. Or is it lemonade?'

'No, he's out. There you are! I told you so.

The moment I talk – It's always the same.'

'Let's talk some more.'

'Well, these bowlers won't get 'em out, so we may as well.'

'Did you hear that?' I whispered.

'Oh, you *are* awake, are you?' said Joan with reproach. 'You're good company, aren't you? That's the first remark you've made for twenty-five overs. Aren't you enjoying it?'

'Yes, we have no banannas,' I replied.

A.P.H.
25.7.1923

-|●|●|-

Gentlemen *v.* Players at Lord's

'R. H. Bettington joined Allen at 283 and had the pleasure of cutting the Yorkshireman to square leg for 6.' – *Provincial Paper*

If Mr Bettington will be so good as to teach us this stroke, we will do our best to show him our on-drive through the slips.

29.7.1925

A Long Day at Lord's

While Hearne was faultlessly batting
  As though he would never cease,
Sometimes cutting a ball and sometimes patting
  The ball from crease to crease,

A gentleman sitting beside me
  (I don't know why)
Poured out, in a manner that somewhat tried me,
  His whole life's history.

I have listened to the unfolding of the dramas,
  Page after page,
Recount by ladies and gentlemen in pyjamas
  On the stage;

I have listened to the story of infelicitous marriages
  And family jars,
In club-rooms, and London and North-Eastern Railway carriages,
  And bars,

But I never yet have heard a gentleman unrolling
  The tale of his life's ambitions and life's rewards
While Hearne (J.W.) was dealing very skilfully with the bowling
  At Lord's.

Between the moment when the batsman had registered fifty
  And the moment when he had registered seventy-five –
Not lavish of strokes to the boundary, but thrifty,
  And sparing of the straight hard drive –

All the wild passions of a youth hot-headed and hearty,
  In many a foreign land
Were vividly narrated to me by the party
  Sitting on my left hand.

Why he chose me as a confidant it is impossible to discover,
  Nor what there was about the level and sunlit grass
That led him to recall himself as a youth and a lover,
  And the gongs of sounding brass –

India, and Africa, and plantations, and coconuts and niggers,
　　And a great deal more of which no memory survives –
But I do know that before Hearne had reached the coveted three figures
　　This man had lost three wives.

All the colour and wealth of the East, the strange mysterious splendour
　　He showed me, an absolute stranger, too frightened to screech
Whilst Hearne was defying the bowling of Holmes, and of Geary and Shepherd and Fender,
　　And Peach.

The telegraph mounted, the runs came exceedingly slowly,
　　The sparrow picked crumbs on the sward,
Apes chattered in forests, *fakirs* were exceedingly holy.
　　Three hundred went up on the board.

I shall never know why this gentleman told me his story
　　(While Hearne was in),
Full of tempestuous striving, and changes of fortune, and fury,
　　And mining for tin,

Under the afternoon sun, which made looking at cricket a pleasure,
　　Especially cricket like Hearne's;
But on leaving I picked up his twopenny score-card, and that I shall treasure
　　Till cricket returns.

Evoe
7.9.1927

=|●|●|=   =|●|●|=

Cruel Cricket

'With the old ball, Tate, in his third delivery, extracted from the dying wicket a vicious kick.' – *Provincial Paper*

Serve him right, knocking it about like that when it was moribund.

6.2.1929

'Before lunch Chapman did some brilliant fielfid-fiinfigfi fiafit mid-off to White's bowling.' – *Provincial Paper*

This seems to us not cricket, but intimidation.

20.3.1929

=|●|●|=

Lord's

August enclosure in St John's Wood Road,
　　Where Willow, peerless Willow, reigns indeed
　　Unchallenged monarch of the well-trimmed mead,
Cricket's stout citadel and famed abode,
Ground of immortal memories of great men
And deeds historic that my artless pen
Lacks virtue to record,
Much treasured piece of earth, most noble sward,
Fain would I visit you and tarry long!
(*Umpires, call softly till I end my song!*)

Where your austere pavilion fronts the lea
　　Dwells one who may most honourably claim
　　To be the chosen handmaid of the game,
The Secretary of the MCC;

There too the wise committee sits in state
And venerable elders congregate
To grieve in whispered pow-wows
That cricket's going headlong to the bow-wows
Now youth plays golf or tennis or ping-pong.
(*Umpires, call softly till I end my song!*)

Oft to this green delectable retreat
  I like a pilgrim wend by underground
  And perch upon that high commodious mound,
Happy to let the fleeting moments fleet,
Happy to bask benignly in the sun,
Munching a simple sandwich or a bun;
There in serene content
I count the idle hours most richly spent,
For summer's all too short and winter's long.
(*Umpires, call softly till I end my song!*)

Old Trafford has its glories, Trent Bridge too,
  Melbourne and Sydney share illustrious fame,
  And many a fair field boasts an honoured name,
But one and all they yield the palm to you;
Here stands the old headquarters, here's the hub,
The home and habitation of The Club,
Where, without raising smiles,
Men still may watch the game in shiny tiles
And sit in grave black-coats the whole day long.
(*Umpires, call softly till I end my song!*)

C.L.M.
10.7.1929

=|●|●|=

'A. W. Carr, in a lounge suite and wearing a soft felt hat, bowled two deliveries.' – *Birmingham Paper*

In thus risking damage to the suite Mr Carr set an example which is likely to have disastrous consequences in many a young batsman's home.

4.6.1930

=|●|●|=

At Lord's: June 28, 3 pm

Sing a song of Woodfull,
  Wiping England's eye;
Thirty-thousand people
  'Neath a baking sky;
When 'Boy' Bradman opened
  The ball began to sing;
Wasn't that a dainty dish
  To set before the King?

9.7.1930

=|●|●|=

Hot Stuff

'In a one-day cricket match the Delhi City Gymkhana beat the Hindu College today by 2 wickets and 64 runs at the College ground. The feature of the game was deadly bowling by Tajammul Hussain, who captured 6 wickets for 19 who was unbeaten with 59 runs. runs only and fine batting by Abid.
    The Delhi City Gymkhana replied with 142 runs for 8 wickets.
    At least 90 Japanese planes and 3 coastal cargo vessels were also destroyed.' – *Indian Paper*

24.1.1945

=|●|●|=

Bodyline Again

'Banerjee taking the new ball at 221 bowled Young three runs later with a beautiful delivery that appeared to break his back.' – *Indian paper*

29.5.1946

DIRTY WORK AT LORD'S.

Aunt (whose nephew has been caught at silly point). "I'm told they put a man in a special
place on purpose to catch Reggie. I don't call that fair, do you?"

Ballade of a Day at Lord's

This is the season when within my breast
  A wild and wilful wanderlust awakes;
Nor will it go to sleep at my behest,
  No more than would that sword of William Blake's
  Sleep in his hand. Most bitterly it aches;
They are light sleepers, wanderlusts and swords.
  I cannot stand the way it heaves and quakes;
I think I'll go and spend the day at Lord's.

This is the season when the golden West
  Seems more than golden; when the youth forsakes
His parents' dwelling, as the bird his nest,
  And through the world his wandering journey makes.
  This is the season when the poet takes
What holiday his slender purse affords;
  I may not fly to the Italian Lakes –
I think I'll go and spend the day at Lord's.

By these low ceilings I am sore oppressed;
  The blistered paint is peeling off in flakes.
The woods and fields are in full foliage dressed;
  Far, far from here the Adriatic breaks
  In a warm bay; the stately cypress shakes
Her swaying head above Illyrian swards
  Where serving-maidens carry wine and cakes . . .
I think I'll go and spend the day at Lord's.

Prince, *you* may go and take the cure at Aix,
Luxuriously cruise about the fjords
  Or coarsely stuff yourself with Irish steaks . . .
I think *I'll* go and spend the day at Lord's.

R. P. Lister
20.6.1951

The Nets at Lord's

'Having provided the young cricketer with the requisite preliminaries to prepare him for playing the game, also with a code of the laws, the next step will be to give him the result of more than fifty years' experience and actual practice amongst the finest players the country ever saw.' So wrote John Nyren, patriarch of all cricket coaches, in his retirement not so very far from Lord's. His benevolent old shade has only a short flight to see his advice yearly translated into reality, a hundred and twenty years later, at the Lord's Easter classes for schoolboys.

The classes were started soon after the first war by Mr Francis Lacey, as he then was, secretary of the MCC. As with many other flourishing projects the start was modest enough and the ground staff was more than adequate to deal with the few boys who attended. But the idea soon caught on and by the beginning of the second war about two hundred boys came daily. The arrangements for the pupils were simple, each batting for half an hour and bowling and fielding for a spell, if so inclined. The only scientific aid at this time was a contrivance invented, I believe, by Mr Lacey and in the nature of a cricketing 'Iron Maiden of Nuremberg'. This, by means of iron bars, confined the back lift of the bat to a strict, not to say restricted, and narrow path, which can seldom have coincided with that of the ball. Otherwise technical problems were solved on the spot by the wisdom and

experience of the staff. There was, for instance, a lad who had every apparent promise yet was clearly unable to fulfil it. A profound study of this baffling state of affairs by Messrs Findlay and Aird, by then Secretary and Assistant, failed to produce a satisfactory answer, so they sought the guidance of that Lancastrian Solomon, Mr Archie MacLaren. After a searching two-minute scrutiny the Oracle pronounced. 'This boy,' he said, 'is a left- not a right-hander.' The subject being rotated on his axis and re-orientated accordingly, was immediately and immensely improved.

Another Lancastrian giant, Mr Walter Brierley, conducted a bowling class, and was to be seen daily striding breast-forward across the ground, a stalwart pied piper, his charges trotting expectantly behind him. What they learned of the 'basic action' I wouldn't know, but they could not fail to see many a spirited demonstration nor hear tell of many a doughty deed. With luck they might even have been given, by way of illustration of their tutor's pristine pace, the alarming instance of the batsman whose boot he struck with such violence that 'You could see *blud coom through bookskin*.' If any pupil acquired no more than Walter's enthusiasm he deserved to play for England.

There was an equally devoted volunteer in a certain Mr Routledge, a schoolmaster from Salop who spent his holidays supervising the nets. As he visited all fifteen in the course of each half hour every day, it is a conservative guess that he walked a distance from Lord's to Bramall Lane and back again every vacation.

The age-groups lay between eleven and seventeen and, naturally, within these margins there was much variation in shape and size. Readers of my generation may recall a young man named Hunter, a somewhat remarkable figure in the Metropolitan Police Force and later the RAF. He boxed for England against Golden Gloves' team from America at 6 foot 10 inches, and something over nineteen stone. When he came to the Easter classes, aged fourteen, he was some inches over six feet and a good head and shoulders above his coach, the redoubtable Bill Reeves. It was not unnatural that Mr Aird, on his rounds, should pause in wonderment at the spectacle of this mountainous figure towering above all about. His fears of optical delusion were abated by Old Bill, who paused in the act of delivering the next ball. 'It's all right, sir,' he explained. 'The boy's queer – Dad's come instead.'

They were, as perhaps one may gather, happy carefree days and no doubt highly beneficial in many cases. The same easy system prevailed for some years after the war, but recently the arrangements have been thoroughly overhauled and, in popular parlance, 'streamlined' . . .

Ian Peebles
30.3.1958

CHAPTER THREE

Political Cricket

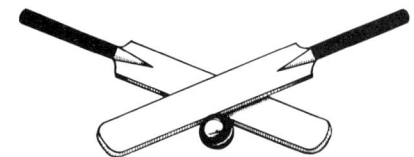

Parliament in Sport
Or, A Meeting in Earnest

('Perhaps the popularity of the competition in national sport between the different parts of the Empire is worthy of the serious attention of statesmen . . . Mr Astley Cooper proposes rowing, running and cricket . . . There is something fascinating in the idea of such a Pan-Britannic gathering.' – *Daily Paper*)

The Speaker, having taken his seat in the pavilion, the Minister for Cricket rose to move the third reading of The Six-balls-to-an-over Bill.

The Right Hon. Gentleman said that the amount of time wasted in changing sides, although the field did their best to minimise the loss by assuming a couple of positions alternately, was very serious – especially in a first-class match.

The Member for Melbourne begged to ask what *was* a first-class match?

The Member for Sydney replied, certainly not a match between Canada and Victoria. (*Laughter*). Now everyone was aware that New South Wales – ('*Question! Order! Order!*') He begged pardon, he was in order.

The Speaker: I really must request silence. The Minister for Cricket is introducing a most important measure, and the least we can do is to receive his statement with adequate attention. (*General cheering.*)

The Minister for Cricket continued, and said that the measure he had the honour to commend to their careful consideration would not only lengthen the over, but also allow cricket to be played all the year round.

The Minister for Football begged to remind his Right Hon. friend that he had promised to consider that matter in committee. What would become of football were cricket to be played continuously? (*'Hear, hear!'*)

The Member for Bombay thought that a matter of no moment. In India polo was of infinitely more importance than football, and he could not help remarking that, in the Imperial Parliament, representing so many sports, and so many colonies, where every great interest was represented, and well represented, polo was absolutely ignored. (*Cheers.*)

The Minister for Aquatic Sports agreed with the hon. Member. Polo was entirely of sufficient interest to warrant the creation of a special department for its guardianship. But at present he was responsible for it. He hoped soon to be able to make welcome a colleague who would make its interests his continual study. (*'Hear, hear!'*)

The Minister for Cricket concluded by thanking the House for the attention the hon. Members had given to the subject, and sat down amidst loud applause.

A division being taken, the Bill was carried by 127 to 96. The majority were composed of Australians and Canadians, and the minority were Africans, Indians, and miscellaneous colonists. The House then adjourned.

6.2.1892

"ALL ENGLAND!"

Captain John Bull (to his "Confederates"). "Ah, my Boys, with such a Team
we'll hold our own against the World!"

Ins and Outs

'Cricket was a far superior game to golf or tennis,' said Lord Knutsford to the members of the Victoria Park Cricket Association; and he went on to tell a story of the first introduction of cricket to Tonga, one of the Pacific Islands. Everybody took up the game so heartily that state affairs were allowed to slide altogether, and at last the King of Tonga had to lay down rules as to the times when the game might be indulged in. 'Even then the Prime Minister was with difficulty prevented from bowling during forbidden hours.' For Tonga read Westminster – where a good deal of *tongue* – ah! – goes on – and we get a result something like this:

'After the usual luncheon interval, the Leader of the Opposition and the ex-Umpire-General faced the delivery of the First Com-

missioner of Stumps and the Scorin' Secretary. The punishment inflicted by the
former on the bowling led to a Cabinet crisis,
ending in the Secretary of State resigning his
office and the leather to the Lord High
Wicket-keep. The result of this change was
soon apparent, for the Leader of the Opposition was clean bowled by a quotation from
Hansard, and his place was taken by a prominent member from below the Opposition
gangway.

'As the score still mounted, the Ministry
decided to apply the closure to the game, an
effort which was resisted by the whole force of
the Opposition, armed with pads and wickets.
During the all-night innings which ensued the
Prime Minister retired hurt, and the Ministry
were finally driven into the pavilion, where
they expressed a decided intention, in consequence of the underhand bowling of their
opponents, of at once appealing to the
country. The Committee of Lord's has placed
its veto on these disorderly proceedings, and
'Down with the Lords' is likely to be the
ministerial rallying-cry during the forth-
coming election.'

3.11.1894

–|●|●|–

The Cricket Crank

Tell me not of Boxer's fables,
  Of the Empress – do not speak.
Summarise the Chinese cables
  Say, once every other week.
    Meanwhile let me, please, peruse
    Every scrap of cricket news.

Does the Boer War still continue?
  Are De Wet and Botha free?
Is 'Bobs' straining every sinew? –
  Oh! that doesn't interest me.
    But minutely tell me o'er
    Every first-class cricket score.

Read me not the turgid speeches
  Of the eloquent MP.
Doubtless he some moral teaches,
  But he only wearies me.
    Tell me then, again, how Storer
    Made his twenty-second fourer.

Crowd the Hospital Enquiry,
  And the leaders dull and solemn,
Court News, and My Social Diary
  Into less than half a column.
    But with every detail tell
    How the Surrey wickets fell.

Is the Empire's glory waning?
  Is our downfall drawing near?
Are our volunteers complaining?
  I have not the least idea!
    But I'm pretty certain that
    Ranji is a clinking bat.

15.8.1900

–|●|●|–

Disbatment; or Some Fun for the Future

Football and hockey, to mention but two of
the famous outlets for rivalry invented by
England, have long been adopted by the Continent, and it cannot be many years now before
the patent on cricket expires too, when Greece
will be challenging Portugal to a Test Match
and Poland will be selecting its eleven to vie
with Spain. Such a consideration has given me
solemnly to think, for with the definitely bel-
ligerent nature that the summer game is now
assuming and the political aspects that appear
to be involved, governments of the future will
undoubtedly have to take a hand, if not a bat;
and it is extremely likely that strong measures
will be needed to secure peace in Europe.
England of course will take the lead; and if
things progress in the manner that they
threaten to it is more than probable that discussions such as the following will frequently
be heard in the House – or the pavilion, as the
House may then be called.

Mr Halma (Soc.): I should like to ask the
Secretary for Foreign Affairs to define a little
more clearly than he has done hitherto the
attitude of this country towards disbatment. Is
the House aware that large orders have just
been placed with Messrs Armstrong-Willows
and other bat manufacturers in direct con-
travention of the Hobbs-Mussolini Plan of
1940?

*Sir F. Woolley (Secretary for Foreign
Affairs)*: The hon. Member seems to be a little
confused. There is nothing in the Hobbs-

THE POLITICAL LADY-CRICKETERS.

Lady Cricketer. "A TEAM OF OUR OWN? I SHOULD THINK SO! IF WE'RE GOOD ENOUGH TO SCOUT FOR YOU, WHY SHOULDN'T WE TAKE A TURN AT THE BAT!"

Lord's and Commons

('Michael Foster . . . was a capital cricketer. He
kept wicket for the first eleven, and (for his age) he
was a wonderfully good bat as well. Most cricketers
will, of course, therefore vote for him. No better
candidate could possible be found.' – 'LLB, BA,
Lond.' in *The Times*.)

O graduates of London, you will all, I hope agree
That Foster is the very man to make our new MP,
For he has played at cricket, and the House of Commons floor
Is just the place, *par excellence*, for people who can score.

Although a man of centuries, he still is far from old,
And though he's bowled his overs, he is never over-bold,
And though we cannot claim that he has never had a match,
It's quite beyond contention that he'd prove a brilliant catch.

He's been a wicket-keeper, and we naturally jump
To the obvious conclusion that he's just the man to stump;
He also is a famous bat, and you will all admit
The man who hits a boundary is bound to make a hit.

And if you would object that he's the last to come upon
The scene of this election, we reply, he's been long on;
In short our gallant cricketer is going in to win,
And though he may have been run out, we mean to run him in.

31.1.1900

Mussolini Plan that forbids this country placing large orders with Messrs Armstrong-Willows or any other firm. The Plan was an agreement whereby England undertook not to pile up bats in excess of the requirements necessary to defend her wickets against possible foreign aggression. (*Nat. C. cheers.*)

Mr Halma: My point is that the required level has already been reached, and that in placing these orders we are not only impoverishing the country in order to put money into the pockets of unscrupulous bat firms who waxed fat on the last Test, but we are encouraging the other nations to bat to an extent that is inevitably conducive to an outbreak of hostilities.

Sir F. Woolley: Encouraging? They need no encouraging. That is the whole point. Is the hon. Member not aware that Germany has already re-batted to such a degree since the Hobbs-Mussolini Plan that the playing-fields of France are no longer safe from menace? Is

he not aware that the Soviet States of Russia have no fewer than ten thousand bats along the international boundary-line? Does he not know that the Czechoslovakian Cricket Office have already broken the Woodfull-Masaryk Pact by issuing body-line bowling booklets to all their crack elevens? Does he not know that Poland is batted to the teeth? Has he not heard that Spain is issuing an ultimatum to Denmark demanding matches to be played to a finish? The dogs of cricket, I would remind the hon. Member, are easily let loose. Europe may soon be at the crease. It gives me no great pleasure to say it, but there are Tests and rumours of Tests.

Mr Ludo (Lib.): I would like to know what concern that is of ours. This country has no wish to see its sons lie bruised and battered in some corner of a foreign cricket-field – sacrificed to the flannelled folly of unthinking Europe. (*Loud Lib. and Soc. cheers.*)

Captain B. H. Lyon (Nat. C.): May I

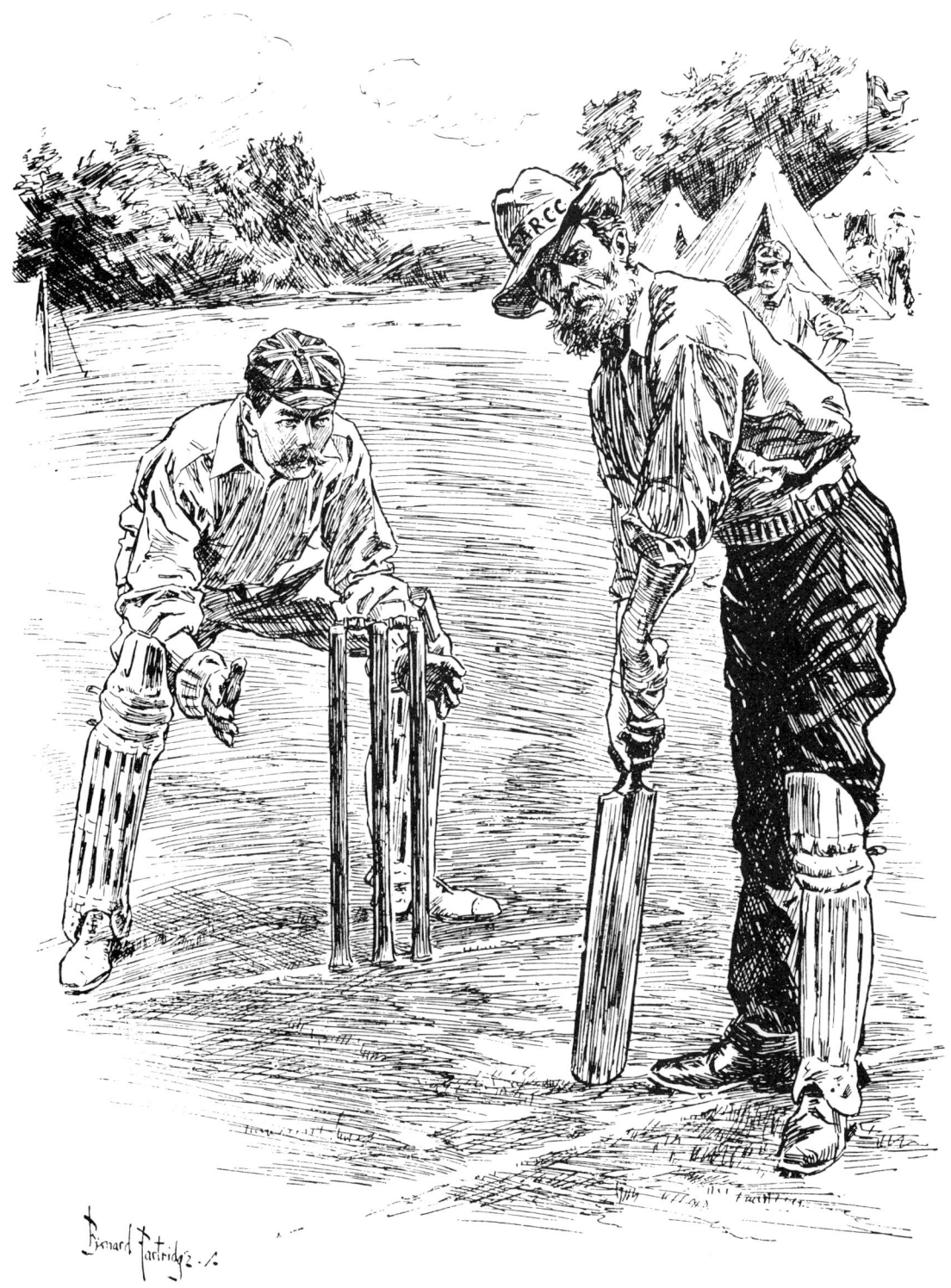

THE LAST WICKET.

Kitchener (Captain and Wicket-keeper). "HE HAS KEPT US IN THE FIELD A DEUCE OF A TIME; BUT WE'LL GET HIM NOW WE'VE CLOSED IN FOR CATCHES!"

remind the hon. Member that in the event of Germany declaring cricket on France we are pledged under the Hammond-Lebrun Agreement to send a reserve wicket-keeper and at least one fast bowler --

Mr Ludo (heatedly): The Hammond-Lebrun Agreement was a scandal and the sooner it is repudiated the better. I know your sort. You're a Test-monger. You won't be happy till the entanglement of foreign alliances has brought the flower of this country's manhood to the wicket once again!

Captain P. Fender (Nat. C.): Cricket is to a man what childbirth is to a woman!

Mr Halma: What! Can the hon. Member say that? And within a few years of the last Test, which was to be a Test to end Tests! Has he forgotten the long-drawn-out misery of those days, the hideous uncertainty of the country's fate, the pitiful questing for the slightest hint of better news, the torturing fears that some of our loved ones might be killed or hit at any moment? Has he forgotten the so-called victory – a victory that was ashes in the mouth? *(Laughter and Soc. cheers.)*

Sir F. Woolley: Hon. Members are wandering a little from the point. I certainly dissociate myself from the views held in some quarters that cricket is necessary and inevitable, and as a member of the last Expeditionary Eleven – the Old Detestables – I emphatically have no wish to renew its horrors. Nevertheless we are

BROTHERS-IN-PADS.

British Lion (to Kangaroo). "HERE'S YOUR HEALTH! YOU'RE GOOD ALL ROUND. YOU HELPED US ON THE VELD, AND YOU'VE BEATEN US IN THE FIELD!"

WINSTON AT THE NETS (QUESTION TIME).
The more bowling he gets the better he likes it.

TRENCH CRICKET ON THE SANDS. THE
RICOCHET FROM THE SIDES INTRODUCES A
COMPLETELY NEW ELEMENT INTO THE GAME.

Wicket-keeper (Mr. CASSEL). "How's that?"
Umpire (Mr. SPEAKER). "Out!"
Batsman (Mr. LLOYD GEORGE). "Rotten antiquated rule!"

["I did not expect . . . that hon. members would go rummaging in the dustbins of ancient precedent to find obstacles to place in the way of these proposals."—*Mr. LLOYD GEORGE on his Budget.*]

Extract from Hun airman's report. "WE DROPPED BOMBS ON A BRITISH FORMATION, CAUSING THE TROOPS TO DISPERSE AND RUN ABOUT IN A PANIC-STRICKEN MANNER."

THE "LEAGUE THEORY."
MR. PUNCH "COME ALONG,
LET'S REFER THIS LITTLE SQUABBLE TO GENEVA."

not always masters of our own destinies. And with regard to the Hammond-Lebrun Agreement, hon. Members should not forget that the clause in question is reciprocal. We are, as I have indicated, heavily out-batted by several of our European neighbours, and supposing Germany, for instance, were to force cricket with us on these shores, might we not be only too glad to take advantage of the French nurseries?

Mr Halma: No! Let England fight her own battles.

Sir F. Woolley: Ah! And will the hon. Member tell me what with? He complains about the orders for new bats and then says, 'Let England fight her own battles.'

Mr Ludo: He meant –

Captain Fender: Cricket is bound to break out –

Mr Halma: I said –

Captain Lyon: In the event of cricket –

The Speaker: Order, please, order! Once again I must remind hon. Members that it is not in accordance with House etiquette to behave in this fashion. Hon. Members must not stand up and interrupt each other in this manner. It simply isn't cric – warfare.

Mr Halma: I should like to ask the Secretary for Foreign Affairs to define a little more clearly . . .

And so on all over again for the benefit of late-comers.

15.8.1934

–|●|●|–

Gentlemen and Players

Between now and the middle of September, when all the solemn things like county championships and League and university matches are fading out, will come all the best cricket.

THE SPIRIT OF THE GAME.
"SO LONG AS I CAN ALWAYS ELIMINATE ANY KIND OF BOWLING I DON'T LIKE THERE OUGHT TO BE NO DIFFICULTY ABOUT CONTINUING THESE FIXTURES FOR EVER AND EVER."

Even Lord's relapses into lovely fixtures between London clergy and Southwark clergy, and all over the country there will be those delightful affairs like Thirteen of Poppleton *v.* Mr Snook's XI, Actors *v.* Plumbers, and Decree Nisi Divorced *v.* Decree Absolute Divorced.

Pleasant as they are, however, I have always felt that from the point of view of the spectator fixtures of this kind tend to be a wee bit disappointing, conjuring up visions which they hardly fulfil. Somebody-or-Other *v.* Jockeys is always quite fun, because jockeys are always small enough for one to *see* that they are jockeys. But for the rest, one would never know that the sides were not just ordinary teams. I defy anyone to say without being told whether the team in the field on these occasions is Lords or Commons or Musicians or Married or Single. They just look like eleven ordinary men in flannels; or, in the case of Married *v.* Single, five men in flannels and six in braces. Teams of Plumbers hasten to the wicket with a complete outfit of gloves, pads and bat. Teams of Mayors and Corporations never interrupt the game to argue about the batting order. Mental Hospitals beat their

opponents by clever declarations at exactly the right moment. Even a team of pawnbrokers which I once saw had so little pride of craft that they played with a single ball and an unenclosed popping-crease. I myself have kept wicket with Mr Ralph Straus and Sir John Squire batting, and would one have realised that the cream of English criticism was performing? One would not. One might have been made faintly suspicious by their tendency to form conclusions about a fast ball by giving it a mere cursory glance, but that was all.

It seems to me that there are two factors which contribute to this disappointingly ordinary effect:

(1) So often representative teams consist of people who are notable cricketers, but not particularly notable Lords or Commons or Actors or what not. It is rare to find such combinations of cricket and critic as Sir John Squire and Mr Straus. Take as a simple example the Lords and Commons. One visualises the well-coached Etonian style of Mr Eden batting on a wicket affected by storms; the long, loose-limbed action and fiery delivery of Mr Maxton; a fighting innings

Mr Aneurin Bevan demonstrating his love for Sir Walter Monckton.

against the clock by Mr Herbert; and constant ringing cries of 'Hozzat?' from a few Lords of Appeal. One visualises Mr Gallacher insisting on coming out of the professionals' entrance and on being referred to as Gallacher (W). One even hopes for some historic score card as –

N. Chamberlain .... not out 337
A. Eden st Churchill b Dalton 50
Earl Baldwin .... retired 70
J. R. MacDonald .... hit wicket 5
Gallacher (W) .... run out* 0
Sir S. Cripps .... not out 0
C. R. Attlee .... c&b Simon 10
D. Lloyd George .... lbw b Brown† 0

The Archbishop of Canterbury, G. Lansbury and A. N. Other abstained from batting.

Supplementary estimates, £2,000,000

Majority 273

* Result of a rash call.
† Out for obstruction. A *very* loud appeal.

But what do we get in fact? Why, simply the old Jones-caught-Bones-bowled-Lones stuff. A team consisting of one man who one has heard of vaguely and ten of whom one has never heard at all. I do not doubt that the people who play for the Lords and Commons *are* Lords and Commons, but I do emphatically deny that they are the best team one could get from a box-office point of view.

(2) People who play for representative sides always seem to be slightly ashamed of their professions and to concentrate on playing the game quite normally, instead of realising that their sole *raison d'être* as a cricket team is that they are not in fact normal. Personally I resent this intensely. I yield to no one in my love of cricket, but I do dislike seeing all the colour and glamour of the Bench and Bar, or the Dumpshire Hunt, or the Inland Revenue Department submerged beneath the sober and uniform white of a rather bad cricket team.

It is therefore with pleasure, slightly mixed with misgiving, that I note that there is to be a match between a company of actors of Shakespeare and a company of actors of Shaw. Surely it is not too much to hope that these sides at least will realise what the public has a right to expect from them? As a member of the cricket-loving and stage-loving public, I ask that this match shall be given a chance to fulfil its magnificent possibilities. Let both sides be cast. Let there be no question of that ordinary-looking white-flannelled figure being 'Mr So-and-so who plays Hamlet', but let him *play* playing Hamlet. After all, people have written books about the psychoanalyses of Hamlet and Othello. Surely a first-rate actor, a man who was really inside his part, could give an interesting reading of Characters in the Cricket-field? Hamlet – a good player in constant practice but undecided about when to declare the innings closed.

25.8.1937

‒|◦|◦|‒

If Cricket Were War

The MCC has disclosed that the Test Match between England and Euthasia is now in its second day. The English team left for their destination somewhere in the Pacific early last week. All have arrived safely. No further information is available. – *BBC*

Our team is in the field. They are prepared to defend the honour of their country. Their prospect of victory is better than ever before. Yet the boastful Britons have not arrived. Do not believe the stories Mr Fry tells you. The glorious innings of your batsmen exist only in his fertile imagination. Where is your English team? Ask your Mr Fry. – *Euthasian Radio*

It is not yet officially confirmed whether England is batting or not. It is learnt from unofficial sources that our opening pair is in. Reports from non-playing countries estimate the score at totals varying from 15 to 300 for no wicket. – *BBC*

The greatest feat in the history of Test cricket has been achieved. Despite subversive criticism and attempted sabotage the whole team, with its reserves and scorer, has been transported safely to its destination without the loss of a single pad. Under the captaincy of a non-playing amateur such unity of purpose and complete accord has been reached between amateurs and professionals at the outset of the struggle as was not established until the later stages of the last Test. In this spirit of co-operation the English team are determined to the last man to see it through – *Speech by the Minister for Overseas Cricket*

We have no quarrel with Yorkshire. Our struggle is with England and to that we will devote our last bail. We have no intention of allowing one small section of our country to fight our battles for us. Let England and Mr Fry shelter behind the Yorkshire players. We, the whole of the Euthasian nation, take the field shoulder to shoulder. – *Euthasian Radio*

"*Never mind the Commonwealth Conference. Go in and knock hell out of 'em.*"

The Ministry of Cricket Information now states that England are batting. Our opening pair have stood at the crease for two days and have now scored 23. This is in accordance with a predetermined plan. The Euthasian wireless claims that their bowlers have mastered the batsmen. – *BBC*

Our batsmen will break their hearts. – *C. B. Fry*

Your great batsman, Hammond, is out for a duck. There remain only two wickets to fall and the score is 91. We congratulate you. Our Leader, in a speech to his mate, praised their skill and daring. 'Whatever tactics the English may adopt in the field,' he said, 'Euthasia knows the rules of fair play. Victory is assured.' – *Euthasian Radio*

Hammond, interviewed in his home today, where he is recovering from the accident that kept him out of the England side, made the following comment. 'My lips are sealed. But you are at liberty to judge for yourself as to whether or not I am at present batting for England.' – *Daily Paper*

The Euthasian Leader has proclaimed that there will be fair play, that victory will be theirs. The monstrous incongruity of the two statements is manifest. We may expect a venomous attack on our batsmen of unparalleled atrocity. Already there is talk of a mechanised outfield. Be sure that it is fact. In the baffled brains of their bowlers other more staggering assaults on the ideals of sportsmanship will doubtless be conceived. Nothing but the grimmest determination of our batting and bowling forces will serve to frustrate for all time this threat to our supremacy. – *J. L. G****n*

ENGLAND	ENGLAND
678	ALL OUT
ALL OUT	87
OFFICIAL	OFFICIAL

Reports continue to arrive from non-playing sources of the desperate tactics to which the Euthasian team has already had recourse.

AFRICAN TEST

"Never mind about the ball—let's get on with the game!"

Fielders are said to be carrying spare balls and bowlers to be throwing the ball without comment from the umpires. It is reported that barracking of the Euthasian team by their own supporters is on the increase. – *BBC*

Despite the rain which your Mr Fry caused to fall during the Euthasian innings, our batsmen piled up a huge score in honour of their country. Against our lightning strokes the bowlers were helpless. The English batsmen are now facing an enormous deficit and have already lost three wickets for a trifling score. Typical of the lies broadcast to the trusting English public is the allegation that our Leader, under various guises, was our whole batting side. There is one thing that impresses us about this ridiculous falsehood: it shows an unconscious recognition of our Leader's greatness – *Euthasian Radio*

It is generally known that facts do not agree with the English. A daily dose of them should be made compulsory, but we cannot depend on our newspapers for that. I have been injecting the English public with facts for half a century with very little evidence of success. In this case they are clear. We are in danger of losing a game which it has hitherto been our privilege to win. Instantly we are full of the most horrid accusations of foul play. This is not playing the game, it is playing the fool, both of which incidentally are national attributes. What is the relative importance of winning or losing a game? If it is a matter of national prestige, then by all means let us at once mobilise our Navy, our Army and our Air Force. It must be brought home to these Euthasians that we are a nation of sportsmen. – *G. B. S**w*

Listeners will already have heard from our earlier news bulletins that England won the Test Match with Euthasia by one wicket after an exciting last day in which the issue was always in doubt. The first full report of the match will be given in our nine o'clock news. Meanwhile the return of the English team was announced today. The captain, interviewed on his arrival, paid a tribute to the sportsmanship of the Euthasian team. 'We are glad to have won,' he said 'and are looking forward to meeting the great Euthasian team over here next summer.' – *BBC*

20.12.1939

Dover Cricket

Here within sight of the cliffs of Calais,
   butterflies out and summer come,
to shake the Hun in his white sea chalet
   are lads from Gloucestershire, chaps from Brum.

Green grass again and the English faces,
   ball on bat as the shadows fall,
and cricketers come from a score of places,
   soldiers and sailormen, comrades all.

Englishmen over the world remember
   what rise of heart the May month brings,
and the long June days till soft September,
   and are one for cricket – and other things.

2.6.1943

CHAPTER FOUR

Feminine Focus

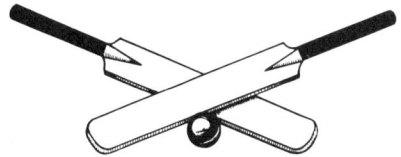

The Cricket Essayist Looks at Women's Cricket

How shall we write of these women, brothers?
 Cricketers, just like men, be they;
Shall we not, as we do for others,
 Make pure gold of the game they play,
In prose as rich as the lime that smothers
 Yellow dust on the summer's day?

Say, shall we strike at the very heart of
 Cricket's mystery? Shall we show
How the flickering figures are but part of
 Something greater, deep and slow,
Slow as time, and deep as the art of
 Life where the age-long graces grow?

No, my brothers, we cannot do it;
 And not the women or we to blame
It's just, well, just as we always knew it;
 Women's cricket isn't the same.
Let 'em play like a book – and they can do too – it
 Won't be cricket. Only a game.

Ande
15.9.1954

–|●|●|–

A WOMAN'S IDEA OF CRICKET (AND OF ARGU-
MENT): The same thing over and over again.

10.5.1873

–|●|●|–

The Martyr of Cricket

'In this case (of breach of promise) £2000 damages
were awarded. The only reason the gentleman
could give for breaking his engagement, was that
the lady did not take any interest in cricket.' –
Liverpool Assizes: Law Report: Stevenson v. *Eccles*

'Not care who bat, or bowl, or field!'
 Growled Eccles to his conscious pillow,
'I'll teach the maid, who will not *wield*,
 That she instead must *wear*, the willow.'

But Miss to lose this Lord demurs,
 Who for Lord's pastime disregarded her;
And so twelve anti-cricketers
 Two thousand damages awarded her!

With tears of pride, Elevens, beweep
 This mulcted martyr to the game:
His memory, like your wickets, keep,
 Oval and Lord's – his earliest flame!

In wives may he yet make a catch –
 Find some *Grace* worthy of his worth –
And when found, may they play a match
 For life, of Cricket on the Hearth!

25.4.1874

–|●|●|–

'Very ungallant,' quoth Mrs R. 'The other
afternoon a well-known cricketer, whose
name,' said Mrs R. indignantly, 'ought to be
made public, actually, as I am informed,
bowled a maiden over, and never picked her up
or apologised!'

1.7.1893

–|●|●|–

The Eton and Harrow Match

(Her Account of It)
Good 'Lord', how changed is all the place!
 That 'Mound' is simply hideous,
Compared – ah, well, I'd best efface
 Comparisons invidious.

CRICKETANA. YOUNG LADIES V. BOYS.

Fair Batter (*ætat.* 18). "Now, just look here, Algy Jones—none of your Patronage! You *dare* to Bowl to me with your Left Hand again, and I'll Box your Ears!"

The saying that 'old things are best',
    A simple truth expresses –
The saying, though, must not be pressed
    In case of hats and dresses.

Still, some with joy the Mound may hail,
    Keen folks who watch the cricket,
Can place the field – as 'Point', 'Leg bail',
    'Long block-hole', 'Cover wicket';

Who dearly love a 'pull to off ',
    Applaud the 'short-pitched Yorkers';
Who jibe at fashion-students, scoff
    At carriage knife-and-forkers!

The X's carriage, by the way,
    (A very ancient queer shay)
I patronised the second day –
    Their lunch was most *recherché*.

I sat some time in Walter's box,
    The place resembled Babel,
And Mabel bored me with her frocks,
    Whilst I – had tea with Mabel.

Love of good things, it may be, tends
    Towards the minor vices –
I own I *did* draw several friends
    For strawberries and ices.

I sauntered, gossiped, lunched and teaed,
    And flirted – or the men did,
Or one did, anyhow! What need
    To say the match was *splendid*?

The cricket? – *That* I can't recall.
    Who cares which side was beaten?
I've only harrowing thoughts of all
    The strawberries I've eaten!

(*His Account of Her*)
A pretty chatterbox! She said
    She loved the game – a sure sign
She is not truthful, I'm afraid.
    Her appetite was porcine!

26.7.1899

He (as the hope of the team goes in). "AH! NOW WE HAVE A CHANCE IF HE CAN ONLY GET SOMEONE TO STAY WITH HIM."
She. "IS HE AS DISAGREEABLE AS ALL THAT?"

Not Cricket

The attempt of the suffragettes last Thursday to seize a pitch for themselves at the Oval was frustrated, stump oratory being no part of the programme for Hayes's benefit. Anti-suffragists, on the other hand, were allowed to enter and get wet. They were distinguished by brooches bearing the initials LBW ('Let's Be Women').

22.7.1908

=|●|●|=

The Eleventh Man
A Cricket Romance

'Marry a man who lives for Ludo?' exclaimed Geraldine. 'Never! A cricketer or nobody for me. You may ask me again when – '

'When I have played cricket for the county?' said Roderick.

'Exactly,' said Geraldine. 'But how did you guess?'

'I know a magazine situation when I meet one,' replied Roderick. 'You shall hear from me in due course. Till then good-bye.'

Roderick was not a cricketer – never had been – but the notion intrigued him strangely. The county – dear old Rutland! . . . He went straight to the Free Library, took out a book on cricket, and, after looking at the pictures, decided to be a bowler.

That was in April. First Roderick mugged up theory. By the middle of May he could draw a sketch plan of a long-hop, with dotted lines and footnotes. Then, early in June, he took a ball into his hand. He practised in all his spare time from sunrise to sunset. His muscles hardened and his face became sun-tanned. Sometimes he practised by moonlight, but the effect upon his complexion was negligible.

Meanwhile, chaperoned by her Aunt Minnie, Geraldine followed the Rutland eleven everywhere. One day, while she was at

"'TIS NOT IN MORTALS TO COMMAND SUCCESS."

Paterfamilias (who has failed to score in the Half-Term "Father's Match").
"These things *will* happen, little girl, no matter how we try."
More or Less Dutiful Daughter. "Well, I hope you'll say the same
when you get a very bad report about me at the end of the term."

OUR SCHOOL-GIRLS.

Anxious Daughter (to parent playing in the Fathers' match). "DON'T FORGET, FATHER, TO STAND *WELL* IN FRONT OF THE WICKET,
BECAUSE IF YOU GET OUT FOR A DUCK *LEG BEFORE* IT WON'T LOOK *QUITE* SO BAD ON THE SCORE-BOOK!"

Appleby for the Westmorland match, the postman brought her a card saying just this: 'Bank Holiday – Huntingdon – Be there!'

Roderick's handwriting! Of course she was there. So was Roderick. But I anticipate.

There was a man named Spallow – Stephen Spallow – who played for Rutland. He was a fast bowler, the fastest in all Rutland. Roderick chose Spallow as the man in whose place he would play against Huntingdon. I'd hardly like to say how he managed it, but all's fair in love and war.

He got in touch with Spallow's housekeeper and found that money lured her. To be exact, five pounds lured her.

So on the day of the match, when Spallow got up in plenty of time to cycle to Oakham to catch the Huntingdon express, he was thrown into a violent rage by the disappearance of his match-trousers, which he put under the mattress to press, as he always did, being very careful of his turn-out.

'Where's my practice pair?' he snapped.

'Not back from the wash, sir,' said the housekeeper.

Spallow snorted, just as he did when a batsman swept him through the slips for six.

'Wear the grey, sir,' suggested the hypocritical housekeeper.

'Don't be futile,' barked Spallow. 'You know Rutland always play in white. Go and buy me another pair.'

'Bank Holiday, sir; shops shut,' said the housekeeper.

'Curse!' said Spallow, who was really of a rather petulant nature. 'Well, I shan't be able to play for the county today, that's all.'

And he went back to bed.

At Huntingdon, as mid-day drew near, the Rutland captain was in a state of panic. No Spallow! – and Huntingdon wouldn't hear of playing ten-a-side.

'Where shall I ever find an eleventh man?' he wailed.

'Here – Rutland born and bred,' said a fresh young voice at his elbow, or rather higher, for Roderick was no dwarf.

Roderick looked every inch a cricketer. He wore white twill trousers with permanent turn-ups, spotless canvas shoes, cream socks, a cellular shirt and a natty belt with tie to match. His hair was all crisply waving under his tri-coloured cap, and his face was, if anything, more bronzed than the captain's own. He had his sleeves rolled up, and in his right hand he carried a bright red ball, stamped 'Match' in gold letters. His left hand held his birth certificate, showing him to be a native of Rutland.

It was wonderful how he had thought of everything.

The captain scanned his birth certificate to see if it was forged.

Then 'Off with your cap,' he said.

Roderick obeyed, and the captain saw the crisply waving hair. This gave him faith in Roderick.

'You'll do. We field,' he said.

'What's your position?' growled the captain on the way out.

'Pupil to an auctioneer,' said Roderick politely.

'At cricket?' snarled the captain.

'Oh, long-stop, please,' said Roderick; 'but I'd rather bowl.'

'Got the right stuff in him,' muttered the captain. 'Perhaps you shall later,' he added gruffly but not unkindly.

Things went badly for poor old Rutland. When the score-board showed two hundred for no wickets, the captain threw one scathing glance at the bowler at the pavilion end and said, 'Here, let Westlake finish the over.'

There were three balls to go. Westlake was Roderick's surname.

Geraldine in her private box now recognised Roderick for the first time. She had never seen him in whites before. They were so different from his Ludo kit – purple velvet with buff piping.

Who will ever forget what followed? Roderick took all ten wickets with consecutive balls, and only an absurd convention stopped him from taking the eleventh as well.

The first man was out to a splendid full-pitch; the second hit right over a straight low sneak; the third was utterly deceived by Roderick's clever trick of bowling with the left hand after setting out with a right-hand action; the fourth – but you may read all about it on a

Nephew. "HE WOULDN'T HAVE BEEN OUT IF HE'D PLAYED WITH A STRAIGHT BAT."
Aunt. "THEN WHY ON EARTH DIDN'T SOMEBODY LEND HIM ONE?"

'Yes, darling?' she murmured.

'Geraldine,' he said, 'have I – have I bowled a maiden over?'

She laughed happily and nestled closer to him. 'Is that original?' she asked.

'No,' replied Roderick; 'but is anything ever original in these cricket stories?'

9.8.1922

–|●|●|–

'HINTS FOR YOUNG CRICKETERS. In the long field a smart spinster who can be trusted to cover twenty or thirty yards at a fast pace in order to save a boundary is necessary.' – *West Indian Magazine*

All the same we doubt whether the introduction of fast young women would be in the best interest of young cricketers.

25.7.1923

–|●|●|–

A Cricket Widow's Lament

O harbingers of household strife!
　　What thrice-accursed brood
First ushered cricket into life,
Condemning thus a happy wife
　　To annual widowhood?

No song from bath or dressing-room
　　Now makes the morning glad,
But unadulterated gloom
And breakfast silent as the tomb
　　If England's start is bad.

His lightest gastronomic wish
　　She seeks in vain to please;
Unchanged the flavour of each dish,
From Larwood, through the soup and fish,
　　To Bradman with the cheese.

In vain she schemes on Saturday
　　Such pleasant things to do –
A river picnic cool and gay,
The movies or a matinee,
　　Or even just the zoo.

But no, whatever be her mood,
　　She sits till shadows fall
On seats that outrage womanhood,
Watching a stupid piece of wood
　　Hitting a silly ball.

commemorative tablet in the smoking-room of the I Zingari Club.

As the tenth man was beaten to extinction by a deadly lob, bowled with both hands at once for the purpose of imparting double spin, a female figure lightly vaulted the rails, brushing aside silly-slip, who had been idly making daisy-chains against the boundary, having nothing better to do, and sped towards Roderick.

The reader is quite right. It was not Aunt Minnie; she was, as usual, asleep. It was Geraldine.

Presently the two were alone.

'Geraldine,' breathed Roderick.

"PITY YOUR BOY HIT HIS WICKET."   "RALPH WAS ALWAYS A PASSIONATE CHILD."

THE OLD GIRLS' MATCH.

Small Girl (in the School Team). "I KNEW THERE'D BE TROUBLE WHEN FATHER WAS ASKED TO UMPIRE. HE'S SO KEEN HE'S ALREADY NO-BALLED MOTHER TWICE."

Wife (encouragingly). "You take longer to get a duck than you used to, dear."

Up, wives, for poor old Hymen's sake,
    And, worm-like, let us turn!
The weapons of our torture take
And one gigantic bonfire make
    These vanities to burn.

Then, to the fiery spluttering
    Of bat and stump and bail,
A million wives will form a ring
And dance around and gaily sing
    The Swan-Song of the Male.

11.7.1934

—|●|●|—

Test Match Wife

Hubby acting funnily these days? Cleaning his shoes the night before, hearing the end of the news, getting sunburnt on a Friday? Then hubby is a cricket lover, and oh dear with these Test Matches that crop up every summer now!

But why not make the best of things and go in for being the Test Match Watcher's ideal helpmeet? It's a fascinating job calling for just that touch of expertise.

Should hubby be getting up early to join the queue, see that his 5 am breakfast is a jolly affair. Chat of the macs the children need, the Liberals' chances, dry rot, family allowances, anything to keep his mind off that old yesterday's paper and yours off putting the salt in the sandwiches. Be clever with sandwiches. Lots of slidey cucumber, and a big flat floppy packet that fits a briefcase and gets squashed flatter by the Thermos. Is he looking for the field-glasses he bought for the last Test series? Be a sport, lend them even if you do miss a rare garden bird or two. As for the special effort of a clean drip-dry shirt daily in case TV camera catches him, all that awful nightly cuffrubbing – what do you mean *special* effort?

Have a few looks at the TV during the day, then you can (a) tell him he could have watched better at home, (b) remark acidly on the number of men with time off on a weekday, (c) know when to start the potatoes for supper. It's when you see E. W. Swanton standing alone in the puddles.

If he does watch at home he'll want the homey atmosphere you can only provide by constantly popping in with the odd remark. Suggested remarks:

'The picture's a bit dim, shall I try?'

'Lunch! Nice and early and it won't keep hot!'

'Come on in children; if you keep quiet Daddy will *explain* cricket.'

Only got the wireless? Two hundred and fifty miles from the Test ground and no evening papers? Then, with the funny old dear so close to the set he can't miss a word, here's your chance to get out the sewing-machine!

Finally, just suppose he spends a Test Match day in the office and rushes home barking 'What was the close of play score?' Keep calm. Stick to facts. 'Someone had a century on the Third Programme then they all got out. Or the other way round and they got out first.'

That's what men mean by the 'glorious uncertainty' of the game. Or, come to that, of women.

11.6.1958

OUR SPORTING WICKETS.

Fond Wife. "HAROLD, DEAR, HAVE YOU TAKEN YOUR TEETH OUT?"

Women at the Wicket

A sure fire conversation stopper, when the men are ruining your dinner party with a post mortem on the last Test, is the casual remark that you yourself are a cricket Blue.

The years have taught me the Olympian detachment necessary for the next few minutes of brilliant male wit. 'Underarm bowling, of course!' '*And* a soft ball?' And the apparently perennially fascinating 'But what did you wear?'

There is no real need to reveal that in Women's Sports playing in the University Side most unfairly earns you only a half-Blue, full Blues being reserved for hat tricks, centuries and fatally wounding the opposing captain. Nor need you cause needless reflections on the standard of the cricket played by going on to tell how you never even reached the 1st XI at school. It was a particularly large school.

Enough that the conversation has been focused back on women and I can always go and poke about on the top of the wardrobe for that incredible photo, if anyone ungallantly demands proof.

The eleven dauntless maidens, one now a missionary, one a prisoner governor, but the rest otherwise normal wives and mothers, gaze at me from the curved and crested cardboard. Ten of us are wearing tennis shoes with our neat white socks, but the prison governor is wearing fierce hard boots. These struck as much terror into the hearts of her own side as of the opposition. She trod on our toes if we dropped catches off her bowling. The photo also reveals another hazard of ladies' cricket – the stiff breeze which blows your divided skirt at the wicket, topples off the bails, and you are given Out, played on.

The carefully posed group however gives no indication of some of the unusual facets of the

Wife of Deep-field. "No, darling, Daddy can't talk to you now; wait until he's dropped this one!"

"The thermos is in the tartan bag, Janet . . . the sandwiches are in the plastic box . . ."

game. There were the peculiarly intricate train journeys to remote areas of Outer London to play matches against London University and its constituent parts, on grounds so far from their colleges that we wondered anyone bothered to play. There were hilarious May Week matches against the men's colleges, who gallantly offered to bat left-handed, but rapidly changed hands after a few balls from the lady in the boots. There were even more hilarious days when we beat them and they took us all out to lunch. We ate sumptuous Match Teas laid on by the steward, which our perpetually hungry friends said were the only reason we played. There was even an opposing team of ladies that played in grey flannels and cricket caps. This enterprising XI from some remote Cambridgeshire village was composed of women, bored with summer Saturday grass widowhood, who had taken as their motto 'If you can't lick 'em, set up in opposition.'

Our coach was a groundsman from John's, who charmingly addressed us as 'Young Ladies', but couldn't maintain this standard of courtesy in our more inept moments. We often wondered what chaff he faced in the College Servants' Club.

So there we sit, immortalised on cardboard in our coveted Blue blazers and white shorts, doomed to give rise to as much mirth as grandmother's boatered and leg-of-muttoned croquet team. Perhaps it would be better not to mention the subject at all.

Anne Haward
17.6.1964

"If Kerry Packer's cricket circus ever needs a clown . . ."

CHAPTER FIVE

Foreign View

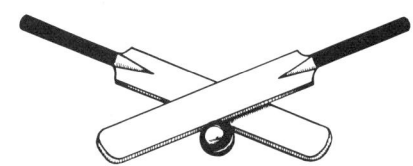

Foreigners and Cricket

What sort of an idea the Portuguese have of the game may in some degree be guessed by the following account of it, which has been translated from a Lisbon paper. There are Englishmen in Portugal as everywhere else, and wherever there are Englishmen of course there will be cricket. Clubs have been established at Lisbon and Oporto, and it was on the occasion of a match between these clubs that a sporting Lisbon journalist thus cleverly explained the nature of the game, for the instruction and perhaps amusement of his countrymen.

'Cricket Match. – Tomorrow there is to come off an interesting game of cricket match between the Cricket Clubs of Lisbon and Oporto. The object of the formation of these societies is the playing of the game of cricket match, an active running, driving, jumping game, which only can be played by a person having a good pair of legs, and in a climate where warmed punch is found insufficient to keep up the animal heat. Does the reader wish to know how to play at cricket match? Two posts are placed at a great distance from one another. The player close to one of the posts throws a large ball towards the other party, who awaits the ball to send it far with a small stick with which he is armed. The other players then run to look for the ball, and while this search is going on the party who struck it with the stick runs incessantly from post to post, marking one for each run. It is plain, then, that it is to the advantage of the party that strikes the ball to make it jump very far. Sometimes it tumbles into a thicket, and the players take hours before they can get hold of it; and all this time the player does not cease running from post to post and marking points. Then those who find the ball arrive, exhausted, at the field of battle, and the one who has been running falls down half dead. At other times, the projectile, sent with a vigorous arm, cannot be stopped, and breaks the legs of the party who awaits it.

'The arrangements for the cricket match include a sumptuous dinner in the marquee for fifty persons, an indispensable accompaniment to every cricket match. We may, perhaps, assist at this great battle, and hope the committee will place us at a safe distance from the combatants, where the principles of the game can be seen with the help of an opera-glass.'

How accurately the Portuguese are acquainted with our habits, and what a true conception they have of our cold climate, if they fancy that warmed punch is insufficient to keep up a right degree of vital heat, and that we are forced still more to heat our blood by the 'active, running, driving, jumping game of cricket match!' How true it is, moreover, that sometimes when the ball is made to 'jump very far,' the players take some hours before they can get hold of it, and all this while the man who hit the ball with his 'small stick' keeps on running between the wickets – we mean to say, the posts – until the scouts 'arrive exhausted at the field of battle,' and he himself 'falls down half dead!' Such incidents as these are, we know, continually occurring now at 'Lord's' (by the way the sporting foreigners who chance to see this name no doubt imagine we play 'cricket match' in our house of peers); and no wonder that we English are looked upon as lunatics by other nations of the world, while they have such true conceptions of the perils of our pastimes and the madness of our sports.

7.6.1862

Motto for French Cricketers

As every soldier has the bâton of a Field-Marshal in his knapsack, so every player has the bat of a Lillywhite in his portmanteau.

Almanack 1868

—|◊|◊|—

'Le Cricquette'
How he will be played – shortly

Offices of the Athletic Congress, Paris

Monsieur,

I am overwhelmed with my gratitude to you and to the generous dignatories, the chancellors of your universities, the heads of your great public seminaries and the principal of your renowned Mary-le-bone College Club for the information they have given me concerning 'Le Cricquette', your unique national game, and I thank you in the name of my committee for your present of implements, – *les wickettes, le boule de canon, les gros bois* (the batsman's weapons), *le cuirasse pour les jambes de longstoppe,* and other necessaries for the dangers of the contest that you have so kindly forwarded for our inspection. But most of all we are indebted to you for sending over a 'ome team of your brave professionals to play the match against our Parisian *'onze'*, for you rightly conjectured that by our experience of the formidable game in action, we should be able to judge of its risks and dangers, and after mature investigation be able so to revise and ameliorate the manner of its playing as to bring it into harmony with the taste and feeling of the athletic ambition of the rising generation of our young France.

A match has taken place as you will see by 'le score' subjoined, which I enclose for your inspection. It was not without its fruits. It disclosed to us, as you will remark, by referring to 'le score' very practically the dangerous, and I must add, the murderous capabilities that 'le cricquette' manifestly possesses. Our revising committee has already the matter in hand, and when their report is fully drawn up, I shall have much satisfaction in forwarding it to you. Meantime, I may say, that the substitution of a light large ball of silk, or some other soft material for the deadly *'boule de canon'* as used by your countrymen, has been decided upon as absolutely necessary to deprive the game of barbarism, and harmonise it with the instincts which modern and republican France associates with the pursuit of a harmless pastime. *Les wickettes,* as being too small for the bowlsman to reach them, should be raised to six feet high, and the umpire, a grave anomaly in a game cherished by a liberty-loving people, should be instantly suppressed. The 'overre' too, should consist of sixteen balls. But this and many other matters are under the consideration of the committee. I now, subjoin 'le score' I mentioned, a brief perusal of it will show you what excellent grounds the committee have for making the humanising alterations at which I have hinted.

AN IDEA FOR OUR SCULPTORS.

ALL FRANCE *v.* AN ENGLISH 'OME-TEAM

All France

M. DE BOISSY(struck with murderous force on the front of his forehead by the *boule de canon*, and obliged to retire),
b Jones-Johnson . . . . o

M. NAUDIN (hit on his fingers, which are pinched blue with the *boule de canon*, and incapacitated), b Jones-Johnson . . . . . o

LE MARQUIS DE CAROUSEL (receives a blow from the *boule de canon* on the front bone of his leg, and is compelled to relinquish the contest), b Jones-Johnson . . . . o

M. BUSSON (receives a severe contusion of the cheek-bone from the *boule de canon*, which is delivered with murderous intent by a swift 'round- and bowlsman')
b Jones-Johnson. . . . . o

LE GENERAL GREX (hits his three *wickettes* into the air, in a daring attempt to stop the *boule de canon* with his batsman's club),
b Jones-Johnson . . . . o

LE DUC DE SEPTFACES (has his *pince-nez* shattered to atoms by the *boule de canon*, and being unable to see, withdraws from the 'innings'), b Jones-Johnson . . . . o

M. CARILLON, M. LE DOCTEUR GIROFLÉ, LE PROFESSEUR D'EQUITATION (all the three being given, in turn, 'out, legs in front of the *wickette*', leave the ground to arrange a duel with the umpire), b Jones-Johnson . . . o

M. DE MONTMORENCY (on reaching the *wickette* and seeing the terrible approach of the *boule de canon*, has a shivering fit which obliges him to sit down),
b Jones-Johnson . . . . o

M. JOLIBOIS, coming in last, triumphantly avoids the 'overre', and is, in consequence, *not out.*

The English 'Ome-Team

JONES-JOHNSON, not out 3276
BROWN-SMITH, not out 3055

So the game stood at the end of the fifth day, when, spite all the efforts of 'All France', even to the putting on of three 'bowlsmen' at once, it was found impossible to take even one of the ''Ome-team' *wickettes*. Yet the contest was maintained by the 'Out-side' with a wonderful heroism and *élan*, for though by degrees, in nobly attempting to stop the flight of the *boule de canon* as it sped on its murderous course, driven by the furious and savage blows of the batsmen in all directions over the field, the fieldsmen, one by one, struck in the arms, legs, head, and back, began to grow feeble under their unceasing blows and contusions, still one and all from the 'Long-leg-off' to the indomitable 'longstoppe', faced the dangers of their situation with a proud smile, indicative of the noble calm of an admirable spirit. So, Monsieur, the game which was not finished, and which, in consequence, the umpire, with a chivalrous generosity, announced as 'drawn', came to its conclusion. You will understand, from the perusal of the above, the direction in which my committee will be likely to modify the rules of the game, and simplify the apparatus for playing it, so as to give your 'cricquette' a chance of finding itself permanently acclimatised in this country.

Accept, Monsieur, the assurance of my most distinguished consideration,

The Secretary of the Paris Athletic Congress

8.6.1889

Cricket in France

Or, Little Lessons for the Little Ones

Maintenant Georges est dans.

Il marche au guichet, prend son chef de train –
milieu et jambe – et affronte le marchand de
vitesse, qui commence à bouler.

Georges ferme ses yeux et fleurit son bat.

Zut!

La balle vole au-dessus des têtes des deux
glissades jusqu'au troisième homme, qui est
un mauvais champ.

'Doigts beurrés!' caserne la foule.

Georges est ravi; il a fait deux.

Il joue la prochaine balle dans la direction de
couvert-supplémentaire.

'Courez,' il crie à Aristide, mais celui-ci est
trop soufflé et ne bouge pas.

Pauvre Georges! Il essaie à retourner mais se
bouleverse.

'Comment ça?' appelle le garde-guichet.

L'arbitre élève son doigt.

Georges est couru dehors.

14.6.1933

–|●|●|–

Mr Peach Plays Cricket

'Talking of England,' said Mr Peach, 'did you
read about the Canadian cricket team over
there this summer? They've been going high,
wide and handsome, and if they're not careful
they'll be asked to play Test matches next, like
Australia and South Africa and India.

'I've often felt sorry there was no cricket
around this district; I'd like to see a game
again. Ever see one yourself?

'Well, neither had I until I played in one.
It's a good many years ago now, the summer Si
Hoskins and I made the trip to the Old
Country. We were staying with an uncle of his,
and one Saturday afternoon there was a cricket
game between his village and one three or four
miles away. Our village happened to be shy
two men, so they asked Si's uncle was it true he
had two Canadians staying with him, and did
he think they'd like a game of cricket? Si's
uncle sent for us, and after we'd been
thoroughly introduced we were asked would
we care to play that afternoon.

'"Sure we'll try it," says Si, "but what sort
of game *is* this cricket? How do you play it?"
"Oh," says the man, "you have eleven men a-
side, and a bat and ball, and – " Si didn't let
him get any further. "A bat and a ball," says
he, looking across at me; "I guess we'll be all
right, then. We've played baseball together on
one team or another since we first went to
school. Why Old Peachy here was the best
short-stop in the High School League." "And
you were the best pitcher they'd had in years,"
I shot back at him. "Why," I says, "believe it
or not, Si here once pitched three no-hit no-
run games in one season!" "Three no-hit no-
run games in one season!" says the man, with
the kind of look in his eyes a fish has when you
get him in the bottom of the boat and knock
him on the head. "Yes," I says, "I've seen
worse pitching in the majors." "In the
majors?" he says, looking glassier than ever. I
could see he was going down for the last time,
so I pushed him right under. "Yes," I says,
"and he's a southpaw."

'Well, you should have seen his face alter.
His eyes cleared and he stared at Si like a small
boy seeing Santa Claus for the first time.
"Why," he says at last, "you don't look so very
red!"

'Now it was our turn to be in a fog, but he
went on: "I take it the Southpaws are one of
the smaller tribes, not so well known as the
Blackfeet and the Mohawks. Do you know,"
he says to Si, "you may be the first Red Indian
ever to play cricket in England!"

'By this time Si was redder than the reddest
Indian who ever scalped a paleface, but when
I'd explained to the man that a southpaw in
baseball is a left-hander he almost made Si
look pale in comparison. Si's uncle came to the
rescue and suggested we discussed something
we all understood, so we did. Several bottles.

'Well, Sir, you should have seen us that
afternoon, all dolled up in white shoes, white
pants and white shirts. It's a swell-looking
outfit, all right, but we were glad there were
three thousand miles between us and the old
home town. If anyone from there had seen us
we'd never have heard the last of it.

'The other side won the toss and went up to
bat first. We were surprised to find they were
only going to play one innings each, but we
soon found out why. Before the two batters

came out – they bat two at a time, one at each end – our captain told us all where to stand. The places had the craziest names; as far as I remember Si was "mid-up" and I was "silly mid-wicket-keeper". Then the pitcher peeled off his sweater and give it to one of the umpires. (The umpires wore night-shirts.) Then he started out on a hike towards the end of the field. After going thirty yards or so he spun round and scratched the ground like a dog or a hen. Then he swung his arm round and round in a circle. By this time we'd have finished an innings in baseball and Si and I were getting restless. Then at last he ran back the thirty yards he'd walked, wheeled his arm over his head and let fly with the ball at the wickets – three sticks in the ground – at the other end. It went past with a foot to spare, and the catcher caught it and sent it back to the pitcher, who then set off on his hike again and repeated the whole performance. He did it six times, and the batter never once tried to touch the ball. Then the umpire who was a parson, called out "over" in the same voice he'd use for "let us pray", we all changed places on the field and another pitcher pitched six balls from the other end. This time they were aimed at the wickets, but the batter just put his bat down so they hit it and trickled away a few feet. This was too much for Si, and he called out to the captain, "Say Cap., when do we begin?"

'Gosh, you should have heard that silence. Every man on that field stood stock-still and stared at Si as though he'd walked into church with his hat on. The captain tried to tell Si the game had already started. "Do you mean to tell me they go on doing this all the afternoon?" says Si. But the captain explained they were just warming up – "playing themselves in" he called it.

'It was my turn to pull a bone next. The ball caught the edge of the bat and was caught by the catcher. At least I thought it did, and so did the catcher, for he let out a whoop and turned to the umpire. But the umpire said, "Not out." Would you believe it, they were playing on as though nothing had happened. So I walked over to the umpire and said, "Lookat here, you big stiff, that was a catch!" and Si came running up with the light of battle

in his eye, and began, "You poor sap, call yourself an umpire? What do you use for eyes?" But now the captain came up and took hold of Si's arm. "One doesn't argue with the umpire," he said. "Not argue with the umpire," says Si, "then what's he for?" The captain looked at Si more in sorrow than anger and said, "It isn't cricket." And that was all there was to it.

'We only got in wrong twice after that. Once I forgot myself and called out to a batter to snap out of it and start hitting, and once Si walked behind the pitcher when he was pitching and was told the batter wouldn't like it. Poor old Si! I could see he was struggling hard, but whether it was to find something suitable to say or to keep from saying something suitable I don't know.

'We also got in a few entries on the credit side. Si did a lot of smart fielding, and once, when the ball was going past at sixty miles an hour, I made a quick jump sideways and just got my left hand to it. It was a darned good catch, though I say it myself, and I'd have been proud of it in a baseball game with a mitt on. But, Lord, you should have heard 'em. They all clapped and said, "Well caught, Sir!" "Lovely catch, Sir!" "Beautiful fielding, Sir!" I felt highly embarrassed. To make it worse the batter came up to me on his way out and said, "Wonderful catch, Sir!" Was I red? And that blamed fool Si had to come up and say, "Me tell Southpaw Chief you heap big cricketer, huh!"

'When our side went up to bat Si and I sat on the pavilion verandah and watched. We were to bat last, naturally enough. So we lay back in comfortable chairs and watched the game, and began to think there was something to it after all. Then Si's uncle came along with cigars, and we decided we really liked it. We sat there smoking and yarning and watching for an hour or so, Si's uncle explaining things as they happened, and we telling him all about baseball. I also told Si a little idea I'd had for pepping up the game. I'd noticed whichever batter could best see the ball called out to tell the other whether to run or not, and I couldn't see why we should tell the other side what we were going to do. So I told Si we'd call "Yes" when we meant "No", and "No" when we

American Visitor. "KIN YOU TELL ME, SIR—HAVE THEY GOTTER MAKE THE BASE OR DO THE ROUND TRIP?"

meant "Yes". "But won't they soon catch on to it?" says Si. "Well," I said, "when I blow my nose we'll change singals and 'Yes' will mean 'Yes', and 'No', 'No', until I blow it again. Get the idea?" Si said he did, and it wasn't long after this before I went up to bat, and Si joined me a few minutes later.

'Si made a swing at the first ball but missed it, and it went straight into the catcher's mitts. So I yelled "Yes!" and pretended to start. Well, Sir, that catcher was so surprised he flung it wildly back in the general direction of the pitcher who missed it, and we got four runs because it went to the boundary. Si hit a foul off the next ball; it skied over his head towards an empty place in the field. It looked safe enough for one run, so I called out "No, no" and we both ran hard. When the fielder running for the ball heard my "No, no" he slowed down from a gallop to a canter, and when he'd picked it up and turned round and saw us running our second run his throw was so wild we got another two before it was safely fielded. But at the end of the over Si came up to me and said he didn't think it was quite the sort of trick to play in that sort of game. "You mean 'It Isn't Cricket'," I said, and he nodded. So our "Yes" meant "Yes" and our "No" "No", for the rest of the game.

'We didn't last very long, but it was great while it lasted. Once I left my bat and had to go back instead of making a run. Another time Si hit four boundaries in a row – sixteen runs in four smacks. And once the pitcher sent me a ball all the way in the air – a full toss, they called it. Boy, oh boy! did I paste that ball! It sailed clean over the pavilion roof, and then there was the sound of breaking glass, the sweetest music I ever heard. The pitcher walked up to me and said, "I hope you'll forgive my saying so, but you're wasted on baseball. The man who can hit sixes like that should be playing cricket." Soon after this I watched him make the ball curve in nearly a foot and knock Si's wickets down while he was hitting the air where he thought the ball would be. "I hope you'll forgive my saying so," I said to the pitcher, "but the guy who can put a curve like that on a ball is wasted on cricket. You should be in big-time baseball." He grinned and I grinned and the score was even.

'But now they were all walking off. "What's all this?" I said. "The game's over," they told me. "But what about me?" I asked. I wanted some more of those full tosses. "You're not out," they said. "Then how can the game be over if I'm not out?" I wanted to know. But Si came up and took my arm. "One doesn't argue," he said. "It Isn't Cricket." '

16.9.1936

-|o|o|-

The MCC – Apathy or Worse

It is now some six weeks since the news leaked out, in a curiously unguarded issue of Moscow's *Soviet Sport*, that the Russians were interesting themselves in cricket.

What steps have been taken by the MCC in the meantime to safeguard our position and tighten up security?

That nothing whatever had been done *before* the disclosure is evident, not only from MCC President Viscount Cobham's bland admission, made at the time, that Russia's interest in cricket was 'new to him', but also from the affair of Tyson's boots which must now, with the fuller knowledge available, be viewed in an altogether more sinister light. The extent to which Russian agents, and their misguided tools in this country, were responsible for the unparalleled series of accidents and injuries that befell prominent English cricketers during the past season will, in all probability, never be precisely determined. But that Tyson's boots were tampered with no one but a fool can doubt. The Northamptonshire fast bowler had only to put them on to fall a victim to crippling afflictions of the heel; and so serious, it will be remembered, did the situation ultimately become that the services of specialists in London were necessary to restore the boots to anything like operational condition.

By these and other less literal acts of sabotage Russia advanced her deadly aim of disrupting the English side. Team-building for the future was set back at least a twelvemonth. The softening up process had begun in earnest, and Russia could look forward with confidence to the time, not far distant, when she would be able to pit her own new-found strength against a weakened and disorganised opposition.

Why then, it may be asked, when so much could be achieved, and was being achieved, by underground methods against a purblind enemy, did *Soviet Sport* reverse the crypto-cricket policy and openly declare its country's interest in the game? The answer is not far to seek. Sooner or later the outward and visible signs of Russian preparation, the stepping up of her imports of heavy rollers, the great bat-willow forests springing up along the banks of the Volga, the constant traffic in copies of the Laws (smuggled out, we need not doubt, by the well-tried route through Prague) – these were portents that must eventually penetrate even the elephantine complacency of the lords of English cricket, sitting aloft in cushioned and pavilioned ease. Not for ever could the rising tide of red flannels be concealed from the dullest eyes. The time had come for Russia, by an apparently frank declaration of her interest, to disarm suspicion, and by extending to British teams (as she did in the columns of *Soviet Sport*) *an invitation to give a 'demonstration' of the game in Moscow next year* to suggest that it would be many years before she could be regarded as a serious opponent. The MCC, already guilty at best of scandalous obtuseness, will lay itself open to a far more serious charge if it allows itself for one moment to be lulled and gulled into the belief that Russia is scarcely as yet even a beginner at the game. Already, in the estimation of competent judges, she may be among the six top cricket-playing countries in Europe.

What, it must be asked again, has the MCC been doing in the last six weeks to set its house in order and counter the designs of a crafty and unscrupulous opponent? Recent events in another sphere have demonstrated afresh the futility of shutting stable doors after the horses are out; and though no one would wish to question the staunch patriotism of the great mass of English professional and amateur cricketers, there is no blinking the fact that there are rats and weaklings in every walk of life. Attempts undoubtedly will be made to get at left-hand bowlers. What is being done about screening? This is a serious question, and it simply is not good enough to reply, as the MCC's Assistant Secretary is reported to have done: 'One at each end on most grounds.' Anything approaching a witch-hunt would be repugnant to British public opinion, but clearly the antecedents and sympathies of some at least of our close-in fielders (a department in which the Soviet Union is expected to be weak) must be carefully scrutinised.

Nor is this all. When attempts at corruption fail, as they surely will, Russia will not scruple to resort to stronger measures. Kidnapping has been tried before and may be tried again. The public will not be satisfied until a full assurance has been given by the Moguls of St John's Wood that adequate counter measures are in hand. Admittedly, the removal of Len Hutton to the comparative safety of a hospital ward is a step in the right direction. But what has happened to the two young Sussex batsmen who went on a day trip to Boulogne at the end of August? Where are Graveney's pads? Is Statham closely guarded? Are the wives of, say, the best thirty cricketers in England constantly being followed? These are questions that must be fully and frankly answered – and at once. It will be worse than useless for the MCC to wait until half the English team are behind the Iron Curtain before issuing a statement that the matter is being kept under active review.

Officially, meanwhile, the Russians themselves are preserving, as might be expected, an attitude of calm inscrutability. A phone call to the Soviet Embassy this morning to ask whether they had anything to say about Tyson's boots, produced only a non-committal, 'Nothing is known of the matter here.' We shall do well not to underrate them.

H. F. Ellis
5.10.1955

–|●|●|–

Punch v. The Hague

The Hague Cricket Club has been playing since 1878. They run five elevens. The children make bowling motions about the house. Their President met us at the Hook in an MCC tie, and later showed this to be no idle boast about taking seven of our wickets. All this is by way of saying that we lost with honour (Het

Punch-team, 203 for 11, declared; The Hague, 204 for 4 declared).

The day was hot, our boots and trousers tight, the British Ambassador present, the ground impressive, with rose-beds on the boundary and two pavilions, one for going out from and coming back to (with gruff comments on the eccentricity of matting wickets), the other for eating, drinking, speech-making and studying photographs of The Hague playing at Welbeck Abbey ('and that's the Duke of Portland'). England, we felt, expected.

There was no language barrier. The Dutch for middle-and-leg is middle-and-leg. Idiom was flawless, particularly 'one for the road'. If the slip-field lapsed into Dutch – well, every batsman knows that mutterings in the slips, whatever the language, are an approved psychological weapon. There had been an earlier attack on our morale the night before, when we were poured over a two-horse *diligence* suitably placarded and driven from the Peace Palace through the public streets to the ground, there to be entertained within an ace of sabotage.

Laughter rang continuously. The Dutch sense of fun is impeccable. 'What happens to *Punch* if the boat goes down?' they cried at midnight, as we went aboard again in a screaming gale. They sang 'For They are Jolly Good Fellows'. They let us kiss their wives goodbye. By the time we left we had seen the canals of Amsterdam, the Rembrandts, the night-clubs, the Royal Yacht Club, the new Rotterdam, Delft, Gouda . . . almost everything but the ball. Our gizzards still humming from the Indonesian 'Rijstafel', we echoed our spokesman's suggestion that the cricket match should be repeated next year, but without the cricket, which had given us our only embarrassment and pain.

But at least it left us victorious in the casualties contest – *Punch*, three knees, two groin muscles and a sprained hand; The Hague, one pulled Achilles' tendon. Sore heads did not count.

J. B. Boothroyd
23.7.1958

The Match at Clonbur

The Irish are, it is well known, the Playboys of the Western World, but what they are allowed to play is by no means so clear. Cricket and rugby and association and lawn tennis are all, they are told by the Gaelic Athletic Association, Sassenach games by which true Gael must not allow himself to be contaminated. The patriotic game for an Irishman is hurley, and this is the more odd since in the middle of the last century, when the Nationalist movement was growing up to strength, cricket was played in almost every village in Ireland, whereas there was in the whole land but a single hurley team – that of Trinity College, of which the mainstay was Sir Edward Carson.

Some years before Carson played hurley for Trinity, Charles Stuart Parnell was the captain of County Wicklow at cricket. He was not a bad bat, with an average of 34, but he was above all a gamesman. The moment that a wicket fell he would whip out his watch to time the incoming batsman. A second over two minutes to the crease and he would appeal to have the batsman out, pulling out from his pocket a copy of the rules to prove to easygoing umpires that they had no option in the matter. They filled his riding boots with claret cup when he was batting for County Wicklow against County Dublin, and when Parnell came out, ill satisfied with an lbw decision, and put on his boots he splashed the claret cup all over his white trousers. The match ended with his chasing the opposing captain round and round the sight screen with a riding crop. Most of the dodges of gamesmanship with which he was afterwards to disrupt the proceedings of Westminster were first learnt by Parnell on the cricket pitches of County Wicklow.

It was the troubles of the Land League that prevented cricket from becoming the national game of Ireland. A village team had to draw some half of its players from the household of the landlord and half from his tenants, and when the tenants started shooting the landlords, whatever the other advantages or disadvantages of that arrangement, it was bad for cricket. Most of the village teams died away.

Yet some survived and some survive even to this day. A light single-line railway used to wind out to the west from Galway into Connemara. Its trains were all marked L in the Irish time-tables, and L in an Irish time-table, as the footnote tells you, means 'perishable train with limited passenger accommodation'. Now, in the name of progress, the line has been closed down and, like all things perishable, the train has perished, but so long as it survived it was used to carry the men of Ballinasloe to play cricket against the men of Clonbur.

This was how the match went in the days of my boyhood.

The captains tossed. Hastily picking up the coin before his rival had time to look at it the visiting captain – a formidable man – announced, 'We'll bat.' The home team then took the field.

'Uncle Henry,' said the home captain to an enormous man, dressed in bowler hat and braces and with a stud in his collarless shirt, 'silly mid-off this end. Silly mid-on the other end. You stand by him, Terence,' he said to his young nephew, 'and when it comes to the over's end, why, just turn him round. The rest of you stand around as may be convenient. Paddy, will you bowl at the end where the horses was last week?'

There then emerged from the pavilion to open the innings for Ballinasloe four batsmen all fully padded: two very old and too decrepit to bat, two young and pink to run for them. One of the opening bats was an English visitor. To him Paddy delivered a maiden over which the Englishman played with conscientious care.

'Over,' said the umpire.

'Turn him round, Terence, turn him round,' said the captain.

Terence picked up Uncle Henry and put him down again in position.

The captain then took up the ball and prepared to bowl.

'Did you hear about the poor Major?' he said to the umpire as he ran up to the wicket.

'No,' said the umpire as the captain delivered the ball.

The ball passed a bat's length outside the off stump. The batsman played no stroke at all

and it lodged into the wicket keeper's pad.

'How's that?' said the captain.

'Not out,' said the umpire. 'What about the Major?'

'His legs turned black in the night,' said Uncle Henry from silly mid-on.

'Well, you can't call that a good sign, can you?' said the umpire.

The captain walked back to pace his run. A shot rang out. Whether it was among the spectators or from just outside the ground was not quite clear.

'Yer a stranger here, aren't you?' said the umpire to the English batsman.

'Yes,' said the Englishman, 'I'm a stranger here.'

'Ah, well,' said the umpire, 'yer not to worry. It isn't often that the boys hit anyone in Clonbur.'

Another ball was bowled.

'Last season, though,' the umpire added, 'I recall that there was a gentleman killed.'

'Season' was clearly the operative word. As a cricket enthusiast he was insistent that the 'gentleman-killing' could properly take place only between the months of May and September.

'There was an English bishop was staying here,' explained Uncle Henry, 'that day when I drove the pigs into the hotel dining room for a bet. He'd never seen such a thing in his life.'

'Ah,' said the captain, who had in the meanwhile been steadily plodding along with his over, 'but I am really sorry about the Major's legs turning black. A very decent old man he was.'

'No ball,' said the umpire.

There was in the pavilion, preparing to make tea, a woman of gigantic proportions who – it was commonly said – had in her youth boxed for Trinity College as a heavyweight.

'No ball, did you say?' she shouted. 'Why, here's a ball for you,' and just as the captain delivered his next ball, a high full-pitch which whistled past the batsman's chin, the Amazon with unerring aim threw another ball from the pavilion which struck him on the pad.

'How's that?' shouted the long leg.

'Out,' said the umpire.

'Out for what?' said the batsman.

'Out for you,' said Uncle Henry.

'It was Biddy's ball that struck me,' said the batsman. 'I'm not going out.'

This defiance was accepted as entirely reasonable alike by the umpire and by the fielding side, and the batsman unconcernedly prepared to receive the next ball. The captain bowled it. The batsman hit it down towards the long leg and called for a run. The runner at the other end, seeing that the fielder had gathered the ball, called 'No!' but neither the striker nor his runner paid any attention to this. Both set off up the pitch at a good pace. 'Get back,' shouted the other runner and both he and the Englishman held their ground. The result was that all four batsmen were at the bowler's end. But long leg in his excitement threw the ball to the bowler. The bowler attempted to throw it to the wicket-keeper, but Uncle Henry with sudden alacrity leapt up, intercepted it, but failed to catch it. The batsman, seeing a ray of hope, decided to make a dash to the other end, but naturally enough all four saw this ray of hope at the same time and all four set off down the pitch together. Their hope was well founded, for by the time that Uncle Henry and Terence had done scrabbling for the ball on the ground and had thrown it on to the wicket-keeper they were all four of them well home at his end. The wicket-keeper was taking no further chances with Uncle Henry. He decided, like a relay racer, that the safer plan would be to carry the ball to the other end himself. He set off with the four batsmen in hot pursuit behind him. But he had the start of them and without much difficulty he reached the bowler's end and broke the wicket.

'How's that?' he shouted.

'Out,' said the umpire.

'Who's out?' said the striking batsman.

'How would I know who's out?' said the umpire. 'If only you'd gone out like a Christian when I gave you out the first time none of this trouble need ever have arisen.'

That was how it used to be; and I cannot think that the Gaelic Athletic Association had much of a case when they said that cricket as it was played at Clonbur was an English game.

Christopher Hollis
10.10.1958

Play! Olé!

Sir Grantley Adams, Prime Minister of the West Indies Federation, said there would be fewer revolutions in Latin-American countries if South Americans were taught to play cricket. – *Sunday Express*

'Yes Señor, we played el cricket here in Paramorela,' said the old man. 'It was a great thing, they were fine times!' His eyes, piercing and coal-black, probed the middle distance as if expecting a long throw-in from some phantom out-fielder. He was tall and still muscular, his faded white flannels patched and stained, his thick llama-wool shirt open at the neck, round which, loosely knotted and greasy, hung a silk tie which might once have been red and yellow.

'They were fine times,' he said again. 'Do you know, señor, what they called me in the tabernas, even as far as San Jiminez de la Fuente?' I shook my head. He drew himself up proudly. 'They called me "Fearless Freddie" García Montalban y Lopez,' he said. 'I was the fastest bowler in South America. Faster than el gran Larwood, as fast as the strike of the Paramorelan mud-hawk!'

'You don't play here anymore?' I asked. 'We do not play here anymore señor,' he replied, drawing deeply at a pipe of asphyxiating Azteblanes tobacco. 'The last game played here was against our deadly rivals, San Bernardino de la Sagrada Botella Gipsies,' he said at length. 'They were the strongest side in the world. *Muy, muy fuerte.* Their opening batsman was Don Carlos de Esteban y Muerte, scorer of seventy centuries and Dictator of Escudaria.' He spat ferociously.

'There was not a place vacant in the plaza,' he went on, 'not in the *sol*, not in the *sombra* – all the youth and beauty of Paramorela was there that day. Ah, the ladies, my Carmencita among them in her black mantilla! *Muy hermosa, muy, muy hermosa!*' He sighed.

'When I went on from the Monastery end with the dust-storm behind me, I sent down a bumper that whistled through Don Carlos' black beard. He scowled at me and at the cañon end his retinue stirred ominously. But I had hot blood in my veins then, señor. The next ball, faster than the pounce of the Paramorelan cactus-adder, struck him between the eyes. He fell to the ground. The next moment a bullet whistled past my head and the umpire fell dead! I drew my knife and grappled with the batsman at my end while the plaza filled with combatants. In ten minutes the pavilion was in flames and artillery had begun to open up from the surrounding hills.

'By nightfall,' he continued, 'the cathedral and seventeen churches were in ruins. With my own hands I rescued from the cathedral our club's most sacred relic, one of the great Doctor's batting pads, carried to our country many years before by a wandering Free Forester. Señor, the war lasted two years and it was a disaster for Paramorelan cricket from which, alas, it has never recovered. Since then, successive dictators have proscribed our grand old game.'

His old eyes clouded momentarily.

'Now, the youth of today does not know a googly from an outswinger,' he murmured sadly. 'All they think of is revolution.'

It was growing late, and I bade him farewell. Looking back through the growing dusk, it seemed that I saw him go mournfully through the motions of one bowling a fast Paramorelan inswinger on the leg-stump.

J. E. Hinder
6.1.1960

–|●|●|–

Tovarich at The Test

After the May Day Parades the BBC reciprocates by relaying the Lord's Test match to Moscow

The time is three in the afternoon, Mackay has yet to add to his one o'clock score and the England captain signals for drinks. E. W. Swanton, J. H. Fingleton, B. Johnston and P. West are interpreting the excitement to television viewers at home while the Russian commentator Y. K. Slobin initiates his countrymen into the mysteries of the game.

FINGLETON: I liked the way Mackay let that long-hop pass safely outside his off stump. Wouldn't you agree, Brian, that Australia are definitely getting on top?

JOHNSTON: Well, it's a bit early to say. Anything can happen in cricket as you well know.

FINGLETON: True. I remember in 'thirty-eight . . .

SLOBIN: English viewers are at present hearing the views of the Australian Fingleton. He is a member of his country's ruling class, his last book was introduced by Prime Minister R. Menzies, the reactionary oppressor of the Canberra Communist Party.

JOHNSTON: By Jove! that was a near thing. Mackay nearly hit that one. Let's ask Jim Swanton what he thought about it.

SWANTON: Pretty good ball. Moved a bit off the seam.

JOHNSTON: I should have thought more than a bit.

SWANTON: A good 'un. Incidentally, I must tell Jack Fingleton that I've just seen in the pavilion an old friend of his, Sir Holtby Humby. Looks very fit.

FINGLETON: All Australians will be pleased to hear that. We remember Sir Holtby when he was Governor of the Northern Territory.

SWANTON: Played for Harrow in 'ninety-eight.

SLOBIN: At one end of the ground there is a fortress called the pavilion. Only aristocrats are permitted to sit in it. The names of all English babies of the ruling class are written down as they are born in the pavilion book. Many of the people who sit there are princes, their leader is the Grand Duke Altham.

JOHNSTON: And Mackay has taken a quick single. Risky in the circumstances. Still four and a half days left.

WEST: My word! Indeed! Yes!

FINGLETON: I think I can see a beard growing out of the press box. It must be.

SLOBIN: No member of the English Communist Party is allowed in the pavilion.

SWANTON: It's Alan Ross of the *Observer*.

FINGLETON: If Mackay doesn't soon get out we shan't be able to distinguish Alan from Father Time.

SLOBIN: Nowhere in England is the mastery of the English aristocracy so perpetuated as here at Lord's field. On top of a stadium there is the figure symbolic of the depressed classes. The Lords who owned this field once seized a serf called F. Time and compelled him to cut grass with a scythe.

JOHNSTON: The Tavern seems to be doing a good trade.

FINGLETON: Probably the press-box emptying.

SLOBIN: In England the majority press is in favour of the cult of personality. Only this morning the *Express* openly encouraged cricket player Trueman with the words 'Freddie! Slam! Wham! Whoosh!' The newspapers like *The Times*, *Guardian*, *Observer* and *Sunday Times* which are the organs of the ruling class all employ journalists carefully conditioned by the University of Oxford.

SWANTON: Our spinners are not flighting the ball as Laker did five years ago. I think Jack Fingleton would agree?

FINGLETON: Well, Jim, as one who was not unacquainted with the pre-war generation of England spinners . . .

SLOBIN: To enter this field one has to pass through the Grace Gates. It is noteworthy that when tribute had to be paid to the medical profession the English chose a man who did not work under their National Health Service. For daring to criticise this and other decisions of the ruling class cricket player J. Laker was recently purged.

SWANTON: Looking through my glasses I can see some very comely young ladies at the top of the open stands. We'll ask Peter West what he thinks. Peter?

WEST: My word! Indeed! Yes!

SLOBIN: The English bourgeoisie are not allowed to sit in the pavilion but use a covered stand. Their spokesmen, the plutocrats Clore and Cotton, slobber as they think of taking-over the pavilion but the Whites will defend their privileges by calling in the Brigade of Guards.

FINGLETON: I prefer the ladies' stand at Sydney.

SLOBIN: Pictured now is the English proletariat herded together in a stand where there is no protection from the snow. They are dressed much as their forefathers were when the novelist C. Dickens visited Muggleton.

FINGLETON: There's one question I should like to ask Jim Swanton – has he ever seen Colin Cowdrey wearing a Harlequin cap?

SLOBIN: Patrolling the nursery and preventing the proletariat from realising their political aspirations are members of the Secret Police. Their uniform explains why they are called White shirts. They are Fascist beasts, the dreaded Lord's PROs.

SWANTON: I've never seen Cowdrey wearing a Harlequin cap.

SLOBIN: English cricket players are either aristocrats or members of the proletariat. The aristocrats used to wear the so-called Harlequin caps but these enraged the masses and the aristocrats now wear them only in the House of Lords.

JOHNSTON: Trueman is taking the new ball. I'll ask Jack . . .

SLOBIN: The expression on the face of English bowler Trueman contrasts strongly with the happiness displayed by our glorious Soviet athletes. Trueman is a member of the proletariat, he is clearly outraged that he should be compelled to carry the cricketing bags of E. Dexter to and from Dexter's hotel. Dexter is a member of the ruling royal family.

FINGLETON: Interesting to see two short legs. Let's ask Jim . . .

SLOBIN: To play cricket at Lord's field a country must be a member of the Imperialistic Cricket Conference.

SWANTON: We haven't seen two short legs since half-past twelve.

SLOBIN: The men and women now debauching themselves is a sure indication that capitalism is working itself out in the Tavern.

JOHNSTON: Well, look who's here! John Arlott having a rest from the old steam radio. Enjoying Mackay, John?

ARLOTT: An amiable man, Mackay, square-shouldered . . .

SLOBIN: English viewers are now hearing the voice of J. Arlott who speaks to those Wessex serfs too poor and exploited to own a television. Arlott was once a member of the State police until he started writing bourgeois poetry.

SWANTON: That was mighty close to a catch at the wicket.

WEST: My word! Indeed! Yes!

SLOBIN: The first full description of a cricket match was written in 1706. That was exactly five years after Peter the Great introduced the game to England . . .

Kenneth Gregory
10.5.1961

=|●|●|=

Boules de Canon

If you have ever wondered what holds Britain together 'in these turbulent times', Coventry's Canon Lawrence Jackson has the answer. Cricket.

Not God, Ted Heath, Maypole dancers, black pudding, or fish and chips. *Cricket*.

That, at least, is what he told the Lord's Taverners when they held their pleasantly boozy spring lunch at the Café Royal last week. The official excuse was that the Taverners wanted to welcome the Australian touring team; cricket, it seems, performs the same useful function for the Commonwealth. But it was really a super, chauvinistic occasion, the kind of do which makes our Australian and European friends realise that superficial appearances are deceptive: we have not really changed at all.

I suppose the chairmen of Arsenal, Chelsea and Manchester City make much the same claim for their own game – and perhaps, with rather more justification. 'The British way of life', after all, has a great many different features. (Do strikes and economic crises, I wonder, qualify as well as Maypole dances and swan-upping? And why must we necessarily assume that the British way of life is superior to, say, the French way of life, or the Italian way of life? Do we simply use the phrase to provide reassurance?)

But let's not quibble. Cricket does inspire some extraordinarily fulsome tributes. Who but a Briton could write of a game (as Alan Ross has done) that it is a 'rite, a ritual of Chinese inscrutability and subtlety, an art form, a balletic background to gossip and drinking, a rural antic, a social event, a conflict reflective of national prestige, a résumé of English tastes, habits, masochisms, a canalisation of the erotic impulse, a species of warfare,

the instinctual man's introduction to aesthetics, an aspect of history'?

The question I really want to raise is this: are we not being just a little selfish in keeping such a unifier from our *fellow-Europeans*?

It is, you will agree, one of the more obvious shortcomings of the European community that most of its members are woefully ignorant about cricket. It illustrates the wide gap which still exists between Britain and the Continent; it also explains why so many Englishmen are bored with the whole Common Market argument.

No, that's not quite fair. The Dutch know how to play cricket. At least they did twenty years ago when Punch took a team across the Channel to play the Hague. Not much has been heard of Dutch cricket since then, and the match may well have killed the game off there.

Attempts have also been made, occasionally, to educate the French. In 1908 Punch published a letter allegedly sent by the offices of Athletic Congress in Paris. (See p. 000) My own view, for what it's worth, is that we shall never succeed in getting Europe to accept cricket unless we put up some convincing reasons. A poll among the Punch staff suggested the following programme outline:

France:

The one thing that the French really envy about the British, curiously enough, is our grass. There was an advertisement in *Paris Match* this month for some grass fertiliser and the slogan read: 'Make your neighbour think your lawn has come from England.' All we have to do is convince the French that, once they've taken up cricket, beautiful pitches and village greens will spring up everywhere. If they wonder why we run up and down with a ball aiming at little sticks stuck in the grass, tell them this is a vital gardening process which makes the grass so beautiful, so flat, and so ventilated.

Germany:

One of the great fascinations of cricket is its statistics – the annual edition of *Wisden* makes the Stock Exchange quotations look like 'O' level maths – and it is well known that the

Germans have a great sense of order and system. They must be persuaded that the main object of cricket is fiddling with numbers, averages, scores and records; the running about with bat and ball is a rather tedious preliminary to the real thing.

Italy:

The Italians must be told that cricket is a game full of passion, romance, sensuality and drama. This may be difficult. In fact, it may be impossible. Instead, tell them that cricket is the English version of grand opera. They both seem never-ending, you never know with either of them what's happening at any particular moment and they're both not as good as they used to be. If this doesn't work, tell them it's much easier to emigrate to Australia from Milan or Turin if you're a top-class leg spinner.

Belgium:

Belgium is one of the great beer-drinking nations of the world. Cricket is the one game viewed from, played near, and centred on, the bar. Need one say more?

Luxembourg:

Luxembourg is difficult, because of the size problem. If you're playing golf there and hit a ball out of bounds, you have to go through Customs to get it back. If cricket was introduced to Luxembourg some other game would have to be banned to make room for it.

There are, one accepts, certain snags in the whole exercise. The indignity of seeing England lose to a German, Italian or Belgian side would be hard to bear. But if we're really serious about Europe, these are risks one must learn to accept. And there could be some interesting side-effects. One is that South Africa would have to think up some new excuses. In Cape Town a few weeks ago Frank Waring, the Minister of Sport, told me that cricket doesn't qualify for their new 'open internationals' policy because 'not enough countries play it'. (Mr Vorster's Cabinet, embarrassed by South Africa's exclusion from international sport, now allows non-whites to play in tournaments providing they have a 'world atmosphere'. 'If there were a world cricket tournament,' says Waring, 'then we would have quite a different approach.')

Meantime, of course, we have Australia. I'm not qualified to comment on the merits of their 1972 offering, but people in the know say it's going to be a super season. 'All that is needed,' says E. W. Swanton, 'is warm, dry weather and positive leadership at all levels to ensure a happy summer.' My sentiments precisely.

Whatever happens, it will make a pleasant change to see newspapers proclaim 'England facing disaster' and know they're only talking about cricket.

William Davis
3.5.1972

-|o|o|-

Opening for Dreamshire or A Yank on the Greensward

All the afternoons of back-breaking practice, the evenings of poring over photos of pace men in action, the nights of buying ale for the captain of the club XI, were about to pay off as I accepted the shiny new ball from my skipper and prepared to open the bowling. At last I had made it. After a dozen years in England, I was a Yank on the greensward. And this was not one of those trick showbiz matches. This was a fixtured club match.

'Over or around the wicket?' The umpire asked.

Now there he had me. Stumped for an answer. I didn't know. All of a sudden I didn't feel like Lord Ted in my new flannels. I felt like a housepainter who had walked into the wrong place.

I'd spent days perfecting that little hopping step which gets you turned side on. The rhythmic flow to the crease I had. The pivotal tension of a Larwood, a Tyson, a Lindwall – it was all there. Hadn't I prematurely aged the dog chasing my fiery deliveries into the bushes? Was there one stretch of my garden which wasn't chewed up by the dreadful thunder of my boots? Real bowler's boots, too. White-washed pit boots with dirty great nails hammered all over the soles. How many summers had I provided innocent amusement for the neighbours by my cricketing antics? These little grey people had suffered their cars dented by wayward deliveries and their flowerbeds trampled as I sought lost balls (my cricket closely resembles golf) – I couldn't let them down.

'Say, ah . . . just a minute there, pal,' I said to the ump and I strode to square leg where my eldest boy was fielding.

'Listen kid,' I said, 'you know I don't go in for the technical stuff. Pace is the name of my game. You don't happen to know whether I go over or around the wicket do you.'

He looked at me in disbelief. Then he threw back his head and laughed. In that instant I was no longer the All-American dad who will even try to learn how to play cricket for goshsakes in order to be a pal to his boy. Suddenly I was some kind of character who his mother had happened to marry.

'You *are* kidding me, aren't you?' he said.

'Sure I am, kid. But just for the heck of it which is which? I got this sort of mental block.'

When I was fourteen and at school in Massachusetts I got a gift subscription to *Punch* and used to stare blankly at the cartoons about cricket. Then you run into the game in *The Pickwick Papers*:

Won the toss – first innings – seven o'clock am – six natives to look out – went in; kept in – heat intense – natives all fainted – taken away – fresh half dozen ordered – fainted also – Blazo bowling – supported by two natives – couldn't bowl me out – fainted too – cleared away the Colonel – wouldn't give in – faithful attendant – Quanko Samba – last man left – sun so hot, bat in blisters, ball scorched brown – five hundred and seventy runs – rather exhausted – Quanko mustered up last remaining strength – bowled me out – had a bath, and went to dinner.

There is a group of pathetic expatriate Yanks who play a debased form of baseball in Hyde Park on Sundays. How can they live in England and not want to have a go at cricket, that most English of sports? They also probably never drink bitter or eat your wonderful traditional old Wimpys. But it was the sight of Brian Statham at Old Trafford which turned me on to fast bowling. And reading cricket writers like Alan Ross.

There are other arts: of flight, of spin, of length as naggingly repetitive as the water-torture. But the great fast bowler's is the final apotheosis, the embodiment of a devilish joy that is at once physical and spiritual, retributive and musical, a rite, a ritual of Chinese inscrutability and subtlety, to which no calligrapher has done justice, an art form, a balletic background to gossip and drinking, a rural antic, a social event, a conflict reflective of national prestige, a résumé of English taste, habits, masochisms, a canalisation of the erotic impulse, a species of warfare, the instinctual man's introduction to aesthetics, an aspect of history . . .

'NO BALL!' The umpire's clenched fist prodding the air. The suspicion of giggles from my own slips. Later in the club bar it is loud laughter. 'You were chucking! Ha ha ha.' Drunken louts. Absolutely the wrong sort of chaps in the club these days. English manhood was saved. The American was no-balled for chucking. A taste of Pommie sportsmanship.

But there is no other summer pastime in England. What better excuse for complaining about the rain? Or for those long, complicated and beery journeys by rail to see a match in a far-off county? Raincoats, sandwiches, field glasses, an out of date railway timetable, elaborate instructions to see Cedric's old mate Bert on the gate at Edgbaston, 'Bert'll see you all right.' Of course it doesn't really matter if he doesn't. Rain will stop play anyway.

A pleasant afternoon of pints in a dripping beer tent listening to stories about something that happened on the third day at Hove in 1934. The story-teller had been there on the day and had almost actually seen the incident he is talking about – he had just that second turned his back to the field to get his round in. Practically a first-hand story the way cricket stories go.

Then the long trip home, finally eating the wife's sandwiches, the sun out at last, picking the trains carefully, making sure they've got a bar, slipping through the quiet parts of strange towns, passing beautiful little grounds, and hearing the news that Boycott has got another century for Yorkshire. Must go to Headingley some time soon. We'll make a day of it. Of course, the rain will go to Yorkshire with us. But it doesn't really matter all that much.

First match – opened the bowling – rock concert – blaring away in next field – amorous labradors – making love at leg slip – street arabs – playing footie at deep fine leg – play stopped – not rain – fire – fire engines on pitch – crowd of several hundred – new flannels all black smuts – no-balled four times in first over – should have gone round the wicket – should have gone Lord's – Lancashire in Gillette final – had the tickets – gave them away when captain asked me to open – had a bath, and drank fourteen pints – best bitter – great game, cricket.

Of course, taking up express bowling at 108 years of age is not the most practical adventure in the world. But in addition to A. K. I also have A. C. and A. S. Reynolds both in nappies and both literally cutting their teeth on number o bats. And so some county Long Room is going to suffer some mighty fine boredom when I am an old émigré Yank leaning on a stick and my boys are opening for Dreamshire.

Stanley Reynolds
6.6.1973

–|o|o|–

The Singular History of Himmelweit

It is my intention to recount the singular history of Himmelweit.

Himmelweit was the only German in the history of the summer game to play first class county cricket.

He played for the county of Somerset from the year 1919 until the year 1921, when he became the central figure in what is known to historians as 'The Incident at Frome'.

Himmelweit came to this country in the year 1916 when his Zeppelin was shot down during a bombing raid on Shepton Mallet – thus giving him residential qualifications to play for Somerset.

He was deposited forthwith in prison – thus giving him residential qualifications to play for Wormwood Scrubs.

He first came to the notice of the cricketing authorities when, in 1918, he appeared in the match of Minor Counties versus Huns.

Minor Counties were skippered by Jas. Humberstone Senior.

Huns were skippered by Thomas Mann.

Mann, a minor literary figure, was later to achieve wider fame as the father and grandfather respectively of F. G. and F. T. Mann of Middlesex and England.

The match took place at Much Wenlock, and Minor Counties won the toss and elected to bat.

The innings was opened by Jas. Humberstone Senior and the former Leicestershire professional, Amiss, later to achieve wider fame as the father and grandfather respectively of the two cricketing brothers, Denis and Kingsley.

The Huns' skipper tossed the crimson rambler to Himmelweit to open the bowling.

Humberstone crouched at the crease in his typical aggressive stance.

As he faced up to the bowling the buckles of his braces flashed angrily, the ferrets in his hip pocket gnashed their teeth and the clank of his steel dentures echoed round the ground.

'Right, Fritz,' he growled. 'Do your worst.'

It was to be a memorable moment in the history of the summer game.

Himmelweit commenced his run.

One stride, two strides, three strides.

It was indeed a fearsome sight as his iron crosses clattered and his cavalry sabre splintered the weak Shropshire sunlight into myriads of sparkling fragments.

Nearer and nearer he approached the wicket.

And as he did so spectators became aware of a curious whistling sound.

Louder and louder it grew. Ghastly. Horrendous.

A banshee howl that caused Humberstone Senior to fling himself to the ground, clasping his ears in agony.

Himmelweit delivered the ball.

It was a masterly delivery.

Full-length, pitched on middle and leg and veering sharply to off with a snake-like whiplash.

Humberstone's castle was wrecked.

The well-known cricket writer, Neville Cardew, later to achieve wider fame as the father and grandfather respectively of the distinguished wit and raconteur, Cardew Robinson, wrote in his journal the following:

'I doubt whether any man alive could have played that ball.

'Even the redoubtable Humberstone at the moment of delivery was stretched on the ground, writhing in contortions of agony, hands clamped tight to his auditory orifices.

'I am of the firm opinion that the perfect pitch and pace of the ball would have beaten his forward defensive prod and caused him forthwith to give no trouble to the scorer.'

Thus did the carnage begin.

The Minor Counties were dismissed for five.

Himmelweit took all ten wickets at a personal cost of one run, all his victims being stricken by the all-pervasive and menacing whistling sound emanating from his person.

The Huns XI, in the persons of their two openers, the Umlaut brothers, A. P. F. and J. W. H. N. S. – the latter known affectionately as Johnny Will Heute Nicht Schlagen – knocked off the runs required in one over, thus winning the match by ten wickets.

It was some hours later during the subsequent fracas in the tea pavilion that the source of the whistling sound was discovered.

Himmelweit with typical Teutonic cunning had affixed to the inside of his knee-cap a device used by the Germans in their howitzers during the bombardment of Beauvais to strike terror into the hearts of the allied horses.

The shock waves of this incident reverberated throughout the game and were the direct cause of what is known to historians of the summer game as the Much Wenlock Amendment:

'The Implements of the Game:

'Note Seven B.

'Articles of ordnance or artillery may not normally be used during the course of the match except by prior agreement of the two captains who must notify forthwith the umpires, if the said articles contain matter of an explosive nature which may cause distress or injury to domestic and agricultural livestock in the immediate vicinity of the ground.'

Despite the various unpleasantnesses which resulted from this match, Himmelweit's services were eagerly sought by all the first class counties with the exception of Yorkshire, who still to this day refuse to allow to play for the county players of German birth or independent nature.

It was left to the MCC to decide that the enforced landing of Himmelweit's Zeppelin on Somerset soil gave that county the right to claim his services.

This rule has been strictly applied to the registration of all overseas players.

Himmelweit's deeds with Somerset require little embellishment from me.

The records speak for themselves.

It is to matters of a more personal nature that we must devote our attention.

Sad to say, it must be recorded that Himmelweit seemed to go out of his way to antagonise both team-mate and opponent alike.

While the majority of players were content during drinks intervals to accept orange squash or grapefruit crush, Himmelweit insisted on a half-bottle of lightly chilled Hock. And on finishing this he would invariably hurl the glass to the ground and grind it underfoot with his spurs – an act which was subsequently found to be responsible for the untimely demise of the groundsman's horse at the Chelmsford Cricket Club.

While most players, too, during the luncheon adjournment were content to take a light salad, Himmelweit insisted on a full five-course meal consisting usually of Bauernschmeiss mit Knackwurst, Sauerkraut mit

Bratkartoffeln, Bayerische Obsttorte, Kaffee mit Schlag and Knoedel au Harry Makepeace.

Himmelweit fell foul of umpires, too, by insisting on appealing in his native tongue.

'Wie ist das?' he would shout in a blood-curdling yell.

And when he came to the wicket to take up guard he would scowl at the umpire and snarl: 'Mittel und Bein.'

Many years later, when talking about the celebrated umpire, George Pope, who was later to achieve wider fame as the father and grandfather respectively of John Paul I and John Paul II, was heard to remark:

'Ahd 'ave let t'bogger rot, if he'd not 'ad t'decency to say bitte schoen.'

It was undoubtedly these indiscretions which accounted for his singular lack of support from both players, spectators and officials alike at the time of the infamous 'Incident at Frome'.

I now propose to recount in some detail the circumstances surrounding this occurrence.

It took place during the match against Lancashire. At that time the red rose county had a team of all the talents including that nonpareil of fast bowlers, the Australian, E. A. McDonald, who was later to achieve even wider fame in the moving kinematograph as the partner of Mr Nelson Eddy.

McDonald was a bowler of awesome speed, a man in the prime of his talents.

Somerset won the toss.

Skipper Bertie Furze deliberated long and hard, but at length decided to bat on a green and lively wicket, expecting, no doubt, great feats later on in the game from his one-legged off-spinner, Mendip-Hughes.

It was a disastrous decision.

McDonald bowling at fearsome speed had the ball rearing and spitting from the very first moment of the game.

Within the space of five overs he had claimed six Somerset wickets and despatched three of his opponents to hospital.

It was at this moment that Himmelweit appeared at the wicket wearing garb of the most singular appearance.

The Lancashire skipper immediately objected.

But on finding that the rule book contained no references to cavalry breastplates, spiked helmets or sabres (Allied or German), play was allowed to continue.

The first ball McDonald bowled to Himmelweit whistled down to a good length and reared like a mortar shell head high.

Himmelweit did not flinch.

Instead of ducking he soared into the air and with a movement of the head muscles that would have shamed the immortal Ralph 'Dixie' Dean, who was later to achieve even wider fame as the father and grandfather respectively of the celebrated light comedienne and chanteuse, Miss Phyllis Dixie, headed the ball first bounce into the boundary.

Incensed, McDonald hurled down a ball of even greater speed.

Once more Himmelweit rose into the air and headed the ball to the boundary.

A six!

McDonald knotted his dark antipodean eyebrows and next ball bowled a vicious delivery that hurtled at Himmelweit's midriff and struck him a sickening blow in the vitals.

Himmelweit stood his ground.

His upper lip curled icily. The sunlight flashed on his monocle.

And then with a sudden movement he made a crucial adjustment to his dress.

McDonald bowled again.

Another ferocious ball hurled straight at the most tender anatomical parts known to man – and sometimes to woman.

Clang!

The noise echoed the length and breadth of the green and rolling hills of Somerset.

Rooks flew up in alarm. Rabbits scurried to their burrows. Hens stopped laying.

Himmelweit did not budge.

Defiant and upright he stood.

But where was the ball?

It was the great Dick Tyldesley who spotted it.

'How's that?' he yelled.

Scarcely had the words left his lips than Himmelweit commenced to run.

'Lauf,' he shouted to his bemused partner, the young Goblet. 'Lauf, Du Englischer Schweinhund, lauf.'

For some time the red rose players stood in a motionless daze as Himmelweit and his

partner commenced to run between the wickets, the ball still attached to the spike on the German's helmet.

Twenty-seven they ran before the immortal Cec Parkin shouted:

'Right, lads, let's scrag the German sod!'

The subsequent fracas was ghastly to behold.

Lancashire players piled themselves on top of Himmelweit who in a cold fury struck out with his sabre.

The gore flowed copiously, and it was not until the arrival of a detachment of the Somerset Yeomanry and representatives of the Frome Fire Brigade that the players were separated.

There was a moment's silence.

And then the immortal Cec Parkin pounced once more.

Pointing at the wicket, he shouted:

'How's that?'

Himmelweit was given out.

And that to my knowledge is the first and only time the dismissal has been written in the score book:

'Out. Iron Cross Hit Wicket.'

But what of Himmelweit?

Of him there was no sign.

Indeed, never again was he seen.

Rumour has it that he was taken under armed escort by the Somerset Yeomanry to London in the dead of the night and there executed on the real tennis courts at Lord's.

But who can say?

One thing, however, still puzzles me about Himmelweit.

No one ever knew his Christian name.

But then I don't suppose he was the sort of man to have one.

Peter Tinniswood
4.7.1979

OUR VILLAGE CRICKET CLUB.

AT OUR OPENING MATCH, SPINNER, THE DEMON LEFT-HANDER, WAS AGAIN IN GREAT FORM. HIS MASTERLY SKILL IN PLACING THE FIELD, AND HIS SOUND KNOWLEDGE OF THE GAME, REALLY WON THE MATCH FOR US.

"ABOUT THREE FEET NINE TO THE RIGHT, PLEASE, COLONEL— THAT IS TO SAY, YOUR RIGHT. THAT'S IT. BACK A LITTLE, JUST WHERE THE BUFF ORPINGTON'S FEEDING. THANKS."

"YOU, MR. STEWART, BY THIS THISTLE. JUST TO SAVE THE ONE, YOU KNOW."

HIS RUSES WERE MAGNIFICENT. WHEN THE SQUIRE CAME IN, SPINNER (WHO HAD PREVIOUSLY HELD A PRIVATE CON- SULTATION WITH THE OTHER BOWLER) SHOUTED, "YOU WON'T WANT A FINE LEG FOR THIS MAN. PUT HIM DEEP AND SQUARE." AND THEN ——

THE SQUIRE WAS NEATLY TAKEN FIRST BALL OFF A GLANCE AT FINE LEG BY SPINNER HIMSELF, WHO HAD CROSSED OVER (EXACTLY AS ARRANGED) FROM HIS PLACE AT SLIP.

CHAPTER SIX

Our Village Cricket Club

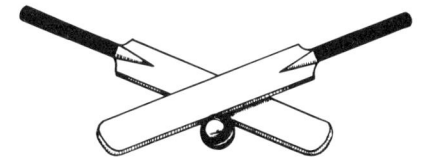

Middlecombe *v.* Paddlewick

I

Philip Renwick to Charles Holcombe
Room 99, XYZ Offices, Whitehall
8th August 1914
Dear Charlie, – Can you possibly turn out for us on Thursday next *v.* Paddlewick? We lost to them rather heavily in May last and are anxious to give them a sound beating. Their fast bowler is playing for them again, I hear, and we absolutely rely on your help. Can you get off for the day?
    Yours ever, P. R.

II

Charles Holcombe to Philip Renwick
Room 83, PQR Offices, Lombard Street
9th August 1914
My Dear Phil, – Thanks for yours. Will try to manage it next Thursday, but am doubtful. My chief, though a capable official, is no sport, and I anticipate difficulties. I had a day off only two weeks ago for cricket. Will do my best. Thine, C. H.

III

Charles Holcombe to Philip Renwick
PQR
10th August 1914
My Dear Phil, – Awfully sorry; no luck *re* Thursday. Boss hopeless. I broached the matter this morning (without actually asking for permission), but I fear the worst. You had better get another man for the Paddlewick match. So sorry.
    Yours ever,
        Charlie Holcombe

IV

Philip Renwick to Charles Holcombe
XYZ
10th August 1914
My Dear Charlie, – We shall be absolutely in the cart without you. They've got an awfully hot fast bowler. Bartram now tells me he can't possibly turn out, and you are the only really decent bat I know. We simply *can't* lose to Paddlewick again – we shall never hear the last of it. (No one need know that you don't play regularly for Middlecombe.) Do try your best, old man. Mightn't your Aunt Martha be seriously ill? Yours ever, Phil

V

Charles Holcombe to Philip Renwick
(wire)
Aunt Martha dying. All well. Boss absent Thursday, so can explain to him afterwards. Holcombe.

VI

Philip Renwick to Charles Holcombe
(wire)
Good boy. Funeral 11.30. Train Paddington 10.5 Lunch 1.30. Draw 6.30. Philip.

Charles Holcombe to Philip Renwick
Room 83, PQR Offices
14th August
My Dear Phil, – I regret that I was forced to leave somewhat hurriedly after the game last night. I have nothing to add to what I told you at lunch as to the identity of the Paddlewick Spofforth with my chief, of whose sporting talent I was in ignorance. But if you should

EXPLAINED.

Our Village Cricket Club, after the Opening Match.

The Young Squire (who, at school, made a century against Harrow). "I SAY SPINNER, I DON'T YET UNDERSTAND THAT FIRST BALL OF YOURS THAT TOOK MY LEG STUMP. WAS I LATE, OR SHOULD I HAVE PLAYED FORWARD?"

Spinner (our demon left-hander). "YOU COULDN'T 'AVE DONE NOTHING WITH IT, SIR."

hear of a good berth going anywhere I should be extraordinarily grateful.

Yours ever,
    Charlie Holcombe

PS – It was doubly unfortunate (in a way) that I should have scored a six and three fours in one over from his bowling.

19.8.1914

=|o|o|=

'CRICKET
Little Snoring Ladies *v.* Little Snoring Lads.' –
Local Paper

This match was played in Norfolk and not, as you might have expected, in Beds.

16.6.1920

Our Village Umpire

It was at the back of last season that Mr Hudgell, our humpire (as he pronounces it, and the aspirate certainly imparts to the word that little extra emphasis that distinguishes Mr Hudgell himself from the ordinary umpire), read a newspaper article by an eminent cricketer on the growing prevalence of the practice of making a loud and concerted appeal on every pretext, however slight, with the object of imposing upon the umpire.

Mr Hudgell cut that article out and kept it, and this season he seems to have made a firm resolve never to be biased in his judgement by the confident and stentorian tone of any appeal. And Mr Hudgell, who draws a

OUR OPENING MATCH.
"I SAY, BILL, YOU'VE GOT THAT PAD ON THE WRONG LEG."
"YES, I KNOW. I THOUGHT AS I WERE GOIN' IN T'OTHER END!"

sergeant-major's pension, is a humpire who means what he says.

Had we been aware of this resolve we should no doubt have applauded his attitude in the matter, for we ourselves had suffered often enough by reason of concerted but unjustifiable appeals. But we should almost certainly have overlooked the fact that Mr Hudgell's mind moves in certain well-defined grooves of its own.

In the first match of the season I lost the toss and we fielded. The very first ball was, to the bowler's surprise, a perfectly straight one. But the batsman mistook it for a leg-ball and stopped it with his pads. A less disputable case of obstruction could hardly be imagined.

'Zat?' bellowed half-a-dozen voices simul-taneously, in no doubt whatever as to the answer.

'Nottout,' replied Mr Hudgell with great assurance.

For a moment there was silence. One could almost feel the incredulity in the air. Even the batsman had the grace to look surprised. As for the bowler –

'*Wot* did you say?' demanded Mr Hudgell, turning and facing him majestically.

'I – I only said I thought – '

'Ho!' boomed Mr Hudgell, 'And oo's humpiring 'ere – me or you?'

'You, Mr 'Udgell,' replied the bowler humbly, retreating a few steps.

'Then I'll do the thinking.'

The general opinion was that Mr Hudgell

Sympathetic Friend (to gloomy batsman, disgusted at being given out for a catch at the wicket). "Wot's wrong, Bill? Was it 'tful?"   *Batsman.* "Dahtful! I should think it was dahtful! I could 'ardly 'ear it myself."

had not been looking, and had given the batsman the usual benefit of the doubt. But in the next over but one the same batsman snicked a ball into the wicket-keeper's hands. It was unmistakable to anybody who was not both deaf and blind. Immediately there was a confident and unanimous roar of 'Zat?'

'Nottout!' answered Mr Hudgell without hesitation.

At that point it became necessary for Mr Hudgell to leave the pitch in order to ask certain of the home spectators if they wanted something for themselves, and during his absence the fielders gathered together and hinted darkly at corruption.

But of course the fault was not in Mr Hudgell's integrity, but in his logic. Having read that nowadays many quite unjustifiable appeals were concerted and confident, he had reasoned that all concerted and confident appeals must be unjustifiable. It is not only on the physique that twenty-one years in the army leave their mark.

A certain theory formed itself in my mind, and I resolved to test it. Pretending not to notice the general astonishment and consternation as I took the ball, I put myself on to bowl at Mr Hudgell's end.

Fortune favoured me at once. The batsman – who had no moral right to be batting at all – chopped my first ball with his bat on to his pads. Of course nobody appealed, and I turned to Mr Hudgell with an assumption of diffidence, and asked in a low, almost apologetic tone.

'Er – how is that?'

'Hout!' roared Mr Hudgell.

3.6.1925

Our Cricket Week

Towards the end of the season we hold our Cricket Week. It consists of a one-day match surrounded by marquees. The fixture is Our Village *v.* Mugthorp. Mugthorp is an old enemy and for days the betting has been fast and furious. After the match a great deal of beer will change hands.

This year we have had the good fortune to secure a star performer, a really Great Man. He wears the colours of all the best clubs. He is staying with the Doctor, who brought him down to the nets last night. The GM didn't actually have a knock because he has been in great form all this year and is rather afraid of getting stale. He stood just behind the net and showed some of our weaker batsmen how to get across to those off-balls, and how not to run away from the fast bowler, and altogether made himself thoroughly useful. He would have had a bowl, but he was a little stiff after such a long spell against first-class batting a day or two ago, and naturally we wanted to keep him fresh for Mugthorp.

Our skipper being a real Tartar, we ended up with twenty minutes' fielding practice. The GM helped us a good deal with advice and encouragement, but a damaged finger (got last week stopping a snorter at silly point) prevented him from actually joining in. His keenness was infectious, however, and we chuckled to think how little the Mugthorpers knew what was in store for them.

We lost the toss, but after a short conference with his umpire the Mugthorp captain unaccountably put us in to bat. The GM and George (from 'The Goat') opened the innings. We had never realised before what a good bowler the Mugthorp speed-merchant was. His first three balls appeared to cause the GM some anxiety. Of course they didn't really. As he afterwards explained, while getting your eye in you can't take any risks. It seems that you should allow any balls to pass if they are not going to hit the wicket. The fourth ball was a half-volley on the off-stump which we expected to see clumped for four, but the GM elected to turn it neatly between himself and

OUR VILLAGE MATCH.

First Batsman. "WHY CAN'T YER CALL WHEN YOU'RE COMING?"
Second Batsman. "'CAUSE I DON'T WANT TO PUT THE FIELDER ON HIS GUARD."

THE CHARM OF VILLAGE CRICKET.

THE CHARM OF VILLAGE CRICKET LIES TO A GREAT EXTENT IN THE STRESS IT PLACES ON THE INDIVIDUAL FACTOR. FOR INSTANCE, ONE KNOWS THAT, OTHER THINGS BEING EQUAL, IF ONE HITS THE BALL DIRECTLY TOWARDS A—

Fougasse

FIELDER IN A CLOTH CAP
ONE CAN RUN A SINGLE—

AND IF HE'S WEARING BRACES
ONE CAN RUN TWO—

BUT IF HE'S GOT ON ONE OF
THOSE FANCY SWEATERS ONE
STAYS WHERE ONE IS.

SIMILARLY, A BELT WITH A SNAKE
IN IT MEANS A SINGLE—

SO DOES A CLUB
TIE—

WHEREAS A GENT'S FANCY
BOW MEANS TWO.

ONE TAKES NO RISKS, OF
COURSE, WITH A HANDKER-
CHIEF ROUND THE NECK—

BUT ONE GETS IN TWO
FOR TROUSERS TUCKED
INTO SOCKS—

STRETCHING IT TO THREE
FOR A STRAW HAT—

AND FOUR FOR A BLACK
WAISTCOAT—

WHILE FOR CUFFS BUTTONED
AT THE WRIST—

OR A DICKEY ONE JUST
RUNS IT OUT.

WITH SMALL BOYS IN SHORTS
ONE NATURALLY TAKES NO
CHANCES WHATEVER—

AS EVERYONE KNOWS THEY ARE APT TO BECOME SO CONFOUNDEDLY ENTHUSIASTIC.

the leg-stump (such a pretty shot) and called George for a run. There was a Mugthorper at short leg, so George was run-out easily, although it was our umpire's end. The GM walked some of the way back to the pavilion with George and gave him one or two hints on running, for future guidance.

Disasters never come singly. The first ball of the next over was a slow full-pitch. The GM played back just too late and was bowled. It is in such moments that great men show their greatness, and the GM went straight across and had the sight screen moved for the benefit of the next batsman.

A sterling display by the Doctor and some free hitting by his groom cheered things up a bit, and we were finally finished off for exactly 100.

Of course the GM went in to bowl first. He seemed to have some difficulty in getting a good foothold on our springy village turf, but after changing his boots and sowing a lot of sawdust he managed to get a better grip. There were two no-balls in his next over, but, as he pointed out afterwards, one can hardly expect village umpires to be up to county standard. The tremendous finger-spin he got on the ball made it come very fast off the bat, and with the score at 64 for no wicket our skipper gave him a rest.

The bowling of Parson and Jasper (George's brother) proved to be so little to the Mugthorpers' liking that we got nine wickets down for 99. The excitement became intense. Parson was bowling and the GM was fielding long-on. I think the skipper should have put a man like him at cover-point; as it was he had very little to do and was obliged to keep on his Old Harvesters' sweater and Blankshire Boosters' muffler to keep him warm.

Parson bowled a fast yorker. The last hope of Mugthorp just succeeded in blocking it and removed a large divot. Parson pitched the next into the divot-hole with unerring accuracy; the Mugthorper made to drive it along the floor past cover-point but lifted it to the long-on instead. Long-on dropped the catch and they ran two. It transpired, as we say, that he was unsighted by a passing bumble bee.

We have written to Mugthorp and asked them to agree to the rule that only *bona-fide* residents shall play in our village game.

4.8.1926

AT OUR VILLAGE FÊTE.
"SEE, AMELIA, THE DEAR VICAR IS JUST PUTTING UP THE HYMNS."

The Young 'Un. "COME ON, IT'S AN EASY ONE! LUMMY, I COULD RUN TWO."
The Old 'Un. "COULD YER? THEN JUST RUN BACK AGAIN."

Village Cricket

Young William on his native green was frolicsome and free,
To watch him bat the village came and sat in ecstasy,
For fielders flinched and bowlers bold recoiled when he appeared
And quivers of excitement ran through every ancient's beard.
Full many a gentle village maiden's heart went pit-a-pat
With longing to walk out with him when he walked in to bat.
He wore no pads, he took no guard, 'twas all the same to him;
He swung a swift and valiant bat and smote the ball with vim.
He smote it oft and hard and high; loud rose the village yells
To peals of ringing merriment from all the village belles.
With last man in and two to win a slip claimed a doubtful catch;
Their umpire took a chance and cried, 'Out! and we wins the match.'
He spoke too soon; the scorer (ours) countered his little tricks
And swore he'd only put down four for William's final six.
So both sides claimed the match and went home happy, which is rare.
Some say it wasn't cricket, but the village doesn't care.

22.5.1939

The Hambledon Touch

In 1948, at the close of his last triumphant tour of his English stamping-grounds, Don Bradman told us what was wrong with our cricket. He said that we were not making the most of our rich natural resources, that our thousands of keen and gifted 'Saturday afternoon' cricketers were denied the opportunity of graduating to greatness because they were condemned to play on poor pitches. We needed pitches on which the ball would come through at a predictable height and would break only when charged with finger-spin. We needed concrete pitches like those found in every Australian park.

Now Sir Donald's statement was, in a way, a pretty compliment to village cricket, though it only confirmed what our village cricketers had always suspected. And it had interesting repercussions. Many clubs invested immediately in bags of cement and loads of rubble; players bought new boots, bats and braces and began to take the game very seriously. At the beginning of the 1949 season it seemed that half the Weald was fighting for a place in the Test team, and for a few weeks, while batsmen padded up to every ball and struggled to avoid a crooked bat, scoring was staggeringly low. Even our most renowned hitters failed consistently, and Elsworth, the 'Lion of Cheapfold', who had never previously worn either pads or batting gloves, was ignominiously lbw three innings running.

I particularly remember our home game with Hartwood Common – always a keen side. When I arrived at the Green shortly after three o'clock I was astonished to find our opponents all present and flannelled although the match was not scheduled to start until two-thirty. Talk about enthusiasm! We batted first and Tickner opened from the compost end. But this was a new Tickner: for years he had hurled his fast long-hops with deadly accuracy, scattering batsmen and stumps at will; now he seemed to spend most of his abundant energy trying to impart lustre to a ball that had already seen service in five matches. For six overs he bowled medium pace in-swingers (or so he said) and was then taken off for the first time in years.

It was in this same match that a Hartwood batsman appealed against the length of the pitch, claiming that it was substantially less than the twenty-two yards prescribed in the Marylebone rules. A tape-measure was produced, unravelled and mended, and the umpires went down on their knees. Later, when we examined the old crease-marks and patches of renewed turf, we realised that a discrepancy of two yards had remained undetected for at least a year and possibly since the club's foundation.

There were other unpleasant incidents – many of them – before the men of the Weald forgot Sir Donald's words, abandoned their pursuit of Test honours and reverted to real village cricket.

What is *real* village cricket? Well, chronometrically it is much more than Saturday afternoon cricket. Village cricket begins at dawn every Saturday with the steady thrumming of finger-tips against barometers –

'I reckon that's put paid to it for today,' says Long-stop. 'Glass is tumblin': it'll rain buckets, drat it!'

'Then you'll not be wantin' your trousers ironed for once,' says his wife. 'A good thing too: I'll be able to get on with my proper work.'

'Trousers? No, won't be needed. Leastways, not unless it clears up. It'll take a lot of wet to spoil the pitch. Bone hard, she was, last night; just right for a few bumpers. Wouldn't do no harm to have my flannels ready just in case. Be a good girl and run your iron over 'em. And get Jackie to dab a bit of whitening on my boots . . .' – and the game isn't really finished until late on Saturday night, when the landlord of 'The Crown' has counted out the last of his cud-chewing customers.

The hours of actual play in village cricket are governed by natural laws and local by-laws. Play begins when the midday meal has been satisfactorily digested or when the inn closes down for its siesta – whichever is the later; the tea interval occurs when the captain's wife announces that the kettle is boiling and lasts until someone volunteers to stand umpire in place of Old Phil, who has suddenly remembered a promise to take his missus to the movies; the game ends when the last wicket has fallen or when the licensing laws make further refreshments available.

The teas, I regret to say, are not up to much. Before the war captains were often appointed on the strength of their wives' skill with a sponge mixture or a sandwich salad; now our provisions are the weekly stock-in-trade and unsaleable returns of the local confectioner. We buy cheaply and sell at a huge profit, and the funds so procured help to keep the club's head just above the waters of insolvency. But I doubt whether Bradman himself would get many runs after an intake of one of our Chelsea buns.

You see? Excuses, always excuses. There, to my mind, you have the essential charm of village cricket. Failures with bat or ball count for nothing: they are so easily explained away. In Test, county, league and club cricket, pitches are good, umpires are neutral, bats are sound and there is little distraction behind the

bowler's arm. But in village cricket the pitches are either sporting or unsporting, umpires are either yes-men or no-men, bats are like hunks of Gruyère, and the zone immediately behind the bowler's arm is always infested with dogs, cats, cattle, children, cars, trees and dark mounds of cumulus cloud.

We do not, of course, suffer from barracking. Most of our spectators have at one time or another been called upon to fill a last-minute vacancy in the team and know that they may be called upon again; and the rest of the onlookers are either 'foreigners' cooped up in their smart cars or ancients who can only mumble ineffectually through their beards. Yet we can never relax: we must at all times contrive to look picturesque and enthusiastic, true heirs of Hambledon and Conduit fields of tradition, for at all times we must be ready to face the cameras of roving press photographers ('Forever England! On Saturday our

I TURN OUT FOR THE VILLAGE CRICKET TEAM BECAUSE . . .

A merry topical quip in my Sunday sermon about the Saturday match keeps my flock happy

In the vac. it's good for the soul to go slumming

I hear things unobtrusively—I shouldn't wonder if I'm made a Sergeant soon

Some of the birds who dish up the teas are dollies

I work for the Squire

There's a binge in the pub afterwards

The Bank Manager considers it part of my job to keep the score for the club

Of the sense of power—like Roman emperor—thumbs down and I can ruin a man week-end

There's a fabulous feed with buns and stuff at tea time

My wife wants me out from under her feet on Saturday afternoons

Tradition, y'know—family inaugurated the local club in 1804 and I'm stuck with it

HARGREAVES

It's a legal way of smashing things—wickets, fingers, bonces. Saturday's a smashing day.

My wife finds jobs for me if I stay at home

I like the kinky gloves and pads

cameraman visited the lovely hamlet of Scronge and found another "Test" in progress. The church in the background is a beautiful example of Norman architecture. It was built in 1135') and withstand the scrutiny of the romantic school of cricket writers ('. . . and suddenly as I emerged from the deep shadows of the ancient almshouses of Scronge a merry sound welled up from the meadows and soared above the flaming copper beeches. It was the sweet noise of bat on ball, of willow on leather. I picked up my skirts and ran, pell-mell, for the village green . . .')

At times our responsibilities are very trying.

I may be allowed to add, in conclusion, that Scronge was not one of the Wealden villages to invest in a concrete pitch. The idea was certainly mooted most energetically and George Stamps, left-handed No. 5 batsman and local building contractor, submitted an uninvited tender; but in the end the scheme was scotched by a carefully worded memorandum from our scorer, Alec Welling. This pointed out that a concrete pitch would disturb the equilibrium between bat and ball, encourage 'safety first' batting, lengthen hours of play and *ipso facto* reduce the time devoted to 'The Crown', penalise bowlers, drive Tickner, our demon trundler, into the arms of our Heddingfold rivals, and cost as near twenty pounds as dammit. It also demonstrated that a club with a natural wicket would (in its home games) enjoy a considerable advantage over teams used to playing on concrete pitches, and might therefore be expected to win at least half its matches – which was something Scronge had never managed to do in all its long history.

Bernard Hollowood
30.8.1950

Alfred, Lord Tennyson Umpires a Cricket Match

So in the leafy heart of June
  I donned, to judge the mimic strife,
  The white coat of blameless life,
And stood, the sunlit afternoon,

Counting the pebbles, fixt in thought,
  And watch'd the battle ebb and flow,
  Where one would come, and lightly go,
Too soon returning, bowled or caught;

And one with keener eye would wield
  The unrelenting blade, and smite
  The flying ball to left or right
In splendid arcs about the field.

With anxious but unerring eye
  I judg'd the careless wide, and spread
  The outstretch'd arms, and o'er the head
Uprais'd the hand to mark a bye.

But, on a sudden, lo! a shout
  About mine ears; and, high upflung
  The eager arms with silent tongue
Made question whether in or out.

I stood; I paused a moment's space,
  And in the sudden hush I heard
  A counsellor that in me stirr'd
And said 'Twere better far to face

The lifted brow and faint surprise
  Of him who waits thy stern decree,
  Than watch the incredulity
Mirror'd in two and twenty eyes.'

I rais'd the finger; as he went,
  The eager crowd, according well,
  Relax'd, and on their faces fell
The silence of a deep content.

G. H. Vallins
1.7.1953

PRECEDENCE AT BATTERSEA.

"Garn! The Treasurer goes in before the bloomin' Seckertary!"

Now that motors are sweeping the children off the roads, the railway tracks remain their only available playground. At least you know where you are with a train.

CHAPTER SEVEN

Kids' Capers

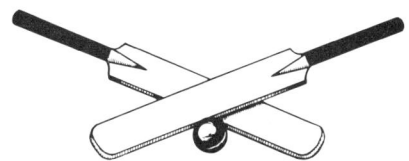

Hants *v.* The Rest

This important match for which I had the honour to be appointed official scorer, was played under special rules promulgated for the occasion by the MCC and laboriously explained to me beforehand by Peter. For example:

1. If the striker play a ball into or through a flower-bed, he shall be deemed to be caught out.

2. A stroke which places the ball anywhere on the grass patch shall count one run, anywhere along the path by the scullery two runs, provided that if it passes the scullery side-door it shall count four runs, subject always to the provisions of Special Rule 1.

3. A ball passing the stumps without being touched by the batsman and hitting the back fence shall count one bye.

4. The names of bowlers and fielders shall be determined when necessary by use of the 'Dickory, dickory, dock, etc.', formula and the jabbing of a pencil in the appropriate page of the score-book, provided always that the jabber must have his eyes shut at the moment of jabbing.

Chapman won the toss for the Rest of England and elected to bat. As official scorer I took up my position on the official chair at square-leg, armed with the official score book and the official pencil, while Hobbs walked importantly to the wicket.

Holding the bat temporarily in his left hand, he hurled the ball against the back wall of the scullery, whence it rebounded on to the field of play. Meanwhile Hobbs had swiftly grasped the bat with both hands and assumed a posture of defence. With the effortless grace of which he is a master he essayed a square cut as the ball passed him, but it went by at least two yards out of his reach and hit the back fence with a thump.

'Bye!' called Peter, momentarily ceasing to be Hobbs.

The Batsman. "TELL YER WOT. YOU BE ENGLAND, AND I'LL BE VICTOR TRUMPET!"

Father. "OH, YES, I USED TO PLAY QUITE A LOT OF CRICKET. I ONCE MADE FORTY-SEVEN."
Son. "WHAT—WITH A HARD BALL, FATHER?"

Bowler. "I'M WARNIN' YER. IF YER STANDS SO MUCH IN FRONT AN' I 'ITS YER, YER AHT—SEE?"
Batsman. "GARN—NEVER MIND ME; YOU 'IT THE BAT. YOU AIN'T DONE IT YET."

A GOOD REASON.

Old Gent. "Now, why do you keep knocking this ball over here?"

The Junior Cricketer. "Because it's six, Sir, every time we 'its it over."

Woolley followed him quickly to the pavilion, neither having scored.

After that most of the others did a little better, but Tate was the only player to reach double figures before shattering a wallflower. All the time, the byes mounted up steadily.

At length Larwood decapitated a geranium and the innings came to a conclusion.

'What's the score?' inquired Peter eagerly.

'Wait a minute,' I said; 'one of these men ought to be "not out", you know.'

'Oh, yes,' he agreed, readily enough. 'Let's pretend it's Hobbs; he's a good man.'

We pretended it was Hobbs and I handed Peter the score:

Hobbs	not out	0
Sutcliffe	c. Kennedy b. Tennyson	2
Sandham	c. Parker b. Brown	0
Woolley	c. and b. Parker	0
Chapman	c. Bowell b. Kennedy	3
Hendren	c. Kennedy b. Bowell	4

I entered one bye in the score-book.

Twelve more byes were added to the score before Hobbs got a ball straight enough to hit. He made a brilliant and characteristic off-drive, which flashed through a flower-bed, knocked off two buds, buckled a tulip and stunned a caterpillar.

'Out!' cried Peter. 'Hobbs – duck!'

Seizing the score-book, he repeated the 'Dickory, dickory, dock, etc.', formula with eyes screwed up conscientiously and jabbed.

'Caught Pothecary,' he announced. 'Bowled Mead,' he added after a second incantation.

Sutcliffe stayed longer and at the end of five minutes the score had been increased by twenty-one byes and two singles. Then he too fell a victim to the flower-bed. Sandham and

Demon Bat. "'Ere, jer fink I'm goin' to let cross-eyed Ginger gimme centre?"

Jack (reading father's expert article on last Test match). "OH, I SAY, DAD—YOU SHOULD HAVE CONSULTED ME BEFORE YOU WROTE ALL THIS."

REPERCUSSIONS OF THE AUSTRALIAN VISIT.

Small Boy. "'ERE, WE CAN'T 'AVE KIDS LIKE YOU. GO AND PLAY WITH YER OWN LOT."
Smaller Boy. "LUMME, DON'T YOU WANT NO YOUNG BLOOD?"

Captain (to bowler). "CALL YOURSELF LARWOOD, AN' GOES AN' BOWLS UNDER-'AND."

Bowler. "SO WOULD LARWOOD IF THE ONLY WAY 'E 'AD TER KEEP 'IS TROUSIS UP WOS BY STOOPIN' DAHN."

Batsman. "AND WHAT'S MORE, JACK 'OBBS ONCE PATTED ME ON THE HEAD."
Bowler. "OH, DID HE? WELL, IF HE SAW YOU PLAY CRICKET NOW, HE'D CLUMP YOU OVER THE EAR."

team was very much better than that of The Rest, principally, I suspect, because Peter was born and has lived all his life in Hampshire. The batsmen were helped too by the removal of the official scorer and his chair to a position directly between the stumps and the deadliest of the flower-beds.

The keeping of Strudwick, however, was immense, and not a single bye was scored. I could picture Livsey blushing painfully in the pavilion.

With ten of the side dismissed, the score was one-hundred-and-sixty-eight and the excitement was electrical, as the journalists say. Mead had scored fifty-two and Brown thirty-nine. Pothecary, the last man, walked slowly to the wicket – a terrifying ordeal for a young player.

The first ball took his middle stump and sent the bails flying.

Hearne	c. Gross b. Boyes	3
Hammond	c. Newman b. Kennedy	2
Tate	c. Boyes b. Pothecary	11
Strudwick	c. Mead b. Parker	4
Larwood	c. Tennyson b. Mead	3
	Extras	137
	Total	169

'Not a bad score,' I said, 'but I'm sorry about Livsey. I've always had such a great admiration for him as a wicket-keeper. What a pity this should have happened in such a swell match! Quite a tragedy for the poor chap.'

'Livsey had a pain,' explained Peter. 'There's going to be a meeting of the MCC now – about the rules.'

He conversed busily with a crimson rambler for a few moments and returned with a grave face.

'The MCC have decided,' he announced, 'that byes are too much of a nuisance, and besides, Strudwick can't have a pain as well as Livsey, and when the ball hits the back fence it won't be a bye – only if it goes right over. The fence is really Strudwick, you see.'

I must admit that the batting of the County

"Don't stop him, darling! It's his form of self-expression."

Small Autograph-Hunter. "Have you got Bradman?"
Smaller Autograph-Hunter. "No, but I've got the signature of a chap that has."

'Out!' I yelled. 'And that's the first man who's been bowled in the match.'

'No ball!' said Peter.

I meekly entered one 'no ball'.

Pothecary slashed wildly at the next ball and missed it.

'No ball!' said Peter.

The third ball shot between the legs of my chair and demolished the last of our tulips. Pothecary was out and Hampshire led on the first innings by one run!

'There's going to be another meeting of the MCC now,' said Peter, and at this moment my wife, in the thoughtless way women have, called me to run out and post a letter for her. I left Peter earnestly communing with the crimson rambler.

When I returned ten minutes later I found that the second innings of The Rest had been completed. Peter handed me the official scorebook with a guilty smirk.

Hobbs	b. Livsey not out	. .	0
Sutcliffe	b. Livsey	. . . . . .	0
Sandham	b. Livsey	. . . . . .	0
Woolley	b. Livsey	. . . . . .	0
Chapman	b. Livsey	. . . . . .	0
Hendren	b. Livsey	. . . . . .	0

Hollowood

"Try a faster one, dear—I think he's beginning to get the hang of it."

Hearne	b. Livsey	. . . . . .	0
Hammond	b. Livsey	. . . . . .	0
Tate	b. Livsey	. . . . . .	0
Strudwick	b. Livsey	. . . . . .	0
Larwood	b. Livsey	. . . . . .	0
	b. Livsey (*sic*)	. . . .	0
	Extras		
	Total	. . . . . .	0

'The MCC decided, you see,' said Peter, 'that there shouldn't be any stumps, but the back fence should be the wicket instead, and they said you needn't dickory, dickory, dock every time, because it takes too long, but do it once at first and pretend it's the same man all the time afterwards. I'm *jolly* glad Hampshire won, aren't you, Dad? By an innings too!'

At any rate I am glad we can pretend that Livsey, who has always been a favourite of mine, is a phenomenal bowler and I can regard him with even greater respect in the future.

10.8.1927

Hollowood

"No, you be Len Hutton and I'll be Neville Cardus."

CHAPTER EIGHT

Mr Punch's Personalities

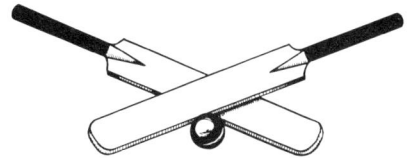

A Century of Centuries

(By scoring 288 in the match Gloucester v. Somerset at Bristol, on May 17, Mr W. G. Grace, now nearing his 47th birthday, made his hundredth innings of 100 runs or over in first-class matches.)

'O Frabjous day! Callooh! Calley!'
Sang *Punch* on the seventeenth instant May,
   With a true Jaberwockian chortle,
As he saw the swipe on the Bristol ground,
Which worked Grace's hundred of centuries round;
   A record ne'er equalled by mortal.

'My beamish boy' – of nigh forty-seven –
There isn't a cheerier sight under heaven
   Than W. G. at the wicket.
When your 'vorpal' bat 'goes snicker-snack'
Punch loves to lie with a tree at his back,
   And watch what *he* calls cricket.

And now, as a topper of thirty years,
After many hopes, and a few faint fears
   (Which *Punch* never shared for a jiffy)
You've done the trick! Did your pulse beat quick
As you crept notch by notch within reach of the nick?
   Did even *your* heart feel squiffy?

Punch frankly owns *his* went pit-a-pat
While he followed the ball and watched your bat
   As the nineties slowly tottled;
And the boys of the Bristol Brigade held breath,
In an anxious silence as still as death.
   But oh! like good fizz unbottled,

We all 'let go' with a loud 'hooray'
As the leather was safely 'put away'
   For that hundredth hundred. Verily,
Now you're the 'many centuried' Grace!
And for many a year may you keep top place,
Piling three figure innings right merrily!

25.5.1895

PUNCH'S FANCY PORTRAITS.—No. 90.

F. R. SPOFFORTH,

"The Demon" or Imp-etuous Bowler, representing Cricket on t'other side of the H-earth.

THE "LEVIATHAN BAT,"

Or Many-Centuried Marvel of the Modern (Cricket) World, in his high-soaring, top-scoring, Summer-day Flight. (Dr. William Gilbert Grace.)

As Champion him the whole World hails. | It takes a week to reach the Bails
Lords! How he smites and thumps! | When he's before the Stumps.
| "Chevy Chase" (revised).

His New Title – Dr Grace, CB ('Companion of the Bat').

15.6.1895

Another Title!! Supplemental Gazette of Birthday Honours – Dr W. G. Grace to be Cricket-Field-Marshal.

15.6.1895

–|●|●|–

A Great Gunn

(Gunn, the great Notts' batsman, playing for the Players of England against the Australians at Lord's, on June 19 and 20, made 228 runs, the highest individual score ever made in this country against the Australians.)

Such calm, graceful batting, of funk as defiant,
    As proof against flurry, deserved the crowd's roar.
'Twas cricket, indeed, when the Nottingham Giant,
    Against the best batting, piled up that huge score;
And the crowd as they watched him smite, play, block, or run,
    Could grasp the full meaning of 'Sure as a Gunn!'

28.6.1890

A PRINCE OF CRICKET.

Mr. Punch. "Bravo, Ranji! Plucky Performance!"

A Song for the Slogger
(*By One who has seen him Smite*)

(During the Scarborough Cricket Week, Mr C. L.
Thornton, the champion slogger of England and
enthusiastic supporter of the sport, was presented
with a silver trophy, representing himself at the
wicket, as a memento of the great part he has taken
in the Scarborough Festival since its institution in
1869. Playing in the second innings of MCC against
Yorkshire, Mr Thornton batted as energetically as
ever, and twice drove the ball out of the ground.)

Great Thornton the slogger, it comes as a jogger
    To memory this tale of your trophy well merited.
Great Scott! how time's flitting.
    Your gift of tall-hitting,
Which no one – save Bonnor – has fully inherited,
    You showed e'en at Eton. It has not been beaten.
You'd whip even Jehu at 'furious *driving*'.
    Not dashing O'Brien could lick the old Lion
Of Cambridge, whose fire is still plainly surviving.
    The pet of the Million, you've cleared the pavilion,
And spanked the ball many times 'over the paling'.

Here's health to you 'Buns!' may you score lots of runs,
    And oft stir the crowd with your spirit unfailing.
How often I'd watch when they 'bowled for a catch',
    And you gave 'em one, truly, but in the next parish!
You'd run up your hundred, while 'all the world wondered',
    In less than an hour, Sir, a pace wear-and-tearish.
Though pedants demur, mighty smiting *will* stir,
    So 'more power to your elbow', great Slogger of Sixes!
Ah! if you should play in the Shades some fine day,
The Elysium Fields, in the old Oval way,
      They must 'spread', and you'll *then* clear the bounds,
      though they're Styx's!!!

8.9.1894

'Our Bobby'
Sung by a Surrey Man

(Robert Abel, the Surrey Cricketer, has already this
season made three successive innings of over a
hundred, one of them topping the two hundred.)

Air – 'Comin' Thro' the Rye'

Gin our Bobby meet a loose one
    Coming, low or high,
Gin our Bobby smite that loose one,
    Won't that loose one fly!

Surrey's Bobby, short and cobby,
    Hath sure hand and eye;
And Surrey shouts when Bob A-bel
    Smacks up a century!

Gin our Bobby hits a hundred
    Three times running – well,
Surrey long time of her Bobby
    Will that story tell!
Ilka county has its crack bat,
    Surrey man am I,
And Surrey's Bobby bears the bell,
    Yells Surrey in full cry!

23.5.1896

Mr Punch's Sketchy Interviews:
Mr C. B. Fry

On entering Mr Fry's gymnasium we found him so absorbed in a game of Wibbley Wob that he was entirely unconscious of our presence. This gave us an opportunity to examine the room, which reflected at every turn the tastes and accomplishments of its gifted occupant. Pens and cricket pads, note-books and footballs, dumb-bells and blotting-pads, parallel bars and press-cuttings, running shoes and encyclopaedias, shorts and short-hand notes strewed the apartment. Over the mantelpiece was a portrait of the Sussex Indian Prince inscribed 'To the best bat of the day, from a better', and on the door was pinned the ten thousand and fourteenth photograph of Mr Fry at the wicket.

"Oh, I write all the time."

"Mr. Fry leaped lightly over our head."

When we had proceeded thus far in our investigation the game of Wibbley Wob terminated, and Mr Fry leaped lightly over our head, bidding us welcome as he passed. While still in mid air he changed his mind and leaped back again. After running up one wall, along the ceiling, and down the other wall, he offered us a chair and subsided gracefully into another.

'This is my Ping-Pong hour,' he remarked, looking at his watch, 'but I'll give it to you instead.'

'Do you play games all day?' we asked.

'All day,' he answered. 'I begin with a Blankley exerciser. Then I row for an hour, bat for an hour at the nets in the back garden, run for an hour, jump for an hour, and play football for an hour. That brings me to lunch. After lunch I play Wibbley Wob, Ping-Pong and Parlour Croquet, and generally spend an hour at the photographer's. This is essential, for you may have perhaps observed that I look quite different every time you see me. Then comes tea. After tea I exercise on the bars, vault, turn somersaults, and use the Indian Clubs. In the evening I play Tiddly Winks, Spillikins, Bumblepuppy and Bridge.'

'But when do you write?'

'Oh, I write all the time. I never use more than one hand for games; I write with the other. While I was playing Wibbley Wob just now I was simultaneously engaged on my weekly Corinthian column for the *Builder*.'

'Can you tell us anything about yourself, Mr Fry? Your name, for example, how did you get that?'

'Well, the Frys are mostly Quakers, and I trace my descent to the inventor of cocoa-nut matting. I was called C. B. after Campbell-Bannerman. One of my first jumps was over his fence. Then, as you know, when only thirteen years old I charged a 17-stone man at Rugby football. He never recovered the shock. At Oxford I studied the classics profoundly, visited Greece in the 'Long' and received the freedom of Corinth.'

'And what are your plans?'

'I have not decided yet whether to stand against Mr Reckitt for the Brigg Division in the Blue interest, to edit *The Times*, or take seriously to Oology. It depends on how the ducks lay next cricket season.'

'Who is your greatest hero in modern life?'

'Ranji.'

'And what is your pet ideal?'

'To make 100 in both innings, get a substitute to field, and write an account of the match simultaneously for two papers. And now you must excuse me, as I have to give my son, already a promising centre forward though only four years old, a lesson in the use of the stylograph.'

7.1.1903

-|◦|◦|-

We think it a pity that several of our newspapers should persist in referring to Prince Ranjitsinhji as 'The Popular Jam'. It sounds so much like an advertisement.

20.3.1907

-|◦|◦|-

W. G.

So W. G. is no more! Cricket itself has suffered the cruellest wounds since August of last year, and now the father of it is laid low. And his place will never be filled again. There could not be another W. G.; there can be, if the Fates allow the game to recover, great cricketers; but there can never be another so immeasurably the greatest, never another not only to play cricket as Grace did, but to be cricket as Grace was.

Cricket and W. G. were indeed one. Popular superstition and the reporters had it that he was a physician, and it is true that, when a wicket-keeper smashed his thumb or a bumping ball flew into a batsman's face, first aid would be administered in the grateful

shade of the 'Doctor's' beard; but it was impossible really to think seriously of his medical activities, or indeed of any of his activities off the field. Between September and May one thought of him as hibernating in a cave, returning to life with renewed vigour with the opening of the season, his beard a little more imposing, his proportions a little more gigantic; so that each year the bat in his hand, as he walked to the wicket with that curious rolling tumbling gait, seemed a more trifling implement.

With the mind's vision one sees him in many postures. At the wicket: waiting, striking and running; and again bowling, in his large round action, coming in from the leg, with a man on the leg boundary a little finer than square, to catch the youngsters who lunged at the widish ball (his 'bread-and-butter trick' W. G. called it). One sees him thus and thus, and even retiring to the pavilion, either triumphantly – with not, of course, a sufficient but an adequate score to his credit – or with head bent pondering how it was he let that happen and forewarning himself against it next time. But to these reminiscent eyes the most familiar and characteristic attitude of all is W. G. among his men at the fall of a wicket, when they would cluster round to discuss the event and, no matter how tall they were, W. G.'s beard and shoulders would top the lot. Brave days for ever gone!

Of late years, since his retirement, the Old Man, as he was best known among his fellow amateurs, was an occasional figure at Lord's. More than a figure, a landmark, for he grew vaster steadily, more massive, more monumental. What must it have been like to have that Atlas back and those shoulders in front of one in the theatre! At the big matches he would be seen on one of the lower seats of the pavilion with a friend on either side, watching and commenting. But the part of oracle sat very lightly upon him; he was ever a man of action rather than of words; shrewd and sagacious enough, but without rhetoric. That his mind worked with Ulysses-like acuteness every other captain had reason to know; his tactics were superb. But he donned and doffed them with his flannels. In ordinary life he was content to be an ordinary man.

DOUBLE GLOUCESTER.

1895 AND 1927.

SHADE OF W. G. GRACE (*to* HAMMOND *of his own county*). "A NOBLE CLOUT ERE MAY IS OUT."

[With a score of 192, made against Hampshire, HAMMOND equalled W. G.'s record of a thousand runs in May.]

Although sixty-seven, he did not exactly look old; he merely looked older than he had been, or than any such performer should be permitted to be. There should be a dispensation for such masters, by which W. G. with his bat, and John Roberts with his cue, and Cinquevalli with his juggling implements would be rendered immune from Anno Domini. Almost to the end he kept himself fit, either with local matches, where latterly he gave away more runs in the field than he hit up, not being able to 'get down' to the ball, or with golf or beagling. But the great beard grew steadily more grizzled and the ponderous footfall more weighty. Indeed towards the last he might almost have been a work by Mestrovics, so colossal and cosmic were his lines.

Peace to his ashes! We shall never look upon his like again. The days of Grace are ended.

3.11.1915

—|●|●|—

Can Nothing Be Done?

Can nothing be done for J. B. Hobbs
To make him sometimes get out for blobs?
Or is he doomed for some dreadful crime
To make centuries till the end of time?
An eminent Harley Street specialist
Says that a nervous action of wrist,
Combined with a lesion of eyes and feet
Which is rapidly growing more complete
Through long indulgence without restraint,
Has at last become an organic complaint,
And only a rest in a nursing-home
And elbow-baths with electric foam,
Or using a bat of exiguous size
And wearing a bandage over the eyes
And batting left-handed after tea,
Can uproot this obstinate malady.

Hobbs went to be 'psyched' the other day,
And the psycho-analyst said to him 'Pray,
Can you remember in early youth
Some terrible shock? Now tell me the truth.'
And Hobbs remembered at last and told
How, when a boy of four years old
And a naughty boy, he was rather fond
Of chasing ducks in the farmer's pond;
And once he chased a particular duck
So far away from its native muck
That it failed at last in wind and leg,
Sat down on the grass and laid an egg;

And Hobbs, triumphant, without alarm
Brought back the egg to show at the farm,
Expecting, of course, to be praised and thanked;
But he wasn't: he got severely spanked.

And the psycho-analyst, looking wise,
Said to Hobbs, who had tears in his eyes,
'It is easy to see how the complex grew
Till a duck became a terror to you.
What you ought to do is go and slay
A covey of wild ducks every day,
Or go and see Henrik Ibsen's play,
Or keep a duck for a household pet,
And dine upon duck's-egg omelette.'

The MCC have at last been moved
To try, if his health is not improved,
To lift from the mind of Hobbs its load
By adding these words to their legal code
Where the ways are mentioned of getting out,
Which do very well for us, no doubt:
'Excepting Hobbs, who must always be given
Out by the Umpire at eighty-seven.'
(A rhyme like that, which is painful to me,
Seems sound, of course, to the MCC.)

But, suppose the amendment does not pass,
Hobbs will be no better off, alas!
Hobbs will go on with both arms aching
For ever and ever century-making.
Unless he follows the doctor's advice,
Or uses a bat without any splice,
Or slippery boots without any nails,
Or ties an invisible thread to the bails,
He will go on for ever enduring the rigours
Of reaching the three ineffable figures.

Can nothing be done for J. B. Hobbs
To make him sometimes get out for blobs?

Evoe
29.7.1925

—|●|●|—

Hobbs the Miraculous

'Hobbs scored 60 out of 14 before lunch.' *Sunday Paper*. Perhaps the scorer had lunched early.

29.7.1925

—|●|●|—

'Fender on Hobbs', says a heading. It sounds like the opposite of the cricket on the hearth.

2.9.1925

Up to Chapman!

(With grateful acknowledgements to the Morning and Evening Press.)

Seldom in history has any man had to face a task of such portentous magnitude as that which will confront the English captain in selecting a team to represent us in the second Test Match at Sydney this week.

It might seem at first that, having triumphed in the preliminary encounter by a margin of 675 runs, the tall young Kent left-hander might rely on the same team as last time. But anyone who knows anything of the difficulty of writing perpetual articles about a Test Match in Australia before the Test Match has begun, will see at once that this is not the case. The former Berkshire player will have to spend many a long hour of earnest perplexity and mental strife (if I can make him) between now and the fourteenth of December. He will have to recollect that in the game concluded last week his bowling was not so thoroughly tested as it would have been if the Australians had failed to get out so quickly and made more runs, or had stayed in five days without making any runs at all. He will have to sit up at night, probably with a wet towel round his head, asking himself what would have happened if Woodfull and Ponsford, as seemed only too likely before the game started, had made about two-hundred-and-fifty each, or if Kelleway had dug his toes in and bitten the wicket-keeper on the pads. Where would Chapman have been then? And what is he to do now?

To answer this question accurately, we must consider the possible bowling talent at his disposal. It consists roughly of the redoubtable Nottinghamshire pit-boy, the Sussex Marvel, the Leicestershire all-rounder, the Kent wizard, the Gloucestershire prodigy, and the Stogumber farmer. In the score-book these men masquerade under the mere pseudonyms of Larwood, Tate, Geary, Freeman, Hammond and White. But it is not likely that Chapman thinks of them, whilst he is making up his team, in such unromantic terms as these.

In the first game he omitted from the side the Kent wizard and the Leicestershire all-rounder. Can he afford to do this again? Yet, if he plays either of them, he must perforce leave out some member of the side chosen principally for his batting strength, or else attempt to play with a team of twelve men, a stratagem which is almost certain to be detected by a scorer, an umpire or by one of the sharp-eyed kangaroos themselves.

Who then is to be omitted? Is it to be the Hampshire stone-waller, commonly known in the barrack-square as Phil Mead? As against this course of action must be set the fact that in the game just concluded the Hampshire stone-waller made a score of seventy-two, which was second top score, exceeding the third top score (namely seventy) by two runs. On the other hand, if the Hampshire stone-waller is not omitted, who *is* to be left out?

At the very moment when I write, Chapman must be bracing himself to attempt the solution of this puzzle. Possibly he is talking to the indefatigable Patsy about it. For he can scarcely leave out the indefatigable Patsy without seriously endangering the rhythm of the team.

Equally impossible does it seem to leave out Hobbs. The Surrey pastmaster is a tower of strength to any side; and these words apply with almost equal force to the Winchester stylist and the Yorkshire virtuoso. It does not seem possible, in view of their previous performances and the names I have just called them, to omit either Jardine or Sutcliffe from the side.

Can the wicket-keeper be left out? Is it possible, in other words, to dispense with the stumper? Chapman of course might don the gauntlets or put on the gloves himself and use Mead as a longstop. But these are tactics which would probably hardly commend themselves to the mind of the English skipper, the last occasion on which a longstop took part in any international encounter being in the game at Melbourne in 1759.

['*Are you sure you have got your facts right?*' – Ed.

'*Absolutely. I looked it up in "Deeds that Won the Empire".*' – Evoe.]

There remains, then, the final course, which is for Chapman to leave himself out, a desperate remedy, from which I earnestly dis-

PUNCH, December 3 1958

Sporting Prints

IV PETER MAY

suade the old Uppingham boy. It is a temptation likely to beset any modest captain, but in view of the number of runs the former Cantab makes and the pace at which he makes them and the number of times that he catches the ball I would seriously urge the young Kent amateur to go on thinking all day and night, if necessary, rather than deplete the resources of his side by falling back upon such a drastic mode of procedure.

A far better expedient is to collect together in a circle all the possible candidates for omission, namely the Surrey crack, the representative of the county of broad acres, the old Oxonian, the Middlesex scoring-machine, the Hampshire mowing-machine, and himself, and use some simple method of counting out, eg:

'One, two, three, four,
Mary-at-the-cottage door
Eating cherries off-a-plate,
Two, four, six, eight,'

and so settle the final composition of the team.

If the lot falls on himself, a contingency which can easily be avoided by a minute mathematical calculation of the number of words in the stanza and a careful choice of the best point in the circle to begin, there is no help for it, and Chapman must hand over the captaincy to the Stogumber farmer, who will no doubt shoulder his responsibilities in a manner worthy of the Western shire whose county town was fortified by Ine in 710. It is worthy of note that the then curate of Stogumber was a prosecuting counsel at the trial of Joan of Arc, and that the pleasant little village now contains a population of 722, is 157 miles from London, nine from Bishop's Lydeard and five from Watchet.

My final conclusion is, may the best team be chosen! And, if I have helped ever so little in choosing it, I am happy to have been of some service to the MCC.

Evoe
12.12.1928

GULLIVER'S TOUR AMONG THE LILLIPUTIANS.
(WITH MR. PUNCH'S COMPLIMENTS TO MR. BRADMAN.)

A Naughty Little Man

(The Australian Board of Control recently reduced 'Boy' Bradman's Good Conduct money from £150 to £100, following the report of Mr Kelly, manager of the touring team.)

'Silence!' a voice was bawling,
'The Chairman's on his feet!'
And order was at once restored
Among the members of the Board
Who'd met for overhauling
Boy Bradman's conduct-sheet.

'I fear the news will hurt you,'
The Chairman then began,
'And add to your anxieties,
But you must know that Bradman is
A boy bereft of virtue,
A naughty little man.

'His nurse, whose name is Kelly,
Reports that he was late
Repeatedly for meals and that
He was disposed to grumble at
His food and leave his jelly
Unfinished on his plate.

'He tore his Sunday knickers
  And soiled his sailor-suit;
    His manner too was rather rough;
    That he was not polite enough
To noblemen and vicars
  Appears beyond dispute.

'Against his morning washes
  His wicked heart he set,
    And nearly always made a face
    When asked by Nurse to say the grace
Or put on his goloshes
  Because the grass was wet.

'He never would perform at
  A drawing-room affair
    When asked, for instance, to recite,
    Nor do what he was told was right
Relating to a door-mat,
  A handkerchief or hair.

'When Nanny asked for less din
  His answer would be more;
    Four hours on end the boy would hide – '
'Enough, enough!' the members cried;
'The ways that he transgressed in
  We very much deplore.

'Our hopes that you'd have shown us
  A model kind of kid
    Are most unhappily destroyed;
    We are, to say the least, annoyed,
And will reduce his bonus
  By just a third.' They did.

C. B.
14.1.1931

–|●|●|–

Frank Worrell's Men

They lined your farewell route in Sydney
  And deafened themselves with cheers,
For you'd made more friends and given more pleasure
  Than most men do in years.

Now you've done it again, and we are happy
  To give you our thanks and praise
For a cheerful and exciting season
  And a few heroic days.

In this intractable, race-torn decade
  Nobody could refuse
To think of the riot that ended the series
  As, for a change, good news.

Much we must lose now you are going,
  But much you leave behind,
Who have done a world of good for cricket
  And something for mankind.

P. D.
4.9.1963

CHAPTER NINE

The Punch Articles of Cricket

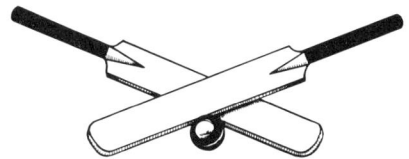

A REMINDER – Mr Edmund B. V. Christian, in *Baily's Magazine*, quoted by the *PMG* last Thursday, complains 'that cricket, the most popular of games, fills so small a place in literature'. Does he forget that Charles Dickens devoted one entire Christmas Book to *The Cricket on the Hearth*?

▬|●|●|▬

Confessions of a Duffer: V. The Duffer at Cricket

To hear my remarks on the cricket, in the pavilion, you might think that I had been a great player entirely, in my day. 'Who is that fine old English sportsman,' you might ask, 'who seems to have been so intimate with Mynn, and Fuller Pilch, and Carpenter, and Hayward and Tarrant and Jackson and C. D. Marsham? No doubt we see in him the remains of a sterling cricketer of the old school.' And then when I lay down the law on the iniquity of boundary hits, 'always ran them out in *my* time', and on the tame stupidity of letting balls to the off go unpunished, and the wickedness of dispensing with a long stop, you would be more and more persuaded that I had, at least, played for my county. Well, I *have* played for my county, but as the county I played for was Berwickshire, there is perhaps nothing to be so very proud of in that distinction. But this I will say for the cricketing Duffer; he is your true enthusiast. When I go to Lord's on a summer day, which of my contemporaries do I meet there? Not the men who played for the University, not the Kennys and Mitchells and Butlers, but the surviving members of college second elevens in the old days of Cowley Marsh, when every man brought his own bottle of Oxford wine for luncheon. These are the veterans who contribute most to the crowd of lookers-on. They never were of any use as players, but their hearts were in the game, and from the game they will never be divorced. It is an ill thing for an outsider to drop a remark about cricket among us, at about eleven o'clock in a country house smoking-room. After that the time flies in a paradise of reminiscences, till about 4 a.m. or some such 'wee short hour ayont the Twal', if one may quote Burns without being insulted by all the numerous and capable wits of Glasgow. Why is it that the Duffer keeps up his interest in cricket, while the good players cease to care much about it? Perhaps *their* interest was selfish; his is purely ideal, and consequently immortal. To him cricket was ever an unembodied joy of which he could make nothing palpable; nothing subject to the cold law of averages. Mine was 0.3 . . .

Cricket is a social game, and its proficients soon give the cold shoulder to the Duffer. He has his place, however, in the nature of things. It is he who keeps up the enthusiasm, who remembers every run that anybody made in any given match. In fact, at cricket, the Duffer's mission is to be a 'judge of the game'; I don't mean an umpire, very far from that. If you once let the Duffer umpire he could ruin the stoutest side, and secure victory to the feeblest. I may say that, at least in this capacity, I have proved really useful to my party in country matches. But, in the long run, my capacity even for umpiring came to be doubted, and now I am only a critic of cricket. There is none more relentless, not one with a higher standard, at least where no personal feelings are concerned. For I have remarked that, if a Cambridge man writes about an Oxford victory (which he seldom has to do), or if an Oxford man writes on a Cambridge victory (a frequent affliction), he always leaves you with the impression that, in spite of figures, his side had at least a moral triumph. These admirable writers have all been Duffers.

27.2.1892

=|o|o|=

Crumbs for Cricketers

(How to report a County Match – Latest Style)

The Wessex v. Loamshire fixture was resumed today, 5,352 paying for admission at the turnstiles. The weather was rather doubtful, and, just before play began, W. Yorker (known to his intimates as 'Piffles') was heard to remark to Bill Stumps, the famous Loamshire bat, that he thought there might be a drop of rain before night.

This version of his utterance, we can assure our readers, is absolutely correct. A quite erroneous paraphrase of it appeared in last night's evening papers. On an important point like this our report, as usual, is absolutely trustworthy.

Talking of 'Piffles', we have exclusive information to the effect that this splendid cricketer has quite got over his old dislike of boiled potatoes. Indeed, he was seen twice to replenish his plate with this form of the vegetable during lunch yesterday. He is still faithful to the same brand of tobacco.

As the celebrated ball-propeller, C. K. Shooter, emerged from the pavilion yesterday, he paused for three seconds at the gate, and then returned to the dressing-room to fetch his handkerchief. Our readers doubtless will remember that a similar startling incident took place in the Wessex and MCC match of two seasons ago.

Good old Bob Thumper urged the sphere to the boundary fourteen times in the course of his sparkling innings. This raises his percentage of boundary hits to other strokes to 14.6428. So his last stroke put him ahead of his rival, Tom Slogger, whose percentage up to date is 14.5873. The crowd was quick to notice this fact, and greeted his triumph with tremendous cheering.

Of the 79 balls sent down by Jim Trundler yesterday, 42 were straight, 31 were outside the off-stick, while 6 were on the leg-side. The longest interval between any two of his balls was 2 minutes, the shortest 52 seconds. These are really notable figures of enthralling interest to all who make a careful study of first-class cricket.

B. Strayer was in great form yesterday. This magnificent bat lives in Sussex, and has played for Loamshire for the last two seasons. Tempting offers, we understand, have been made to the celebrated amateur by the Rutland Club. He has been given the refusal of a sinecure post with an income of £700, but is waiting, as he humorously put it to our reporter, to see whether Loamshire 'will go one better', before making up his mind. It is by such players as Mr Strayer that the glorious traditions of amateur cricket are kept alive.

Dick Stumper accounted for two batsmen yesterday, and this fine wicket-keep has now assisted in dismissing an average of 3.4 batsmen per match since the beginning of the season.

By the way, we believe that the match about which we are writing, Loamshire v. Wessex, was finished in the course of yesterday's play. We have no idea which won, and no doubt the readers of our columns will pardon this ignorance. No one cares about petty details like this nowadays.

28.5.1902

=|o|o|=

The Tea Interval

On this most important feature of first-class cricket much can be said. In the old benighted days, when the most noteworthy figures selected for hero-worship were the Graces, A. G. Steel, C. T. Studd, A. N. Hornby (to name these only), luncheon was the only meal partaken of during a match. Bearing this fact in mind, it is of course no matter for surprise that cricket was what it was – a pastime almost wholly neglected by the newspapers, creating no popular interest in the County Championship, offering little employment to photographers or statisticians, and with hardly a single first-class player criticising in print the matches in which he took part.

Fortunately we have changed all this, and the game has now taken its right place in the affairs of the country. On inquiring into the cause of this salutary alteration, by which the cricketer has become a public character, second in fame only to a music-hall artist, we find that it synchronises with the introduction, so long and dangerously delayed, of the tea-interval.

In the advance of the cricketer from the monophagous to the biphagous stage, the scientific historian of the game will not fail to note the advent of the crowning phase of its evolution. What was once a monotonous display of animal endurance, lasting from a quarter to three to half-past six, is now pleasantly broken at half-past four by an adjournment to the pavilion for a cup or cups of the refreshing beverage of China, Assam or Ceylon. Tastes differ in this matter, as in everything else. Mr C. B. Fry finds Orange Pekoe with a dash of Oolong the most stimulating variety, not only for the game but for the many literary labours connected with his innings. Mr P. F. Warner prefers a syrupy Souchong. Mr Jessop is a pronounced adherent of Gunpowder. Prince Ranjitsinhji favours a blend of Indian leaves. Mr Maclaren swears by pure China with a slice of lemon in it. Mr H. K. Foster will not look at cream. Albert Trott, curious to relate, prefers brown to lump sugar.

It is pleasant for the historian to be able to record that cricketers are reviving some of the graces and amenities with which tea was taken in the days of Pope. Now and then, it is true, one is distressed to see a professional pouring the steaming liquid into his saucer; but for the most part the exponents of the game of games (as it has been called) empty their cups with charming delicacy and *espièglerie*. And this reminds us that some very dainty porcelain services are now to be seen in the County pavilions, which vie with each other in a friendly contest of ceramic taste. Sussex is famed for its Sèvres, and the Wedgwood set at Old Trafford has not its equal in the kingdom. On the other hand it is an open secret that the inadequate tea-table equipment of one of the Midland Counties nearly led to the discontinuance of several of their most attractive fixtures. The difficulty, however, has been happily surmounted by the princely munificence of a local magnate, who recently presented the County Club with a superb service of Crown Derby, a set of apostle spoons, and twelve exquisitely embroidered hem-stitched table-cloths.

22.7.1903

–|●|●|–

Pickwick Up-to-Date

(The following is an attempt at the style in which Charles Dickens doubtless would have written one of his chapters had he been able to utilise the classic idioms of the modern cricket-reporter.)

ALL-MUGGLETON DISHES DINGLEY DELL!
PODDER PROPELS THE PILULE!
PICKWICK PATRONISES THE PAVILION!
JINGLE'S GENTLE JAPES!

(Special and Exclusive Report)
A mighty smart crowd it was which sweltered in the reserve seats to witness this annual fixture. Pickwick was there, Snodgrass was there, Winkle was right on the spot, and knocked them every time with his caustic comments. And the great Jingle, button-holed by our representative, took the cocoanut with the following opinion:

'CAPITAL GAME – SMART SPORT – FINE EXERCISE – VERY!'

At eleven o'clock the fateful coin was jerked towards the azure, and the fickle jade gave All-Muggleton the right of first knock. Mr Pickwick was heard to question the Muggletonian skipper upon his policy.

'Bound to get 'em,' explained Mr Dumkins. 'Wicket like bloomin' concrete. We'll let daylight into the bowling, give you my word we will.'

Mr Pickwick was evidently about to enquire into the nature of this optical phenomenon

when the tinkle of the pavilion bell bade Skipper Dumkins depart to

DON HIS SHIN-SAVERS,

since he and Podder were to open the Muggletonian credit-account. And this they did to
some tune. The Dingley-Dellers entrusted the
rolling-up of the sphere to Luffey and Strug-
gles, but their deliveries were far from being of
a rot-making order, and the batsmen promptly

TOOK TEA WITH THEM.

In the second over Podder wafted one out of
the ground for six, while Dumkins quickly
materialised with a touch behind cover for a
quartet and a sylph-like push to the on-
boundary. At the same time it must be con-
ceded that neither willow-wielder would have
enjoyed a protracted sojourn had the fielding
of Dingley Dell been a trifle less moth-eaten.
At an early stage of the proceedings Podder
offered Luffey

A DOLLY C.-&-B.,

– which, however, was declined without
thanks. For an hour or more there was no
slump in the run-getting, Podder being particularly noticeable with his dreamy hooks,
while his Co. twice patted the pilule into the
ladies' enclosure. The second century had
long since whiffled into the forgotten past
when at length the Dingley-Deller stick-
custodian found Podder not at home.

'BRAVO – CAPITAL START – TOUCHED 'EM PRETTY!'

– was Jingle's timely comment as the ousted
wood-handler trickled through the pavilion
gate. Nor was Mr Pickwick himself slow to
express his approval. 'Permit me to congratulate you, sir,' he remarked. 'So remarkable a
display of skill in a manly and health-giving
exercise justifies, I believe, an offer of at least
half-a-dozen glasses of brandy and water, to be
consumed by you at my expense.'

Mr Podder was understood to refuse this
offer. His innings, as he explained, had
certainly given his average a useful heave, but
anyone could knock the stuffing out of the ball
when the bowlers were just lolloping up baby-
soothers. 'It's a very different show,' he

explained, 'when you have to conciliate hum-
ming-birds on a wicket like stick-jaw'; a
phrase which Mr Pickwick carefully wrote
down in his note-book, while replying with a
rather puzzled expression, that the game
under these conditions must be very different
indeed. 'And you do not anticipate that your
opponents will defeat you on this occasion?' he
added. 'Well,' said the Muggletonian
representative, 'they *might* bring off a real
hair-raiser, but I don't believe myself that they
have

THE SLIGHTEST EARTHLY.'

And the result proved Mr Podder's estimate to
be correct.

20.7.1904

–•|•|•–

How to Save Cricket

WHAT IS TO BE DONE?
WHO WILL DECIDE?
While *Mr Punch* reserves his own opinion as to
the necessity of making cricket more alluring
and of the seriousness of the tragedy of the
small attendance at the Derbyshire v.
Hampshire match, he has had, in common
with the emotional editor of the *Daily Mail*,
such a mass of correspondence on the subject
that he cannot but print a selection; first,
however, informing those of his readers who
may have missed the point of the attack that
the batsmen of England are on their defence
for daring to make any but boundary hits, the
bowlers for ever sending down a maiden, and
the players generally wasting time by changing
over, taking refreshment and beginning at any
hour after sunrise or finishing before dark. In
short, the modern spirit condemns the game.
What then is to be done? Read and see.

A CAUTIOUS VETERAN

Sir, – No one can yield to me in admiration of
the grand old game of cricket; but I am with
you in your noble attempt to bring it into line
with the times. I remember all the best players
– Harris, Nyren, Lumpy, Lambert, Mynn,
Pilch – and not one of them ever took a tea
interval. Did they play any the worse for it?
No. They played, if possible, better. It is true

that they did not always make a big score, but that was not because of any wish to disappoint the public or bring cricket into disrepute (as with players now), but purely on account of a certain uncertainty in the game.

Yours, etc., Centenarian

Deductions for Non-Scoring

Sir, – It is not enough to stop the tea interval, and begin earlier, and so forth. Cricket must feel the knife if it is to live. Fine the batsmen who do not hit. Give them 2 for every single, and 4 for every 2, and 8 for every boundary; but if they let a ball go by and do not score deduct 1 every time. An umpire also should now and then be burnt alive.

Yours, Root and Branch

To Rival the Cinema

Sir, – In order to bring cricket up to the high level of the cinema or a music-hall as a spectacular entertainment certain things must be done and done quickly. First and foremost, all tedious batsmen must be forcibly discouraged, and the best way to do this is to make a rule that every batsman who fails to make a 4 in his first two overs automatically ends his innings. This simple if drastic measure would instantly transform the game into precisely that eventful spectacle which the wise public wants, for there would of necessity either be wickets or boundaries, and what else interests anybody nowadays, except a few fossils in the pavilion?

Yours, &c., Reformer

5 Stumps and 4 Bails

Sir, – The three-day match is undoubtedly a farce, and should be curtailed. I suggest that the wicket consist of 5 stumps and 4 bails; this would give the bowler a better chance, and at the same time test the merits of the batsman to a greater degree, besides providing more excitement for the spectators.

BRIGHTER CRICKET.

The present system of double innings should be abolished in favour of a single innings for each side, and all matches should be played on a Monday or a Saturday and finished in one day. By these means we may be able to attract to our cricket matches crowds similar to those that witness football matches.

One Who Knows

A FEW SIMPLE SUGGESTIONS

Sir, – How to make cricket more exciting? It is merely a question for the younger bloods of the MCC. They have but to draw up new laws. For their guidance I suggest a few:

Extend the over to thirty balls; or do away altogether with changing over by placing the field in some position of compromise suitable for both ends. Still further time (so precious to a busy public) might be saved if every bowler were required to keep wicket and every wicket-keeper to bowl.

Insist upon the next-man-in standing by the umpire so as to be ready the moment the previous wicket falls.

Or, in default of this, establish a motor-car service between the pavilion and the wicket.

Enforce captains to give preference to sloggers and black-list the patient men.

Abolish the lunch and tea intervals.

Reduce the time between the innings to two minutes.

Exclude the press.

The above suggestions, it will be observed, do not interfere in any way with the fundamentals of the game or the liberty of the batsmen. Everyone must still get out as before. I object utterly to changes that curtail an innings in any arbitrary way.

Yours, &c., K.C.

THE TATTERSALL'S RING CURE

Sir, – I have been giving the question of the decadence of cricket much attention and I find from study of the old records that it was for many years a great betting game, England being, in spite of our national disapproval of gambling, the happiest hunting-ground in the world for all commission agents. Would it not be a popular move to bring wagering back to Lord's and thus not only brighten the game and get it nearer to that far more perfect

pastime, football, but have every seat filled? Mere betting on one side or the other would, of course, be too tame; but a system by which each member of each side was backed for this performance or that could easily be worked out, while there could be betting on the averages, too, and the championship table.

I will gladly give you any support in my power to bring about this.

Yours, &c., Joe Straight
Vevey, Switzerland

AWAY WITH THE UNCERTAINTY!

Sir, – One is always hearing parrot-cries about the glorious uncertainty of cricket. If the foolish persons who used the phrase would only pause to think for a moment they would see how very far from glorious this is. So far indeed that it is cricket's ruin. Why are matches neglected? Why do cricketers strain themselves to play for keeps and get not a single hand? Why are the coffers of the counties impoverished? Entirely because of this idiotic uncertainty. Make cricket certain and you will see the difference. Go to every length to ensure the success of the popular men, and spectators and money will again roll in. It is quite simple. You advertise, for example, that Jessop will make 100 on Wednesday afternoon, and you see that he does it. That is to say, the bowlers will bowl right, the fieldsmen will field right, and Jessop (who is an honourable man) will hit right. Result: delight of everyone present and plenty of cash for the club.

Yours, &c., Business Man
26.6.1912

The Curse of Cricket

Woolley stepped out and leaned against the ball, and it shot past cover to the boundary. This is the sort of cricket I can enjoy quite easily by myself, but the man on the bench below was afraid I might be feeling lonely. He turned round and introduced himself with the remark, 'They're using the long handle.' When a stranger says that to you at Lord's, you know at once that your day is spoilt. You can get up and leave the ground, or you can stay and talk to him; you can't watch cricket anymore.

'Yes, they're taking the long handle to it this morning,' he said again.

'Why are they doing that?' I asked innocently.

'They want to declare, you see; that's what it is. Oh, well fielded, Macartney. That's Macartney, that little fellow at mid-off.'

'I like that stouter man behind him better. Who's that?'

'The one who's just going to bowl? That's –'

'No, the man quite close to the wickets. He's wearing a white coat.'

'The umpire?' he said in astonishment.

'Yes, who's he?'

My new friend explained at length the duties of the umpire at cricket, and how it was that they had to have two, one at each end.

'Yes, yes,' I said; 'but the one at this end – who *is* he?'

'Oh, I don't know his name,' he said carelessly. 'Some old cricketer.'

'Because he looks rather like a man I used to know at Leamington,' I explained. 'I suppose his name isn't Carruthers?'

My friend looked at his card. 'Moss and Street,' he read out.

'No, this was just Carruthers alone. I haven't heard from him for a long time, and I should have liked to meet him again.'

'Funny thing, likenesses,' he said shortly, and turned to watch the game.

For two minutes I had the cricket to myself, and then he began again.

'It won't be like this when Australia goes in,' he said. 'They'll play for keeps.'

'They ought to play for something,' I agreed.

'I don't know about Macartney. He generally goes for the gloves.'

'Yes, we must get him to go for those if we can.'

'Wonderful bat, Macartney. He's the only man who's made a thousand runs, you know.'

'Fancy!' I said. 'A thousand! Is he really the only man who's ever done it?'

'This year, of course.'

'Oh!' I tried hard to keep the disappointment out of my voice, but I am afraid he noticed it.

'You'd never think a little chap like that could hit the ball so hard,' he went on. 'It's timing, that's what it is – all timing. Look at Jessop.'

'But I thought he wasn't playing.'

'Ah, and why isn't he? They never ought to have left Jessop out. If I were a selector, I should always say, "Give me Jessop, and then you can put in who you like."'

'Then I should put in Carruthers. He made a century for Leamington once. And he bowls too – slow benders.'

'But that's Fry all over. He's a bad captain. Why doesn't he declare now? We've got 300 on the tins.'

'Perhaps he hasn't noticed it,' I suggested.

'Some people call him a good bat, but *I* don't. Not what I call first-class. Good against bad bowling, but no good against the best.'

'Like me.'

'I should always make Warner captain at Lord's. He knows every blade of grass on the ground.'

'By name?' I asked with interest.

'And then Warner knows the Australians.'

'Ah, well, there's not so many of *them*.'

'You see – Well fielded, Smith! Fielded, sir! That's Smith; he's a great footballer.'

'I thought he was a wicket-keeper.'

'Oh, that's *our* Smith. The Australians have got a Smith playing too.'

'Are they relations?'

'Not that I *know* of,' he said as though allowing that they might have arranged something privately. 'There! Fry's declared at last. Now the Australians have got to sit on the splice for the rest of the day. The question is, can they do it?'

He asked this so fiercely that I didn't like to give an opinion. 'Just as you think,' I said modestly.

'Well, *I* say it depends how the wicket rolls out. If it doesn't roll out easy, and if Fry has sense enough to start with Barnes and Foster –'

'Barnes and Warner, surely?' I said. 'Because if Warner knows all the different blades of grass and all the different Australians –'

He looked at me with compassion.

'Warner doesn't bowl,' he said kindly.

'Don't see much cricket, do you?' he added.

'I'm afraid I don't get as many opportunities as I should like,' I said truthfully, for there are black days in the week when I have to stay away from Lord's and work.

'I thought p'r'aps you didn't. Now I've watched it for thirty years. Ever seen Grace?' he asked with the air of one who had an anecdote to tell.

'I don't *think* so,' I said. 'What's he like?'

And that gave it away. He looked at me with sudden suspicion, and then slowly reddened. He turned away and buried himself in his paper. But his spirit was undaunted. A newcomer took the seat next to him, and my friend, having taken a glance out of the corner of his eye, introduced himself.

'I suppose,' he said carelessly, 'they'll play doggo?'

A.A. Milne
3.7.1912

-|●|●|-

To Save Cricket

The regrettable dispute between Middlesex and Yorkshire, which may, it is feared, end in the cancelling of their two matches next year; the sparse attendance at Lord's and the Oval all this season, and the general feeling of depression caused by Hobbs's super-caution in the Gentlemen and Players contest, cause much disquietude and thought among the friends – not of cricket, which can always take care of itself and is flourishing on its true home, the village green, as never before, but – of those exacting and important persons, the cricket crowd. Are they to be permitted to abandon the game without a blow being struck in their defence? No. Their good opinion must be recaptured at any cost.

After much thought I have perfected a plan to save the situation. By this plan the cricket of the future will be put on a sound and stable basis and the public will at last get what it wants.

Now, one of the reasons why football is so much more popular than cricket is the fact that there is intense activity and excitement compressed into ninety minutes. Cricket suffers by its leisureliness and by the timidity of

batsmen who are solicitously desirous not to return yet to the pavilion. Reduce the time of a match from three days to three hours, and remove the cause of the batsmen's prudence and tremors, and you have an ideal entertainment for Wembley. Bowling and fielding have little interest for the crowd; the crowd goes to see big hits, and, if there are no big hits, it remembers that it will never, never be slaves, and boos. Without the crowd first-class cricket cannot live, and moreover, if the counties are going to quarrel and refuse to meet each other, there will be little point in continuing the first-class championships, anyway.

Therefore the first-class game may as well go, and its ordinary practitioners return to normal life and play only on holidays in smaller matches. But what of the batting cranks? By my plan they will be kept as star turns for the Wembley Stadium and other suitable arenas.

I have it all mapped out in the manner of the Rodeo. The management will announce a series of hitting displays and secure the services of Hobbs, who will then recognise no just impediment to opening his shoulders, Hendren, Woolley, Sutcliffe and others of the more famous bats, together with some of the more adventurous sloggers of the day, the men who, by reason of their aptitude as bowlers or wicket-keepers, now cheerfully lash out at everything, such as Tate and Parkin and Murrell. Perhaps some amateurs may be persuaded to join too – Mr Mann, Mr Gilligan, Mr Haig, Mr Fender, Mr Blaikie, Mr Carr, Mr M. D. Lyon, and so forth. Only bowlers who send down half volleys will be employed, cutting and leg-glancing and such subtle strokes having little spectacular value; and everything like defence will be under a ban. What the crowd wants is big hits into the air, if possible out of the ring; and prizes will be offered every afternoon for the longest efforts.

But we have not yet touched the heart of the matter. The special attraction, the certain lure, will be the undertaking that, no matter how often he is caught or bowled, the batsman will continue his innings for a definite space of time, say half-an-hour each. This will at once enchant the spectators and by liberating the batsman's mind from all petty restrictions and

Friend (to Professional Cricketer). "I SAY, OLD MAN, THAT WAS A SPLENDID ARTICLE OF YOURS IN LAST SUNDAY'S *HOOT*. WHO WROTE IT?"

fears will enable him to do his best and deserve the applause that I am sure will be constant and cordial. There will be a few fieldsmen, but only for the purpose of returning the ball, like the boys at Wimbledon; and of course, as at Wimbledon, the bowlers will have a plentiful supply so as to save time. And there will, of course, be no running, because that would fatigue the batsmen and divert them from the real business of the day.

I can visualise a poster:

SIXES AT WEMBLEY

On Monday at 2.30
in the Stadium
Hobbs will hit sixes for half-an-hour against the worst bowling in England. Followed by Hendren, Woolley and other giants of the bat.

No disappointments,
No tiresome science,
No kill-joy umpires
and
More comfortable seats than
in 1924.
&c., &c., &c.

Don't you think this is a very good way of bringing popularity back to this unfortunate game? It is now at sixes and sevens; it will then be only at sixes – the magic figure.

E.V.L.
30.7.1924

–|•|•|–

So You Want to Be a Cricket-Journalist

First, you require a thorough understanding of the art of batting. Off what balls should a batsman attempt to score?

I cannot think of any. He might, perhaps, open his shoulders to a no-ball.

None others?

What others *are* there? He must never nibble at anything outside the off-stump. He must never be tempted by anything wide of the leg-stump. And what more suicidal than to try a scoring shot in front of the wicket?

But a long-hop or a full-toss?

Cunningly baited traps, both of them. In each case a classic defensive stroke is indicated.

You appear to have mastered the rudiments of batting. What would you say of a batsman who ignored these rules?

That he was recklessly throwing his wicket away.

But supposing he played with tireless patience, and by his sound defence in a crisis ensured a draw?

I should have no alternative but to say that he had killed all interest in the game by a stodgy and unenterprising display, when if only he had attacked the bowling a definite result might have been obtained.

I find your answers so far show a shrewd knowledge of the game. Let us now turn to bowling. What is the first duty of a bowler?

To bowl with the fire and the great heart of a Maurice Tate, attacking the stumps all the time and forcing the batsman to –

Think again.

I beg your pardon. To close up one end. To keep down the runs with a great spell of defensive bowling.

What is your opinion of defensive bowling?

It slows down the play. It is contrary to the true spirit of the game. It is not to be wondered at that counties complain their gates are falling off.

Now to personalities. What did Hobbs and Sutcliffe do?

They stole cheeky singles.

What was Woolley's method of scoring?

He leaned gracefully against the ball and it sped to the boundary.

Describe Hammond.

Majestic.

Good! Tell me, now, what does a batsman do when he scores a century?

He does many things. Primarily, he gives the selectors a hint.

What else?

He shows up the limitations of the attack. He tames the bowling. He wins golden opinions. He finds his form. He makes merry.

How is he dropped?

"IS IT NECESSARY FOR THE BOWLER TO TAKE SUCH LONG RUNS?"
"NOT EXACTLY NECESSARY, BUT IT'S VERY FORTUNATE. IT GIVES THE BATSMAN TIME TO THINK OUT HIS PRESS REPORT."

Expensively.

What are the bowlers doing while he is putting together his mammoth score?

They are toiling and spinning.

And the fielders?

Leather-hunting.

How does a captain declare?

He applies the closure.

And what does the rival captain do in such circumstances?

He refuses to accept the challenge.

What is your judgement on any Test team before the match?

The selectors have done a good job. They have shown imagination in picking what is undoubtedly our strongest XI.

And after the match?

Drastic changes must be made. The selectors must acknowledge their errors and make a clean sweep.

Discuss the inclusion of a youthful player in a Test team.

It is a grave mistake to throw a young player of promise into the grim atmosphere of big cricket before he is ready for it.

And the exclusion of such a player?

Utterly incomprehensible. Our policy should be to build for the future and 'blood' our youngsters as early as possible.

With reference to a Test match, what are our eve-of-Test prospects?

They are bright.

Kindly give your expert forecast.

Much will depend on the state of the wicket. Winning the toss may also prove an important factor. It must be England's strategy, if we win the toss, to pile up a big score and then dismiss our opponents cheaply. If we lose the toss, our tactics must be to dismiss our opponents cheaply and then pile up a big score. If we exceed our opponents' total in both innings, then I think we can win. If, on the other hand –

Thank you, you need not continue. Would you care to say something about the effect of rain on the pitch?

The pitch was treacherous after rain, and took any amount of spin. Balls popped or kept disconcertingly low. What a harvest our own bowlers would have reaped on such a pitch!

That, of course, is when we are batting. Let us now suppose that we are in the field.

Oh, the rain has rendered the pitch dead and lifeless.

I am pleased to inform you, sir, that you pass with honours.

Thank you. May we even say, sir, that I have given a hint to the editors?

Colin Howard
29.8.1951

–|●|●|–

Cricket: A Plea for Plain Speaking

One thing to get clear, before the team of journalists to tour Australia is finally picked, is that it is no use sending men who will fob us off with veiled hints. We had enough of that in the West Indies. To this day it is far from clear to me what actually happened out there. There were Ructions, certainly. It wouldn't surprise me at all to learn that there were Goings On. But all is surmise. 'Unhappy incidents' and 'misunderstandings, both on and off the field' – such was the pigeon's milk served up by my newspaper. Nobody ever told me, in plain words, who threw what at whom.*

One is expected, I dare say, to read between the lines. But you have to have the trick of it. I can read between the lines of a police-court report, having some knowledge of original sin; and in much the same way, I suppose, those who have been on cricket tours have only to see the word 'misunderstanding' to know that one or two of the wilder spirits have been putting sawdust in the captain's boots again, or scribbling bad words in the score-book, or whatever it is that constitutes an unhappy incident on tour. Those who have *not* been on cricket tours, a considerable majority even of

the readers of my newspaper, are at a loss; we can only stand about with ears agog, as we did in the old days when our parents were guardedly discussing some neighbour's downfall, and give our imaginations free rein. This, on *omne ignotum pro magnifico* grounds, is unfair to the tourists.

My own favourite cricket writer has a particularly annoying habit, recently acquired, of writing as if there could not by this time be a single reader in ignorance of what it is he is writing *about*. 'Everybody is agreed,' he will say, 'that the lamentable occurrences of the West Indies tour must never be repeated.' I do not care for the feeling of isolation, of being out of the swim, that this gives me. He goes on, as a rule, to point out that cricketing ability is by no means the sole requirement in a member of a touring team; an equable temperament, ability to mix easily, a personality acceptable to his fellows are no less vital qualifications; one misfit in a side can fatally impair . . . and so on. This also maddens me, because it seems to imply that he has one or two names in mind, which ought to be in my mind too, and it thus accentuates my growing conviction that I am too naive and untutored to be a fit reader of his column. I cannot take the allusions.

What is worse, it cuts the ground from under my position as a private selector. It means that I have wasted all the time I have spent this season, in common with millions of besotted Englishmen, in pitting my wits against the official selectors. I have been theorising without knowing all the data, a capital mistake. All the thought and energy I have devoted to the question of Higgs or Briggs (to assume a couple of names at random) has in all probability been so much spindrift. I have weighed up their rival bowling abilities on soft wickets and on hard, on dead wickets and on sticky dogs, against left-handed batsmen and against right-handed batsmen. I have evaluated their worth as tail-enders. I have considered Higgs's renown as a close fielder and balanced it against a certain loss of accuracy in throwing-in from the deep if Briggs is omitted. I have thrashed the matter out in bars and buses from Islington to Kew. And to what end? Higgs, for all I know, may have hit Hutton cross-batted during the tea-

---

* Except, of course, that some West Indians threw bottles at the umpire. But that was a side-issue.

interval at Georgetown. Or Briggs, more likely, makes golloping noises with his porridge and was never even considered.

Well, it is too late to do anything about that now. The MCC team has been chosen, and what happened in the West Indies can now, as my favourite cricket writer says, be forgotten – an easy task for some of us. But should anything untoward occur during the Australian tour – and when seventeen hot-blooded young men are touring together for six months, closely pursued by twice that number of journalists, it is inevitable that cries of 'Yaroo! You beast! Leggo!' should occasionally be heard coming from the dressing-rooms – let the thing be hinted at in a manly, straightforward way, so that at least I can make a guess at what my newspaper is getting at. I don't ask for details; all I really want is the culprit's name, tactfully revealed: 'After an unusually noisy lunch interval, Hutton reverted to a defensive field, Wiggs eventually moving back from extra cover to deep extra.' Something on those lines will do; the word 'eventually' will be enough. I can then write 'sulky' against Wiggs's name, and scrub him off my list of possibles for next summer's Tests against South Africa.

H. F. Ellis
4.8.1954

The Hash England Made of the Ashes

The somersaults turned by cricket correspondents after the Test match at Adelaide have prompted our own carping correspondent to deflate the English team before they start the final Test at Sydney:

Yes, England has won the Ashes, but like almost every other cricket expert sent out by the press to Australia I consider that everything Hutton did was wrong. I feel so strongly about this that I cannot bring myself to call him Len. What right had he to lose the toss at Adelaide? Surely Hutton has been playing cricket long enough to know that the first duty of a captain is to win the toss. He should have had a double-headed coin and a double-tailed coin; anyone with as many strokes at his service as Hutton should possess enough sleight of hand to use them effectively. The argument that such a trick would not be cricket is out of date. Cricket is not cricket today except when the Authors and the Publishers dabble about in the rain at Vincent Square. And even if cricket were still cricket a Test match would not be cricket. A Test match is something between trench warfare, mounting a bus in the rush hour, and waiting for a train on British Railways on the evening of Bank Holiday.

"Private Johnson—About-turn!"

Hutton has had two first-class fast bowlers, but he used them as if they were playing a game. When one remembers what Jardine could do with the body-line bowling of Larwood it was surely not too much to expect that Hutton with Tyson and Statham at his disposal would have made sure that not a single member of the Australian eleven left the field alive. The excuse that the weather was too hot on the first day to think what anybody ought to do next will not stand examination. Noël Coward once made it perfectly clear to the rest of the world that mad dogs and Englishmen enjoy rushing about in the sun. Yes, but England won the fourth Test. I prefer to say that Australia lost it, which is not the same thing. If Australia had won should we not all agree that England lost?

Hutton made a big mistake before he muffed the toss by not playing Bedser. The fact that England won without Bedser is no answer. It was a grave error of judgement not to play Bedser, as most of the armchair critics at once pointed out. It is not fair to sneer at armchair critics. They are in a much better position to judge what ought to be done than men playing in a temperature of 110°. They see the struggle as a whole and can cable home to their papers an objective view of it.

Why did Hutton tell Cowdrey to use his nose to stop a ball at short-leg? Cowdrey is a stocky young man but he is not an elephant, and a cricket ball is much harder than even the buns at the zoo. Cowdrey may own the auspicious initials MCC, but that does not mean he can perform the impossible. Would Hutton ask the Mayor of Pudsey to field with his nose?

Then there was that six when Wardle hit the ball at a lady among the spectators who had to receive first-aid from the ambulance men. If Wardle wanted to hit a six why did not Hutton tell him to aim at the press box? Your carping correspondent, and every other carping correspondent, like London, could have taken it.

Dickens' Mr Wardle would never have behaved like that. Even if his sister had been sitting among the spectators at Muggleton with Alfred Jingle's arm round her waist Mr Wardle would never have tried to hit her with a cricket-ball. The only conceivable occasion on which one could forgive Wardle for such unchivalrous behaviour would be if he heard George Formby singing 'My luve is like a red red rose' to a female spectator at Old Trafford when Lancashire were winning.

Whatever Hutton did he was wrong. After he was out at 80, when any moderately good captain would have hit a century, he apparently told Compton and Cowdrey not to make any runs at all for two hours. That is not the way to win even a Test match. Yes of course I know that England won. But why did Hutton allow the kangaroo to wag its tail by putting on something like a hundred runs for the eighth wicket? Hutton may argue that the tail of a kangaroo is a much more efficient organ than the kinked tail of a bulldog, but that only goes to show he should have played Bedser and Loader. In justice to Hutton it must be pointed out that the MCC selectors picked the wrong team to send out to Australia, as was only too painfully apparent at Brisbane. Another mistake Hutton made was in letting some of his team off to go and watch the Davis Cup tennis matches between Australia and the United States. Any one of them might easily have cricked his neck, and nobody can play good cricket with a cricked neck. Fortunately, no harm was done, but Hutton took a serious risk in allowing his players time off to watch tennis.

However, in spite of all that Hutton and the touring side did to prevent it, England has the Ashes, and your carping correspondent can only wish that the ash-bin in which they rest were not quite so badly dented. Yes, England has won the rubber, but I hope people at home realise how much they owe to the cricket correspondents whose cool, confident, friendly and always infallible advice has made Hutton's task a sinecure.

Compton Mackenzie
23.2.1955

–|●|●|–

The Tweakers

There is one score upon which I will defend the batsman. It is that he is frequently blamed for dull and dreary play when it is really the fault of the bowler.

There are in fact more dull bowlers than dull batsmen. They run an inordinately long way to deliver the ball at an inconvenient pace to an inaccessible place with unerring accuracy. They count their success in terms of maiden overs, frustration, and exasperation. And their evil influence extends beyond the scope of their actual operations, for now, if more than four are gathered together on the on-side, the ball has but to pass outside the batsman's legs for him to switch his skirts away and assume an air of persecution. The whole muddled scene is then resolved by the addlepate in the outer who deafeningly directs the bowler to 'Baowl at the shockin' wicket'.

But these, as Holmes was heard to remark, are deep waters. Let us rejoice that there are still some very interesting bowlers. The brightest innings we have seen 'down under' was played, appropriately, by Peter May and was against New South Wales. For this he justly received full credit, but the bowlers seemed to get scant recognition for the large part of the entertainment which they had supplied. It was because they were such an interesting lot that May was enabled to exercise his full artistry.

They were led by Australia's new fast bowler, Rorke, a blond giant whose majestic approach to the crease is something between a buffalo charging and Siegfried's journey to the Rhine. On arrival he is liable to skid several feet past it and, in moments of excitement, his action is more enthusiastic than orthodox. His pace is tremendous and his variation of direction so generous and unpredictable that assistants as far afield as gully and short leg, who normally look at the bat, are well advised to keep a sharp eye in his direction, with a view to taking instant evasive action. His wicket-keeper gets the same amount and type of exercise as a tumbler on one of those spring mattresses. Nary a dull moment here.

Above all there were three leg-breakers, Benaud, Philpott, and O'Neill, to keep the proceedings alive throughout the day. Typically, Philpott, a big spinner of the ball, beat May decisively for a start, and in the same over was smacked for three whistling fours for his pains. Whatever his faults the true tweaker is never repressive or boring. In truth, the greater his faults the less so he is likely to be.

I am not concerned with the impeccable Barnes or O'Reilly, who turned the ball from the leg, but with the devotee who curls his wrist up in the region of his flask pocket and, with bared teeth and countenance distorted with effort, gives it all he's got. What matter if it doesn't land quite in the right place, so long as it bursts like a bomb in a beehive; this is art for art's sake – even if some captains do not appreciate the point. If this ball is belted far into the most expensive seats the occupants at least have had their money's worth. If the next one drops in the right place to puncture an inflated batsman, thrashing furiously in the wrong direction, they have had a handsome bonus. That is the true tweaker, the optimist, the sanguine gambler; the serpent among bowlers, venomous but vulnerable.

The bias from the leg was, of course, the original and natural one in underhand days, but its application by the overarm bowler called for a complicated and rather unnatural technique. That grand old Middlesexian, Billy Williams, used to say that he had invented this while bowling to an early Australian team in the nets. But even as a fellow clubman I am unable to support this claim in the light of history, and it is more likely that the modern leg-break evolved from a technique similar to that of W.G.'s round-arm top spinners. It was pioneered in international cricket by A. G. Steel.

The greatest innovation in the era of over-arm bowling came with Bosanquet's invention or discovery of the googly. The impact of this on the uninitiated must have been akin to that of Lamborn's newly-invented underhand off-break on the All-England Eleven on Broad-halfpenny. 'This new trick of his so bothered the Kent and Surrey men that they tumbled out one after another as though they had been picked off by a rifle corps.' To the decently brought up batsman the first off-breaking leg-break must have smacked of the Indian rope trick.

It would seem that the inventor was not among the greatest practical exponents, but succeeded chiefly on grounds of novelty. It was the South African school, Vogler, White, Faulkner and Snooke, who brought the leg-break-cum-googly to its highest pitch of perfection. Schwartz was another sort of phenomenon in that he could only bowl the googly, and the more he strove to master the leg-break the more he turned from the off.

Faulkner was my first employer, and a rare good bowler when I first knew him in his late forties. He spun abundantly, disguised the wrong 'un from all but the hawk-eyed, and was remarkably accurate. But he himself said that Vogler was the best of the breed, over medium in pace, with a knife-like wrong 'un. In fact, Faulkner ranked him in the best moments next only to the great Sydney Barnes. Slightly later came Pegler, the last of the great South Africans.

Their mantle blew across the Indian Ocean to alight on the shoulders of an Australian dentist named Hordern, who, in a losing series against England, took 32 wickets for 24 apiece with slow flighted spinners, which he delivered from a longish run. He was succeeded by Mailey, who spun the ball more than anyone could remember having seen it spun before, and revelled in its every rotation. He recalls in his book a Sunday during a Test Match when he and I spent an enthralling hour, bowling a ball to and fro on a stately Lancastrian lawn. Reprimanded by a cagey manager for blowing State secrets, Mailey replied that this was art and, as such, international! With him in the press box last week was Clarence Victor Grimmett, who, now approaching seventy, complained that he had lost his nip off the pitch.

Without ever rivalling the great Australian school England has had her moments, but now the tweaker is almost non-existent. Nor is he likely to return so long as our green and pleasant land tends to be brown and dusty, or black and muddy, so far as cricket pitches are concerned. I wish we could subsidise him, for in his absence the game is that much duller.

Ian Peebles
25.2.1959

Batting from Memory

Cricket in wartime is unreality in a setting of lunacy. It is itself a form of warfare without (as a rule) bloodshed: the real – bloodletting – form robs it of conviction. In any case, cricket then was a parade. The below-named would – according to what had once been the team-selection sheet – parade at HQ at 10.30 on Sunday to play in a match in aid of Red Cross funds. The prospect looked unattractive through the dry eyes of night duty.

The clerk who typed the names of the required men was too security-conscious to mention where the game would be played. The coach driver, however, set off as if he knew: so, we assumed, would the local population expected to pay for the privilege of watching us. But curiosity gave way to sleep and solo whist until the coach hissed up a gravel drive to the steps of a handsome and un-war-scarred mansion which had obviously not been taken over by the services. Her Ladyship welcomed us at the portico with hands spread like an actress responding to her public, and at once demonstrated both her hospitality and her ignorance of the habits of cricketers by leading us to a bar of imposing stocks by the standards of any time. At about the second drink the captain approached me with 'Have you ever played here before?'

'No.' A lame reply to give as the first man consulted.

'I thought you'd played against every bad club in the county?'

'So did I, but I didn't even know there was a ground here.'

A look of shrewd doubt came into his eye. 'Let's go and look at it.'

We identified the pitch by the presence of a marquee and some flags. My captain was not normally a verbose man but some uncharacteristically violent words jerked out even before we went through the gate on to a field of grass part shorn, part torn but largely soaked and smeared down like an urchin's hair. As we approached the strip identifiable as the wicket by being slightly less heavily grassed than the rest, he produced some pearls of blasphemy which never reached their promised high peak because, at a rustle behind us, he swung round

man. Throughout his career he has waged constant war against the airs and graces of the snob cricketer. His task has been made easy in that next to the zebra the snob cricketer is easily the most identifiable animal in the world. He is likely to wear a multi-coloured striped cap, hold up his trousers with a multi-coloured tie and when thinking about a single often addresses his partner thus: 'Just the jolly one on this occasion, Charles, I think.'

There is a famous Trueman story about his encounter with just such a cricketer. It occurred in Trueman's sapling days when the sight of a snob cricketer made him bowl twenty miles an hour faster than normal. This particular young man faced Trueman and was completely beaten by a delivery of such pace and venom that it reduced his stumps to a smouldering ruin. As he passed the scowling Trueman he remembered his manners and said: 'That was a jolly fine delivery, my man.' Trueman glowered at him and then said: 'Ay it was that. But it was bloody well wasted on thee.'

It is not everyone who remains as dedicated to the battle as Trueman. Some cricketers sell out and attempt to join the snob set. In the main the attempts have been disastrous. The first sign that a cricketer is about to go over to the enemy is when he starts speaking posh. I played for a team in Yorkshire skippered by a man who was never the same after standing in a lift next to E. W. Swanton. From that day on he dedicated his life to becoming a snob cricketer. Unfortunately he couldn't afford elocution lessons and his attempts at self-education were laughable. He simply didn't know what to do with his aitches. He stopped play in one game with an example of his own version of the Oxford accent. The incident was provoked by a slow left-arm bowler called Alf who was notoriously cowardly against attacking batsmen. Even on wickets that suited spin he would revert to medium pace seamers if his opponent seemed likely to chance his arm against the slow stuff. On this particular occasion he was bowling the slow stuff on a wicket taking a lot of spin. In desperation one of the batsmen made a couple of suicidal strokes and scored two desperate boundaries. Immediately Alf started bowling at medium pace. Our

captain watched this tactic with growing impatience and finally bellowed: 'H'oh for 'eaven's sake h'Alf give 'em some bloody h'air . . .' A long pause while captain and Alf glowered at one another and then: 'H'idiot.'

Fred Trueman tells a similar story of a Yorkshire cricketer who began to get ideas above his station after being awarded his England cap. The trip to Lord's changed him completely and he returned to play for his county entertaining thoughts of marrying the daughter of the President of MCC. On the morning of his first match with the county after playing for England he looked out of his bedroom window and said: 'The rain is terrestial.'

His team mate looked dumbfounded.

'Surely tha' means torrential,' he said.

The new England player shrugged his shoulders. 'It's all imperial to me,' he said.

Any serious-minded student of snobbery in cricket will learn most of all from a close study of the Marylebone Cricket Club, sometimes referred to as the Marylebone Clodpoles Club. This quaint and lovable institution has done more than most to foster the idea that cricket is the birthright of young men of impeccable manners and breeding who will eventually, if nature runs its course, grow up to be committee members of MCC. Browsing through an old book the other day I came across the perfect cricket snob philosophy as preached by Lord's. The book is called *The Right Way to Become a Cricketer* and is written by Major John Board. The first chapter states: 'Apparently the game fails to appeal to the Latin, the Teuton or the Slav. It may be and probably is that those races are incapable of assimilating the true meaning of sportsmanship as understood by the Anglo-Saxon.' A sentiment which although written many years ago would even today bring loud hurrahs from a meeting of MCC members.

The curious thing about snob cricketers is that for all they preach about good manners and sportsmanship they can turn very nasty when aroused. As a very junior national service officer in the Army I once captained a team of Other Ranks against a team of Senior Officers. My team included a fast bowler of homicidal tendencies from Sheffield who went berserk at the sight of a snob cricketer. Unfortunately the adjutant who opened for the Officers XI was a snob cricketer in glorious Technicolor, a figure of peacock finery as he strode to the wicket. Predictably his opening over from the fast bowler contained four deliveries aimed straight at his head, one which threatened his breastbone and the final one which struck him full toss on what is laughingly called 'the protector'. After rolling around in undignified agony for five minutes he retired from the field of play.

The fast bowler was well pleased with life and believed he had chalked up a notable victory against a representative of snob cricket. His joy lasted until next morning when he discovered he had been posted in rather mysterious circumstances to a remote island in the Indian Ocean. Which only served to confirm what I had always believed about snob cricketers: you can't beat them and you really wouldn't want to join them.

Michael Parkinson
16.7.1969

—|●|●|—

There's a Breathless Hush in the Close Tonight – Seven to Four and the Last Man In

'Ladbroke's are to open a betting shop at the Test Cricket ground at Trent Bridge. Cricketing punters will be able to bet on the top-scoring batsman, a player to score a century, the bowler taking most wickets, and the number of runs scored in a session.' – *Evening Standard*

Say what you like about cricket, it brings out the best in people. Take Little Isadore Nachschlepper. Normally, you ask Little Isadore the time of day, he'll tell you it's two-thirty-three when it's really only two-thirty, on account of he figures you owe him three minutes' interest on a deal like that. Tighter than Little Isadore you won't find. But yesterday I'm standing around outside the Lord's Tavern, fingering the scorecard and wondering what I fancy for the afternoon session, when who comes up to me but Little Isadore, in a very chic mohair suit, you can tell

it's imported, and wearing this big smile on top of his MCC tie.

'Hallo, Little Isadore,' I say, very cautious, not wishing to push off with any enquiry, such as How's tricks? on account of it could end up costing.

'Skinny Al!' cries Little Isadore, pumping my fin and flashing the gold molars like I just rode in with news his brother-in-law dropped dead, 'What a day, what a day!'

It is while Little Isadore is pumping that I notice this large lump to the right of his bespoke tailoring, and I immediately deduce that Little Isadore has been a recent source of grief to the bookies at the Nursery End. The little item in question notices my eye.

'The seventh wicket partnership just came home at 33 to 1,' says Little Isadore. 'Intikhab and Long put on 110, which is somewhat less than yours truly collected for recognising quality when he sees it.'

Since I personally have just taken leave of twenty large ones for having judged Fred Titmus capable of wiping out the aforementioned Surrey pair in short order, I am more than somewhat impressed by Little Isadore's coup, and I tell him so.

'Thank you,' he says. 'I am deeply moved by your appreciation, Skinny Al, and will return the gesture by offering you a tip which will bring security and fat smiles to you and yours for many years to come, viz., Parfitt to remove the tail-enders with a personal tally of 5 for 80. Past the post. Money in the bank. No argument.'

'Parfitt?' I say, overcome that Little Isadore should be giving away such information, if genuine, when I personally know Parfitt to be a nice long price, owing to the boys having looked him over in training and he is having a pretty lousy net and sweating too much, and generally looking like a citizen ready to hang up his boots in return for steady work in Gamage's sports department. 'They tell me Parfitt is off-form.'

Little Isadore looks very hurt.

'Who is this they of whom you speak, Skinny Al? Listen, this is Little Isadore Nachschlepper speaking, never knowingly undersold, and I am informing you that if you want to put fifty on Parfitt right now, you will be counting your way through five grand by the tea interval. I know the man who oils his bat. I know the man who makes his supporters. Better information you won't find.'

'But these are very good outsiders he is matched with, Little Isadore,' I say. 'Tail-enders they may be, but word is this Pocock is a very good striker of the ball, and in his last outing at Somerset he is driving a considerable number of balls through the covers and making many wallets on the premises look very sick indeed.'

Little Isadore shrugs.

'Do not say I did not tell you, Skinny Al,' he says, somewhat distant. Then he's gone, with a dame she's a head taller than he is, and real class, a genuine Lebanese masseuse, works for only the best. I tell you, this year you got a different class of people at Lord's altogether. The cream.

So, anyway, I think, what can I lose? So I do Parfitt for a pony, and may I be struck dead if he doesn't lead from the off and come home at 66 to 1! Like a three-year-old. By four pm he's back in the pavilion with 5 for 69. Like Little Isadore says, no argument.

Naturally, this makes me somewhat happy, and as I am not fancying nothing in the next, it being the Middlesex opening partnership on which nobody has any information, I decide to stroll into the Tavern and put down a couple of long ones, when who should I see but Soft John Arlott and Each Way Swanton poring over the scorecard at the next table, accompanied by a silent midget in bi-focals. I edge my chair closer, since these are clearly people in the know.

'I am strongly in favour of laying negotiable lettuce on Murray to make the ton,' says Soft John, casually picking up a piece of paper which happens to be blowing across the table. 'He will be long odds on account of his crummy showing at Old Trafford last time out.'

'I am made somewhat nervous, Soft John,' says E.W., 'by this recent tendency of Murray to poke at slow rising balls outside the off stump. Does he not remind you of the weaker moments of E. Hendren?'

'I am a great believer in the form book, Each Way,' says Soft John, very soft. 'When was the last time a right-handed Middlesex wicket-keeper going in at number seven during the third week in July under a Conservative government with the wind blowing from West Nor'West scored a century, Bill Frindall?'

The midget citizen whispers something into his glass.

'That's good enough for me,' says Soft John, and the three knowledgeable characters move off, very fast.

This incident prompts me to peel not a few tens off my winnings in short order, with a view to converting them into something with which I can organise a swell funeral for a citizen who has been leaning on me somewhat heavily of late on account of my warm affection for one Big Freda, an elegant dish who has not as yet had the pleasure of meeting Mrs Skinny Al, and I make very good time to the Ladbroke End. When I get up to the stands, they are very crowded and it is all I can do to squeeze into a place among a number of Sicilian cricket-lovers in long black overcoats and silk mufflers, to whom I am very civil.

The Surrey side is already spread all over the pitch, and I am just focusing my glasses to assess what shape the opposition is in, when the Middlesex opening pair come down the pavilion steps, and the Mediterranean supporters around me begin whistling and stamping their feet. I look at the two batsmen, and am somewhat surprised to notice they have their pads on backwards and seem to be carrying their bats upside down. I do not recognise them at once, and I am a citizen who has seen many cricketers, around and about.

'They do not seem to be the usual openers,' I murmur, very polite.

'Issa new pair,' says the fan on my right. 'Issa Napoli Joe Fromaggio an' Glass Eye Ginsberg. Issa coupla gooda boys wotta we persuaded Middlesex to try.'

At this, there is much good-natured laughter on all sides, in which I naturally join, on account of having better things to do than end up off Waterloo Bridge in a concrete kimono.

'I hope they make a century,' I say warmly, and the next thing I know, most of me is clutched up against the spectator on my left.

'Iffa they doan make a coupla ducks,' says

this citizen, whose garlic is meanwhile remov-ing the gum from my toupee, 'they gonna get took dead.'

'We gotta lotta money riding on thissa open-ing bowler from Surrey,' says his neighbour, 'so you obliging us to shutta your face.'

'You erd wotty say,' says the other phil-anthropist, putting me back in my seat and wiping his hands on his muffler.

At this point, the Surrey bowler comes on, and he is a cricketer I am not seeing before, and I know this for a fact because I am not a citizen to forget a fast bowler with a wooden leg in a hurry. I am aware that my neighbours have not allowed this interesting item to slip by unnoticed, either.

'That ain't the regular Surrey opener,' mut-ters the one on my left. 'Thatsa Stump Finkel, wotta used to drive for the Fray twins.'

'Someone gotta to the Surrey Committee!' shrieks the fan on my right.

Hands start going to inside pockets, and I am about to commence crossing myself when Glass Eye Ginsberg takes guard with his inverted bat, and Stump Finkel begins his hop to the wicket. After some minutes, he arrives at his destination, coughing more than somewhat, leans on the umpire, and lobs the ball down the pitch underarm. It rolls to a halt half-way down the wicket, whereupon there is a lot of silence all of a sudden. Glass Eye Ginsberg squints at the ball for a while, then turns round, kicks down his wicket, and begins walking back to the pavilion. At this, the Sicilians break out cheering.

'Thassa wot I call bowling!' screams my neighbour, and he is too overcome at pulling off the first leg of his treble to notice that the stand opposite, which is filled with six-foot-square citizens in lightweight worsted, has become somewhat chastened at the batsman's failure, from which I deduce that the Fray twins and their loved ones have reckoned without this sporting talent of Stump Finkel, demon bowler. This becomes even clearer when an individual across the pitch gets up and puts a megaphone to his mouth.

'We got your old lady, Reg Foskett!' booms the megaphone.

'Whosa this Reg Foskett?' mutters my neighbour.

'No ball!' shouts the umpire.

'Thatsa Reg Foskett,' mutters my neighbour.

I do not stay for the subsequent proceed-ings, since I am wearing a normal string vest and the air is suddenly filled with a lot of stuff I recognise as forming no part of a healthy citizen's diet. And, anyway, I have this very hot tip for a Kent slow left-arm spinner who is just about due to come out at Tunbridge Wells.

And I want to get some money on before they give him a saliva test.

Alan Coren
28.7.1971

-|●|●|-

Death to the Flannelled Fools

I have a friend, W. Rushton, an actor like myself, a creature of the dusk who earns his living lampooning Prime Ministers on the Box. I came upon him the other afternoon in a meadow, dressed all in white, a forlorn uneasy moth of a fellow unaccustomed to the daylight and in boots which seemed to be causing him discomfort. He was, he affirmed, playing cricket for money: the fact that he wasn't going to get the money himself didn't seem to disturb him as it surely would have done on a more normal occasion.

Living as I do in Berkshire, I am used to oak trees displaying posters advertising charity cricket matches – indeed am grateful for the warning not to approach too closely on such occasions – but Rushton, not for the first time, had caught me unawares. I withdrew hastily. I would rather watch a man at his toilet than on a cricket field, but such is the madness of the players that in time they come to believe that the spectacle they make of themselves dressed in white wielding a willow (to use their own revolting phraseology – and why not?) is some-thing their betters should pay to see.

'Car Park two shillings' the posters pro-claim. 'All proceeds to HRH Duke of Edinburgh', and blow me if the public don't drive their cars through the gate over the cart tracks, park in the cow dung, wind down the windows, turn up the radio and tell each other that they are getting a bit of fresh air.

It is not of course everybody who rolls up on these occasions, mostly people who still have drawing rooms and take the *Telegraph* and *Punch* and who like myself were brought up in the shadow of The Awful Game.

I have never got over the shock of seeing my first cricket ball. I simply couldn't believe that there was anything so dangerous loose in what up to then had seemed a safe sort of world. A terrible master at a terrible prep school introduced us. 'This is the bat, Morley,' he said, 'and this is the ball,' and flung it at me. A small red leather bomb, which for some reason failed to explode. I have lived in terror of the thing ever since. In vain I pleaded to be allowed to continue playing with a soft ball. 'I might even learn to like the game,' I told them, 'if I played with a soft ball.' Of course I lied. I had already played with a soft ball and hated it. My governesses were always urging me to join up with other children standing in front of groynes or spread out over the pebbles while Father bowled. (Never my Father, thank God.)

Blind in one eye, I discovered early on that I was never to stay long by the breakwater. While others made a meal of their innings, my own were brief to the point of incomprehension. A moment of top dogmanship holding the bat, a quick swing and back to Long Stop for the rest of time. Later at my Public School I used even to hasten the process by taking guard and then before the ball could reach me knocking down my wicket. A protest which enraged the jolly cricketing house captain, who beat me nightly in the bathroom.

Right-minded boys were supposed to like cricket. The masters used to read out the scores of the county cricket matches after prayers. They believed in a God who liked cricket and prep schools named after his saints.

Not being of the faithful I particularly dread the Test Match season, always fearful that switching on the radio or television I shall be exposed to a cricket commentary by Mr Arlott.

I cannot explain why I dread being told that Sun Yet San has now bowled more overs in his sweater from the gasworks end than any other fool in cricket, but I do. Readers may think me mad if they wish. I am but I am also brave. The other day, taking some of my old phobias out and examining them, I decided to go back to cricket for the day and to see what really goes on at Lord's during a Test match. When I arrived nothing whatever was going on. It had been raining and although the sun now shone, the wicket was covered over with what appeared to be collapsed sight screens, and a number of mackintosh sheets of various sizes and colours were laid out to dry on the turf. Someone had obviously been shopping at the army surplus supply stores and were now keen to display their trophies. No one seemed keen to play cricket. While I watched two men in blue took the field with the measured tread of police officers approaching an incident which they trust will have sorted itself out before they get there. 'Umpires inspecting the pitch,' one of the custodians informed me. They go in for custodians at Lord's. Sports which were once the privilege of the few are still run by the gentlemen of England. Polo, cricket, racing concentrate as far as conditions still permit on the 'enclosure within the enclosure'. At Lord's there are stands marked Members Only and others bearing the legend Friends of Members. Always one to dramatise my situation, I asked how I could make a friend. 'It's no use today,' the custodian informed me, 'friend or no friend, it's another fifty pence.'

By now the Umpires had reached the centre of the ground, cautiously lifted one end of the tarpaulin and sniffed. I wondered what they were looking for, could it be wet grass? Inscrutably they returned to the Pavilion. I bet Mr Betjeman likes the Pavilion, I bet he likes cricket. 'The Players,' announced the public address system, 'will take lunch . . . another inspection will be made at two thirty.'

'But I've paid,' I told the custodian.

'You should read the small print.' No one having asked me to lunch, I lingered by his side while he reminisced about the time when as a boy they paid him sixpence for eight overs. 'Who paid sixpence?' I asked. 'Why the players, of course . . . we were glad of the money in those days. Cricket is dying,' he went on, 'it's been dying ever since I can remember.' I went over and read the menu outside the restaurant. Everything was cold. I was cold. I took a taxi and went to an Indian restaurant up the road. If I wasn't going to watch them playing cricket at least I could watch them cooking my lunch.

When I got back they were ringing bells, just like they used to at St Christopher's. An Indian stood outside the Tavern shouting at one of the players coming out to field. 'Encouraging him?' I asked. 'He is my kid brother, he insulted my mother, now he can never go back to India. I shall cut him in small pieces.' He insisted on buying me a gin and tonic. 'Keep the bottle to throw later,' he advised. He was a very cheerful fellow.

I sat down beside a man who knew all about it. He had spent a lifetime playing and watching the game, a helpless hopeless addict. Perhaps he was happy, perhaps they were all happy, even the little man in a turban who bowled and kept rearranging the fieldsmen and seemed more grown up than all the others.

The Father figure on the sands, he bowled all through the long afternoon, slowly, cunningly, patiently, and the children got out one after another trying to prolong their time at the wicket, not really scoring, just staying there so they shouldn't have to field in their turn. Nothing had changed. Halfway through the afternoon I found myself almost enjoying myself. It was the bars I suppose. Lord's is full of bars and barmaids. I always like barmaids. 'We come down from Lincoln every morning,' one of them told me. 'We enjoy the change.' If they could why couldn't I? The very last ball of the very last over bowled Edrich. He had stopped trying to score half an hour earlier. He wanted to bat another day. I was glad he went.

I watched them all go home, the old men and the boys, the mothers and the custodians, the waitresses from Lincoln, the decent quiet people of England – and, oh my God, you should have seen the filth they left behind.

Robert Morley
11.8.1971

–|●|●|–

Indian Cricket – The Way to Truth?
Miles Kington's armchair guide to this now fashionable ancient cult

Cricket is nothing new in this country. For many years there have been small clubs all over Britain devoted to this ancient belief, where the few devotees could meditate and do their exercises in the privacy of deserted stands and pavilions. And over the last half dozen years it has actually won a certain mass popularity, thanks to Sunday afternoon TV performances and knock-out competitions. But according to the experts, this kind of cricket is a crude and sensationalised version of the true mystical art.

'It's just a lot of clever tricks,' says Guru Ristspinna, one of India's top practitioners. 'Always, the Western world takes something like Kung Fu or Karate and sees only the flashy, sensational side of it, chopping wood in half with the hand or lying on beds of nails. Many folk in Britain now think that cricket is a matter of clouting a ball immense distances, and bowling as fast as possible. But true

Bedi, the God of Spinners, here seen flighting the ball, making it turn, finding the pad and asking for L B W

Devi, the Umpire Goddess. With her eight arms she can simultaneously give a man out, signal the scorer, take a jersey, hold up play, inspect a bat and, if necessary, count an Australian eight-ball over

cricket is all about the control of the body. Cricket lies in the mind.'

A team of Indian cricketers is in Britain at this very moment, demonstrating the true art to a public who have probably never seen the real thing before. Much of it is based on the Venkataraghavan, the sacred book of Indian hand movements, which describes the 105 different positions for the fingers. A master of the art can use his fingers to control the cricket ball and make it do anything he wants – a true master can perform such difficult feats as Moving It Both Ways, Finding the Edge, Beating the Bat and Lifting It Off a Length.

'A truly great bowler,' says Ristspinna, 'enters into an almost mystical relationship with the ball, and they become one. He delights in using as many variations as possible, unlike most English bowlers, who think that sheer speed and aggression is the secret. It is only when he rids his soul of aggressiveness and learns the subtlety of the slow spin that he becomes an entire man. The deity of Indian bowling is the god Bedi, who is reputed to have been able to bowl the ball slowly, yet still evade the batsman, the wicket and the wicket keeper. This is known technically as Bedi byes.'

But the main difference between our crude form of cricket and the true creed is that the British still see cricket as a martial art, as something to be won. The basic ritual of cricket is the 'match', a stylised game. The English try to beat the other side; the Indians go beyond that.

'An enlightened cricketer is not interested in winning or losing – he has already rid himself of such primitive emotions. The true cricketer thinks the important thing is not to win or lose or even to take part but to be a better person afterwards. He may easily go into a trance while at the wicket; some top flight batsmen seem almost motionless, lost in contemplation of some distant object such as a spectator, or two spectators, if there are two.

'Time, remember, has no meaning for the real cricketer, which is why we disapprove so strongly of your Sunday afternoon travesties.

Bringing on the light roller

One of the most important parts of the ritual is the creation of symbolic patterns by positioning the eleven devotees on the open ground, or Placing the Field, and this alone could take all day. It is said that the ancient Indian hero Gavaskar stood motionless for three years on one leg, his chin sunk in his hands and his brow furrowed. On the first day of the fourth year, he opened his mouth suddenly and said: "And a man on the square leg boundary."'

Not a martial art, then, though a skilled cricketer could no doubt do tremendous damage with the lethal three-foot-long 'bat'; not a religion, as Sikhs and Hindus can join without abandoning their own creed; not a philosophy, even. What is it, briefly? A way of life? 'More than that,' says the Guru. 'It is man's only way of expressing eternity.'

Some ancient Indian books on the art of cricket:

The Venkataraghavan. The sacred book of hand movements, written in marvellous medieval Hindu prose. 'And the second finger shall be laid along the seam like a lion stretched out at the watering place when the blood-red sun of the Ghats goes down behind the . . .'

The Perfumed Wicket. A loving disquisition on the little-noticed erotic side of cricket. The unknown author finds sensual delight in everything from the tying on of the pads to patting and stroking the pitch, for which he describes thirty-one different techniques.

The Tale of Chandrasekhar. Long, involved epic describing a mythical cricket game lasting six years in which each delivery is narrated in some detail, with ten side-chapters on the Mogul Invasion that held up the match for two years. The hero is the engaging slow-right-arm off-spinner elephant god, Chandrasekhar.

The Poems of Prasanna. More lyrical than practical, these five hundred and eighty-five poems dwell on the glory of the morning dew and how to make the ball rise sharply off it.

Some mystical terms used commonly in cricket:

Googly: the state of mind in which one expects one thing and receives another.

Chinaman: a person from China, hence a hostile presence, an alien spirit, a man who shouts 'Somebody wake up the batsman and tell him there's only five days left!'

Wisden: the state of grace towards which all cricketers strive.

Draw: the outcome of a meeting between an irresistible bowler and an irremovable batsman, the conflict between good and evil.

New ball: symbol of rebirth and regeneration.

Rain stopped play: in the parched heartlands of India, the whole year is geared to the moment when, after months of suffocating dry heat, the heavens open, the monsoon arrives and the losing side gratefully secures a draw.

Boundary: the imaginary circular line which encloses all civilisation and beyond which lie only hecklers, transistors and men with no shirts.

Forward defensive stroke: the basic position in cricket, a simple exercise which a batsman repeats for an hour or two until he feels in the exalted state of mind where he may attempt some more exotic movement such as the sweep, hook or cut.

Umpire: an all-present, all-seeing deity who is basically benign but always aloof.

Miles Kington
19.6.1974

Success

Like health, success is harder to describe than failure (or sickness). We rarely reflect on the former until we experience the latter. We notice adverse criticism more keenly than favourable; we're sensitive to failure while we tend merely to wallow in success.

What, then, is it like for a batsman to be 'on the go', in the right frame of mind? He is, of course, absorbed in the activity and feels completely alive. In my case, I become wide-focused; aware of all sorts of things around me – the flight of a bird, interactions between fielders, and the bowler and his ball. One is resilient to minor setbacks. John Edrich batting against New Zealand at Leeds, on a pitch that helped seam bowling, played and missed on average one ball an over. But he shrugged off these little moral defeats, received the next ball with an uncluttered mind, and scored 310.

At times, especially between 1974 and 1977, and again last summer, I have had a similar attitude at the crease. I have relished the contest. When in difficulties I have, like a toddler learning to walk, picked myself up and carried on without self-criticism, and scored runs when below my best. I enjoy the bowler's skill. When Robin Jackman bowls a ball that pitches on middle stump and veers away over the top of off-stump, I appreciate the delivery for what it is. And I still look forward to the next ball.

In such a mood one can almost (but not quite) hope that the bowler stays at his peak, so that the pleasure of the competition remains intense; one can certainly be grateful to him for it afterwards. After one classic fight for the world middle-weight title in 1948, Rocky Graziano and Tony Zale fell into each other's

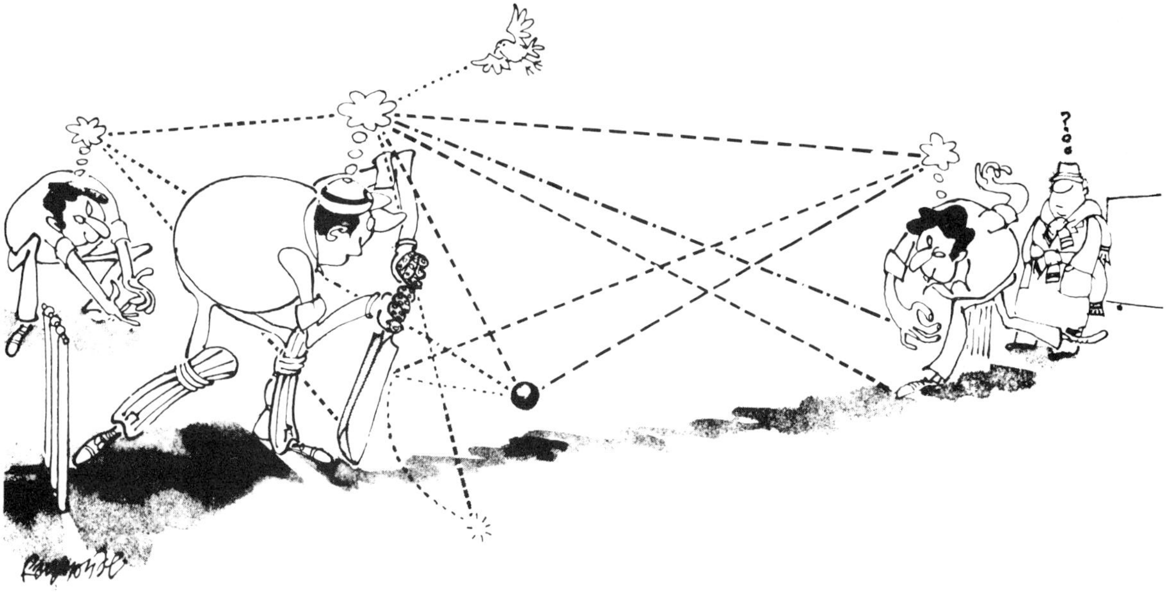

arms. Similarly, batsmen and bowlers need each other's skills so that the action, the drama, can come alive.

The first time I batted against the Indian off-spinner, Eripalli Prasanna, was in a relatively unimportant match at Ahmedabad. He bowled only a few overs at me and I scored few runs. But there was what struck me as a peculiarly Indian flavour to our interaction. I noticed that after I played each ball Prasanna would look at me and catch my eye. Sometimes he wagged his head a little. Always he looked shrewd, and knowing. I enjoyed this, and started to join in his game. He had an engaging appearance, short and plump with big round baby's eyes. The messages were, I think, instructive about the source of much of cricket's pleasure. The exchange, if verbalised, might have gone as follows:

PRASANNA: Did you notice how I drew you forward there, and made you reach for the ball? A bit slower, you see, but the same action.

ME: Yes, indeed, I noticed it. Beautiful bowling. But though I had to watch you, I didn't let you fool me. I waited for the ball to come and quietly dropped it down.

PRASANNA (*after another ball*): Ah, you thought of driving that one, did you not? But no doubt you also saw how foolish it would be to take such a liberty with me.

ME: Yes, I probably could have gone through with my shot, but couldn't quite trust myself on this pitch. Wait until I get you on a true wicket.

The mutual appreciation in this sporting dialogue is crucial. Each of us liked having an opponent it would be worthwhile getting the better of. We both enjoyed the other's knowing that we were playing well.

Such knowledge need not be only between the contestants. The crowd, and those other onlookers, the fielders, can to an extent share it. I once saw Ravi Shankar play the sitar in Delhi. Around him on the floor sat his closest acolytes and apprentices. Again there was the expressive shake of the head from the performer and the initiates' encouraging response: 'A player like you needs an audience like us who appreciate you as we do.'

The character of the sporting interaction varies, and few fast bowlers indulge in the head-wagging and subtle eye-contacts of an Indian spinner. But the essential features remain. Moreover, as a batsman, I often find that the slight physical risk presented by a fast bowler increases, if anything, the liveliness of my concentration. Again, the bond is enhanced by mutual respect. The logical fact that batsmen and bowlers are necessary for there to be a game at all is paralleled by the psychological fact that batsmen and bowlers have an absorbed interest in each other's activities.

This unity of the protagonists is, paradoxically, derived from their confrontation. One fundamental pleasure of competitive games is getting the better of someone else, whether individually or as a team.

The urge for success may get out of hand. Jardine went too far in his strategy for containing Bradman. Ian Chappell, going beyond an admirable identification with his own players, has turned cricket matches into gang warfare. But the opposite is more common; when an often unacknowledged uneasiness about our own aggression may make us both less successful than we should be and less capable of enjoying whatever success we do achieve.

I have seen England players, overwhelmed by the aggression of the opposition, lose touch with their own combative powers and surrender to the legend of Lillee and the Perth pitch. There's a fear, too, that showing one's own aggression will invite even fiercer retaliation. But one may also be afraid of one's own destructiveness. Some individuals (and teams) let their opponents off the hook when they have them at their mercy. They fail to ram home an advantage. Some find it hard to play all out to win; if they did so, they might be revealed as nasty and unlikable. We dislike our own barely suppressed tendency to gloat. A tennis player often drops his own service the game after breaking his opponent's, perhaps feeling guilty at having presumed so far; while the opponent, his guilt now assuaged, is stung into uninhibited aggression. The sportsman, like the doctor, should not get emotionally involved with his 'patient'. Len Hutton's advice to me on the eve of the England team's departure to India in 1976 was, 'Don't take pity on the Indian bowlers.' Respecting an opponent includes being prepared to finish him off.

Cricketers are now less inhibited about showing pleasure at their own and their colleagues' successes. During a stoppage for rain in 1977, we watched the film on television of Jim Laker's match at Old Trafford in 1956. After a few dismissals, Derek Underwood, incredulous, said, 'But they don't seem to be *pleased* about taking wickets!' The reactions of the players certainly looked, to our eyes, rather low-key. The bowler might allow himself a modest hitch of the trousers as he sauntered down to the group of fielders, whose 'creams' were unlikely to be sullied by any mark of mud or grass. It was all in the day's work.

Whereas we! – we've not yet started widespread kissing, but hugging is commonplace and I've seen cheeks chucked. David Shepherd, the rotund Gloucestershire cricketer, was fielding at third man when an important catch was caught at wide long-on. He set off at his usually single-gear chug, reached the cluster of congratulatory fields and arrived back at his corner of the ground, the 300-yard round trip completed, just in time for the next ball.

I used to get huffy letters from Colonels in Surrey about all this palaver. 'Dear Brearley, must we have all this hugging and gloating? Is not taking wickets and holding catches what you chaps are paid for? The captain's hand on the shoulder and a quiet "well-caught" should suffice. Yours etc. . . . .'

Behaviour that seemed outlandish to such writers felt quite natural to us. We were not, usually, gloating; just delighted. And the fact that we are paid to play does not mean that we don't play for the love of it, or that our emotions on the field are different in kind from those we felt when at the age of six we 'became' our heroes in the local park.

The dramatic improvement in fielding that one-day cricket has caused encourages the sense that each fielder is an integral member of a unit, not a casual bystander in a scene enacted between the protagonists. Underwood was surprised not only at Laker's lack of exuberance, but also at the nonchalance of the fielders. Cricketers now train before and during the season. A track-suit is not, as it was fifteen years ago, a pretentious irrelevance. I suspect that the common effort required in training and fielding practice has shifted cricket slightly in the direction of the team game. It is now inconceivable that a bowler would have to fetch a straight-drive off his own bowling; but in Alan Moss's early days, when he came in one evening with the second new ball, and the batsman drove it back past him he looked round to see the ageing Jim Sims, at wide mid-on, edging towards square leg and saying, 'Sorry Al, but you'll have to go.' So he went, and picked up the ball in front of the pavilion.

Authoritarianism is out of fashion, in cricket as elsewhere. The view that everyone has the right to a say in how his group is run is matched by the idea that each has a responsibility to see that it is well run. Mutual motivation is essential for the success of a team. I nicknamed Graham Gooch 'Zapata', not only because of the moustache and sombrero, but also because of the impression he gave in the field of being ready for his siesta. We used to get at him for this soporific air. Now Gooch looks lively, and encourages the bowlers more than most.

The successful sides that I've been involved in all seem to have been robustly humorous. Like a steam-roller, a cricket team is composed of atoms that continuously bounce against each other, but unlike the roller its atoms are complex and variegated. The rivalry within a side, which can become bitter and selfish, is often richly productive. And certainly no one is exempt from his turn as butt. One of Ian Botham's contributions to the England side has been to prevent others, including Geoff Boycott (and me), from taking Geoff Boycott (and me) too seriously. I trust that someone is doing the same for him.

Mike Brearley
25.2.1981

Lif' Dat Bail

The very work *cricket* is, of course, itself of orig. uncert., of etym. dub.: the best bet is Swahili, the likeliest connotation sexual, perhaps to describe an organ, perhaps the act of deploying that organ, who can be sure? Possibly a small noise made during. Certainly, the other semantic arcana have their seedy origins in unsavoury sexual puns: *gully, short leg, long stop, over*, for example, may still be found in virtually pristine use along the Lourenço Marques waterfront – 'You want gully-gully, mister? You want short leg-over, very clean, you want nice long stop?' – and the fact that *googly* and *Chinaman* are synonymous comes as no surprise to the experienced stoker, for whom, in a lonely port, they unfortunately amount to the same thing.

No fixed date, obviously, can be established for the beginning of the modern game, but most experts agree that it had its origins on slave plantations, where cotton and sugar workers, to relieve their wretched lot, would get up crude matches using a cotton boll and a whippy length of sugar-cane, the boll being *bolled* at three pieces of implanted bamboo in an attempt to *knock down de wicked*, since the game was also deeply steeped in the fundamental religious beliefs held by the unfortunate slaves. The simple homiletic message of the early game is, of course, clear, and those origins retain their echo today in the name of the spiritual home of cricket, Lawd's.

Gradually, after the American Civil War, the game grew more refined. The slaves, naturally not able to afford the sophisticated equipment in use today, improvised with whatever they found lying around the battle-fields of the defeated South: the small cannonball, for example, introduced the hard missile to the game, the musket-stock replaced the sugar-cane and ushered in the characteristic bat-shape, and very soon, teams of freed slaves were touring Dixieland and playing improvised games against local sides to the delight of dancing, drunken, finger-snapping crowds, whose modern counterparts may be observed today, from the Lawd's Tavern to the Hill at Sydney.

It was probably at around this period that the name stuck. There is no contemporary record of exactly when and how this happened, but the romanticisation of the incident in the film *The Birth of the Blues* (the story of the first Oxford vs Cambridge Match) is probably fairly close to the truth. In that, you may recall, the young English undergraduate (C. Aubrey Smith), while on a visit to South Carolina, notices a group of slaves playing in the grounds of his host's ante-bellum mansion, and calls one of the *bollers* over to him with the words:

'I say, boy, what do you call that stuff?'

To which the young black (Stepin Fetchit) replies:

'Why, boss, we calls it cricket!'

Within a very few years and with the increasing mobility of the newly-freed negroes cricket moved off the plantations and into the towns around the Delta. Hardly surprisingly, it was not yet received into the better circles of society, so that many young cricketers learned their trade playing in the brothel districts, like Storyville. The madames found that waiting clients would drink more if they had a cricket match to watch, and for the unemployed young negroes, this was a Godsend. This is from an interview with the distinguished old batsman Jelly Roll Hammond, recorded by Alan Lomax:

'Ah fust started messin' wid a bat when ah wuz in de Gravier Street Orphanage. Cricket wuz a way of keepin' us kids off de street. Ah din have no formal trainin', an' even to dis day ah still cain't read a scorecard, but that din make no never-mind, ah jes' picked up dat ole bat an' ah impervised. Pretty dam' soon ah foun' ah could handle tricky stuff like de short risin' ball outside de off-stump etcetera, an' one day after ah hit 134 befoh lunch agin de Big Eye Louis Sutcliffe Hot Seven, dis high yaller butter-an'-egg man come up to me an' he say "Ah like de way y'all play dat stuff, kid, how's about y'all come to work on mah groun' staff?" Turn out he wuz jest about de top ponce east o' Memphis! Pretty soon, ah wuz playin' out back o' De Square Leg Cat House, Noo Orleans, ten dollars a match an' all de gully ah could git, heh-heh-heh!'

The reference to the Hot Seven is particularly interesting. In the early days, teams were very small: Satchmo G. Grace, for example, started off with only five – himself at cover,

Kid Ponsford at deep fine leg, Blind Lemon Bosanquet at silly point, and Baby Hobbs behind the stumps. Bunk Larwood had to boll continuously from both ends. But he soon found that this basic ensemble was too restricted, and the team was implemented by two more players, the most important addition being a slow-tempo boller to relieve Larwood at the other end. After six bolls were bolled, Satchmo would cry: 'We'll take a break now, folks!' and Mezz Titmus would come on and send down his off-spinners from the other end. This traditional cry was soon replaced with 'Over!', partly because it was shorter, but mainly because the lewd overtones made the crowd fall about, particularly if it had been a maiden.

By the end of the Great War, white men had begun to take an interest in the new game: not only did cricket move up from the Delta towards Chicago (a fairly direct result of the Volstead Act and the enormous boost it gave to the drinking with which cricket spectators have always been associated), but the first travelling team was formed. The all-white Original Dixieland Test Eleven arrived to play in England in 1919, but the tour was a complete fiasco: the rudimentary English game was played according to very different rules, and the local variations in pitch and rhythm entirely defeated the ODT XI. They found the bunny hop and the turkey trot totally unplayable, and after three or four ill-attended matches they packed their bags and returned to Charleston.

In Chicago itself during these Prohibition years, black cricket still dominated the scene. It was the era of the giants, and consequently of the legends: of men like Wingy D'Oliviera, who had lost his right arm years before in a car crash, yet still became a great all-rounder, hitting a double century against the Mound City Jug Cricketers and, in the same match, taking 6 for 40 with his tricky one-arm-round-the-wicket leg-cutters; of men like Miff 'Sobers', whose nickname derived from his habit of getting through all-night net sessions on two gallons of moonshine and then being carried out to the middle on the following morning and hurling down his murderous

bouncers at batsmen whom his captain had told him had signed the pledge. Sadly, his career came to an abrupt end when, in 1926, he killed both opening batsmen for the Temperance VII, and received a 10-to-30 stretch in Alcatraz on a Murder Two count. However, his brain was by this time so befuddled by alcohol that he went to his prison grave happy, still believing that his final figures had been 10 *for* 30.

And who amongst us who love the game will ever forget that other great nickname, Clarence 'Pine Top' Close. Perhaps the finest silly mid-off ever, certainly the dumbest, Close fielded so short that batsmen were terrified to hook, for fear of breaking their bats on his forehead. Of all the wonderful anecdotes about Close that have become enshrined in cricket's annals, perhaps the one nearest to the spirit of the man concerns the match against the Fletcher Hendren Big XI, played at the Metropole Oval in a thunderstorm in 1929. Just before tea, Close was struck by lightning, losing nine teeth, and immediately cried 'Howzat?', believing he must have caught the ball in his mouth.

And then there was Bix. Leon Bismarck 'Bix' Washbrook, star of the famous 1930 movie *King of Cricket*, hero of Dorothy Baker's fine book *Young Man with a Bat*, Bix was the first white cricketer of any stature, so poor that he often walked out to the wicket with his bat behind him to hide the holes in his flannels, yet so rich in the affection of crowds that as soon as each ball left the bowler's hand, the pavilion would rise as one man, and shout: 'Oh, play that thing!'

He died, at the height of his powers, in 1931; but for lovers of the man and the traditional game, this tragedy was lessened by the knowledge that cricket was now taking a road he would have hated. The Swing Era had begun, and with it the rise of the Big Teams. For vulgarisation and commercialisation had struck the great game: to attract vast crowds, ignorant crowds, managers were now including anything up to five or six swing bowlers in their huge sides, not to mention dozens of crude sloggers, simply to appeal to the lowest common crowd denominator. Finesse, subtlety, originality vanished; the improvising solo player was no more. The boring pattern of short-pitched balls and haymaking hoods ruled supreme: Artie Bradman's XXXV, for example, beat Benny Hutton's All Stars at Carnegie Bridge in July 1937 by 164 runs, all of them wides. As for Glenn Ramadhin and his endless, worthless search for innovation, it almost ruined the game altogether with its culmination in an ensemble of eight wicket-keepers, four seamers bowling in harmony, and sixty-two men in the offside trap.

It was left to the caring black man and, oddly, the old-fashioned English amateur, to drag cricket back from the brink and remind it of its roots and true genius. On the one hand, virtuoso players unconcerned with wealth and mass-appeal emerged (Coleman Bailey, Lester Lindwall, Thelonious Spofforth), and the small team reappeared (the Modern Cricket Quartet, the Zoot Laker Trio Plus Two); and on the other, in bumpy fields behind quiet English pubs, keen village sides started to come together under Humphrey Compton and Cy Dexter and Ottilie Martin-Jenkins to revive the traditional game. Crude they were, yes, and unsophisticated, often pitifully derivative; and yet, travelling the country in broken-down Dormobiles and playing to enthusiastic kids for rent-money, it was crick-eters of that brave kidney who kept the old game alive, and, indeed, still do.

As to its future, who can say? Cricket has come a long way from the African slave ships and the chain gangs and the cotton plan-tations, and the roads have not always been smooth nor the conditions clement. Once more it is undergoing a somewhat fallow spell, and there are those Jeremiahs, as there have always been, who say that this time it may not recover. And yet, surely, as long as there are sassy kids about, the tough little Fat Bothams, the plucky Young Meade Lux Gowers, prepared to grab a boll and an old piece of sugar-cane and an advertising director from a cigarette company, does any of us really believe that this great game will ever die?

Alan Coren
1.6.1983

Rock Botham

Frank Keating recorded the actual words. It was Maundy Thursday in Jamaica and Ian Botham – at the end of his disastrous captaincy of England's even more disastrous tour of the West Indies – was being told a joke. Naturally enough it came from *Punch*. The article con-cerned spring, and how (apart from actually remembering the date of the vernal equinox) it is possible to be certain that the season of renewal has come round again. One of the proofs that the daffodils were about to bloom concerned cricket. 'Somewhere very hot and very far away, England will be batting to avoid an innings defeat in the final Test.'

Mr Botham was not amused. 'God, you bloody pressmen!' said Ian with dismissive despair. He said he'd heard from home some of the things the British press had been writing about him. 'And I thought they were friends of mine!' Relations deteriorated.

Ian had 'menaced' the Old Etonian journal-ist, Henry Blofeld, at a stopover in Bermuda during the team's flight home. Blofeld had written in the *Sunday Express* that Botham 'captained the side like a great big baby'. Ian wanted Henry, languid and elegant, to step outside and repeat the charge to his face.

It is not the duty of this column to make judgements about the character and conduct of cricketers, though it has to be said – as a commentary on professional journalists rather than professional cricketers – that Mr Botham's reaction to the 'joke' was typically naive. The camaraderie of drinks after the game and gossip behind the early morning nets is, no doubt, a pleasure which both players and commentators enjoy. But only in a world less complicated and competitive than Fleet Street could it turn into a multiple friendship that protected the cricketer and inhibited his critics.

But all that happened in 1981. And since then Ian Botham has, no doubt, learned a great deal about journalists. For he remains the centre of their summer attention. They overstate his failures and exaggerate his suc-cesses. They rejoice with him in triumph and in defeat they treat him as if he has wilfully let them down. 'After all our industry,' they seem to say, 'he still insists on being human.' And they take a terrible revenge for having been proved wrong.

Tony Lewis of the *Sunday Telegraph* demonstrates the dangers of being told – and believing – that men can become gods.

The selectors will now have to believe their own eyes and apply mundane judgements to a great player who has come down to earth to compete with mortals. There was a time when he could amble on stage at any old weight to perform his art. Now he must succeed and that depends on just how much he himself wants to succeed.

In Mr Lewis's paragraph of strictures you can actually hear the wax cracking and the wings falling off – even though we are not told who it was that convinced young Ian that he could fly all the way to the sun.

Of course Mr Lewis quickly recovered his confidence in his own initial judgement. '"There's only one Ian Botham!" the overspill football fans chorused down at the Tavern' – and 'for once the message carried the emotions of us all.'

At any rate it carried the emotions of the cricket writers in the Sunday papers. Even the ranks of the *News of the World* could scarce forbear to cheer. To be fair to the paper, they actually cheered more loudly than any of their competitors. But then, the decibel count of their booing had been correspondingly high in previous weeks.

At Leeds (at least according to Pat Weaver who attends Test Matches for the *News of the World*) 'Ian Botham, in a moment of macho madness, put the immediate cricket future of England and himself in grave peril . . . The sad fact,' he continued, 'is that Botham has not looked even a good first change England bowler this summer. And his batting lacks the responsibility to command a specialist position.'

And things got worse. By July 3rd Mr Weaver had turned sympathetic. 'Problems pile up for Ian Botham. Already suffering from back trouble, weight worries, hay fever and lack of form, he missed yesterday's match at Taunton with a groin strain. Now the star all-rounder who flopped in the World Cup . . .' But I end the quotation in mid com-

miseration lest you should be overcome by so much tender concern for the welfare of the fallen idol. No doubt Mr Weaver was almost as distressed by writing the article as Mr Botham was by reading it. Fortunately, Mr Weaver has marvellous powers of recuperation.

By the Sunday of the Third Test Match he was able to write a piece that justified the headline 'Botham Hits Back' – though it discreetly avoided saying against whom Botham's retaliatory blow was struck. His story of the Botham innings proclaims that 'Ian Botham can eat three Shredded Wheats again. England's all-wrong all-rounder rediscovered his appetite at Lord's yesterday.' It ended, 'When he had reached his half-century, he dipped his sunhat and bowed in the direction of the Press Box. We will allow him such ego acts if he continues to play like this.'

Exactly. The newspapers will continue to idolise Botham when he is on form. And by doing so will actually reduce his chance of producing consistently high standard performances. They will encourage his fatal inclination to believe that he is above the normal disciplines of the professional cricketer's life. And they will intensify the feeling of bewildered resentment which surfaces during moments when he loses his form and makes his ugly complaints against professional cricketers turned journalists who 'never had an off-day, never lost form, never got out for a duck – at least to hear them talking'.

In fact, one of the most distinguished players to turn pundit has treated Ian Botham with a courtesy which is rarely enjoyed by anyone who has been hammered by the press. Denis Compton has actually admitted that he was wrong. 'I know,' Compton wrote on August 7th, 'I have been more critical than most about his disastrous loss of top-level form . . . I have even suggested that the shock of being dropped might be the jolt he needs.' But he went on to change his mind in public.

The date of the volte-face is important. Denis Compton revised his opinion of Botham the week before the England all-rounder rose from the dead. By now I doubt if the occasionally unheroic hero needs any advice about triumph and disaster from the sort of impostor who comments about flaws in outstanding players. But I recommend that he does not think Denis Compton a friend just because of one Sunday's support. All that can be said for Compton's conversion to Bothamism is that he changed his mind because he knows more about cricket than all the Botham detractors added together.

Roy Hattersley
24.8.1983

–|●|●|–

Saint Geoffrey

We had been discussing the possibility of making a biographical film. I had a final note from him just before he left for South Africa at the end of the summer. In his twirly-youthful, ballpoint longhand, he has always been a prompt, meticulous, businesslike correspondent but, to me anyway, he will always sign-off differently and jokily. This one ended '. . . All the best – Your old Fruit 'n' Nut Montgomery.'

Once, years before, I had dubbed him in print as 'old Fruit and Nut' after sitting next to him on a Guyana-bound aeroplane during which time he had consumed, solo, one of the largest bars of Cadbury's I had ever seen. 'Aye, good for energy is chocolate.' The name 'Monty' also stuck for bit, suggested by his habit in faraway, foreign, deserty places of seldom socialising with his fellows after play and retiring to the 'caravan' of his hotel room, ordering a healthily frugal and lonely room-service, reading, writing letters, sipping ginseng tea, plotting his campaign for the morrow and, at early lights-out, dreaming his recurring dreams of 'roons and more roons'.

The nickname that stuck most readily through his career in the English dressing-room was 'Fiery', an ironic, grudging testament to his monumental, patient and diligent concentration at the crease.

When Geoffrey Boycott left for a brief trip to South Africa last month he obviously knew that something had to give – but probably grinned his wonky grin to himself at Heathrow, secure that his 4,000 runs for Yorkshire in the last two seasons would keep his place snug for another summer at least, and that the man who would go was his rival, the player-

manager Raymond Illingworth. Their barneys had become legends in every cricketer's lunch interval. Between them they were bringing disputes into disrepute. Someone had to go. But this time Geoffrey misjudged the pace of the pitch.

A fortnight before, at Chelmsford, he had played, unknowingly, the last of his 720-odd innings for Yorkshire. It was a grey, wind-blown morning, but he had all day to make the 61 runs he needed to post his 2,000 for the season and so offer Illingworth a farewell V-sign. He was lbw to Phillip of Essex in the second over of the morning. He stared hard at the umpire, furious, then scurried off with that almost sheepish matelot's walk. In the pavilion, still livid with himself, he carefully folded his blue cap, badged with the white rose, and buried it in his bag. At once, he combed carefully his precious, expensive, sewn-in, Sinatra-style strands of hair, then untwined the sticky wads of Elastoplast from the bottom joints of his right thumb and forefinger; he unbuckled his white knight's armour and, naked, he went to shower.

The final rituals of his 21st season with Yorkshire were done. Who could have realised then there would not be a 22nd? And so ended Boycott's last rites for his beloved and beloving, infuriated and infuriating, divided and divisive county. Or did they? Whatever happens, can any one man, in any walk of life, here so split an English county as Geoffrey Boycott has split Yorkshire.

Town Halls are packed to the rafters in his support. Other Town Halls are filled to castigate him. The last eruption was in 1978 when they dismissed him as captain. On that occasion the *Guardian* sports pages organised an 'Ode to Sir Geoffrey' poetry competition. Hundreds entered. Some were unprintably venomous. Others were too droolingly adoring. Few were simply good fun. The winner was a Mr D. Cleaver, of Oldham, who twigged the ridiculous solemnity of the hoo-ha as well as the high-grade humour:

> 'Twas evenin' time in t'Vatican and
> t'Pope 'ad gone to bed.
> 'E were laid there readin' *Newsweek* wi'
> 'is skullcap on 'is 'ead.

Frank KEATING Saint Geoffrey

At around about ten-thirty a knock came
    at front door
An' there stood a tiny errand boy all
    breathless an' footsore.
'E stood there, eyes all wet wi' tears, 'is
    voice about t' crack,
'Tha'd best raise t'gaffer right away –
    Geoff Boycott's got the sack!'

We recalled that verse with laughter, before
the balloon went up, when Geoffrey and I had
a last supper of the 1983 season – though I
must admit there was just a gleam, a passing
glow from his Coventry-blue-tinted contact
lenses, that wanted to agree, earnestly, that
the poet had a point. If Boycott was a Catholic,
some part of him would be looking already for,
well if not quite a canonisation yet, at least a
beatification to be going on with.

We dined in a posh, sweet-trolley, ice-
bucket, provincial Trust House hotel
restaurant with menus like Town Criers'
scrolls and waiters like unctuous gendarmes.
No, Geoffrey didn't want any wine, only some
hot water for his ginseng teabag and a bottle of
mineral water. Perrier? No, certainly not Perrier, go out and get some Ashbourne water –
'I'm English, aren't I? Support home
industries, that's me.' They went out to find
some Ashbourne water. He didn't bother with
the menu – 'I just want an 'unk of that *Dutch*
cheese!' You never quite know where you are
with Geoffrey.

Nobody has ever known. Except perhaps
his beloved mother, the widow of an always
coughing-sick miner who was latterly badly
injured in an underground accident. His
mother died just two weeks before he was
sacked as Yorkshire's captain in 1978. 'That
was the worst month of my life.'

I nudged him to remember what was surely
the best day of his life – when he had walked
serenely through the milling throng, moist-
eyed, and sheepish grin more skew-whiff than
ever, in the starling-shrieking, jabbering cock-
pit of that tumbledown stadium at Delhi on
Christmas Eve in 1981. Five minutes before,
Boycott had meticulously tucked the slow left-
armer, Doshi of India, to the midwicket fence
to become the most prolific batsman in the
whole long, grand, history of all Test Match
cricket.

This complicated, self-absorbed, warrior–
hero–friend had now scored more runs under
pressure than the founding-father, W.G.;
more by far than the Doctor's sparkling
apprentices like Jessop or Trumper or Fry or
Macartney; more than 'the Master' called
Hobbs; more than the twinkle-toed, narrow-
eyed bully-boy of bowling, Bowral's Bradman; more than the languid, liquid-moving,
laughing cavalier called Sobers; more than the
mighty Hammond, the debonair Compton,
the accumulating Hanif, the three wondrous
Ws, more than May or Cowdrey . . . more,
many more, than predecessors in his same
rose-blue cap, the smarm-haired, ever-sound
Sutcliffe and the un-racy rationalist of batting,
Hutton. (Boycott's all-time hero, oddly, had
never been either of those latter two fellow
Tykes: when he was getting his eight O-levels
at Hemsworth Grammar School, the great and
graceful Wessex whiffer Graveney was, to the
squinting, lonely mother's boy, the
non-pareil.)

For the next two days in Delhi, Geoffrey
was on a high. In public he was modesty itself,
insisting that his hundredth at Headingley
meant more to him. But the dreamy, faraway
mists would not leave his eye. On Christmas
Day he was a hit at the fancy dress party in
which the theme was 'Heroes'. Boycott went
as Prince Ranjitsinhji. (Ian Botham went as Sir
Geoffrey Gandhi, but that's another story!)

Then, calamitously for the new champion, a
gruesomely depressing reaction settled on his
mind and spirit. We moved on for the next
Test in Calcutta. Geoffrey closeted himself in
his room for a week. He finished the massive
novel *Shogun*, but mostly had his face turned
to the wall. He complained of 'utter listless-
ness', cried off in the middle of the Test and
flew home where, 'with the whole world
turned against me', he organised the rebel tour
to South Africa.

My theory was that, having become statisti-
cally the most successful batsman in history,
his very driving motor simply conked out. His
unlikely – impossible – ambition of 30 years
had been achieved (his later, refound, greed
for Yorkshire runs was to show Illingworth
which of them was indispensable), and there
was nothing left.

It was well over a quarter of a century before that a ludicrous – indeed laughable, on the few occasions he divulged it – determination had gripped the lonely little lad with bad eyesight who was fed up with being teased in the playground. He was going to be the best bat in the world. And so, once he had passed his 11-plus, for night upon night after school, through springs and autumns and the slush of winters, he would make two changes on the bus to travel from the family's tiny Coal Board house at 45 Milton Terrace, Fitzwilliam, to Johnny Lawrence's indoor cricket hut some 20 miles away. When he could, his cricket-loving uncle would accompany him. But the dream was Geoffrey's. 'They can laugh now. They won't when I'm the best there's ever been.'

His first, grown-up, senior League game was for Hemsworth in 1954 when he was 13. He went in No. 9 against Knaresborough, who had been bowled out for 119. Hemsworth had struggled to 85 for seven when the boy marched in – in spectacles, short trousers and cumbersome pads. At 118 for seven he put his left foot down the wicket and coldly drove the winning boundary . . . and his dreams that night again determined him in his course.

His nightly bus journeys continued. One Sunday, in his late teens, he was batting again for the local club, relentlessly moving towards another century. Play was interrupted with a message for him to report next day to Head-ingley to attend the Yorkshire first team nets. He left the field at once, pursued by the opposition captain.

'Is it not courtesy to ask permission to leave the field in the middle of an innings?' Boycott fixed him with a withering glare. 'I've finished with your class of cricket,' he sneered. And he went on his way.

Half a dozen years later he was walking out with Dennis Amiss to open the batting for England. 'Good luck,' said Dennis as they went to their respective ends. 'It's not luck,' snorted Geoffrey, 'it's skill.'

On another occasion, on a perfect Test wicket, Amiss accidentally ran out his partner early on. Boycott came back seething. When, an hour later, the rest of the England players on the balcony applauded Amiss's half century, a distraught Geoffrey shouted above them, 'They're *my* roons, y'clappin', *my* roons!'

In India a couple of winters ago, at one of the interminable official functions that must be attended, the small talk of a sudden was turned off dramatically. The gathering froze. H. M. Bateman could hardly have bettered the tableau. A diminutive Indian banker, ming-ling enthusiastically till then, had had the temerity to ask one of the England tourists, 'And what, good sir, is your name, may I ask?'

The famous wonky grin sought to cut through the horrified silence. The blue eyes rolled and blazed. The little banker wobbled. Finally one of the greatest of living English-men spluttered a reply in his Yorkshire accent: 'W. G. Grace! what's yours?'

We all laughed, but Geoffrey wasn't done – 'And what's more, unless I'm crackers or something, I've scored a bloody sight more roons than that bearded old bugger, too, I'm telling you!'

And so he had. And whatever happens, wherever he ends up – all the best, old Fruit 'n' Nut Montgomery! The one sure thing is that we've not heard the last of him.

Frank Keating
26.10.1983

CHAPTER TEN

International Engagements

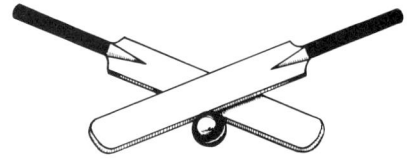

From Mr Warner's book, *England v. Australia*:

'Barnes had bowled 9 overs, 6 maidens, for 3 runs and 4 wickets; surely a most astounding and scarcely creditable performance.'

Rotter – to throw away three runs like that.

12.6.1912

-|●|●|-

The Australian Eleven *v.* MCC

The Australians came down like a wolf on the fold,
The Mary'bone Cracks for a trifle were bowled;
Our Grace before dinner was very soon done,
And our Grace after dinner did not get a run.

8.6.1878

-|●|●|-

Birds of a Feather

(Lord Hawke's team of Cricketers were beaten at Manheim by the Philadelphians by eight wickets whereat the *Philadelphia Ledger* cockadoodles considerably. The Britishers, however, won the return match somewhat easily.)

The Yankee Eagle well might squeal and squawk
At having licked the British bird (Lord) Hawke.
But when that Hawke his brood had 'pulled togethe
That Eagle found it yet might 'moult a feather'.
Go it, ye friendly-fighting fowls! But know
'Tis only 'Roosters' who o'er conquest *crow*!

24.10.1891

The Philadelphians

(*By One who wishes them better luck*)
(The Cricket Match between the Philadelphian team and Yorkshire at Sheffield, June 28–30, was wholly spoilt by rain, and on the third day, when barely half played, had to be left unfinished.)

AIR – 'Off to Philadelphia'

In weather wet and weary
It is anything but cheery
    (Though good cricketers the elements seem scorning)
To sit in the Pavilion,
When 'tis one chance to a million
    That we'll see the Philadelphians play this morning!

    With my macintosh on shoulder,
    I'm a weariful beholder
        Of Yorkshire and the Yankees idly yawning;

And I've got a gloomy notion
Good Lord Hawke won't make a motion
　　To score off the Philadelphians this morning!

These Yanks, it is well known,
With the bat can hold their own,
　　Wood or Cregar any team would be adorning.
But they all look sad and weary,
When the wickets soaked and dreary,
　　Gave no start to Philadelphia all the morning.

　　With his bat across his shoulder,
　　Sure no slogger could look bolder
　　　　Than Lester; but the rain came without warning,
　　Till the wickets, I've a notion,
　　Are much like the German Ocean,
　　　　And it's 'off' with Philadelphians this morning.

Such gloom would dull e'en genial Grace!
He strove to keep a cheerful face,
　　Like batsmen bold, bad luck and weather scorning.
But 'tis hard to 'buck up' cheery,
With the wickets wet and dreary,
　　When you have to 'draw the stumps' on the third morning.

"HOW'S THAT"—FOR CRICKET COSTUME?

"THE LATEST NOVELTY IN CRICKET TOURS IS A TEAM OF FIJIAN PLAYERS, WHO PROPOSE VISITING AUSTRALIA DURING THE COMING WINTER. . . . THEY WILL BE LED BY RATU KADARU, THE REIGNING CHIEF OF FIJI. . . . THE FIJIANS WILL NOT PLAY IN CONVENTIONAL CRICKET ATTIRE."—*Daily Mail.*

But though top-coats grace each shoulder,
And it wetter grows and colder,
From Sheffield the bhoys start, bad omens scorning.
And some day I have a notion,
I shall feel a proud emotion,
    To see the Philadelphians *win* - one morning!
                                    10.7.1897

STUDY OF A " TRIANGULAR " TEST MATCH.

The Fifth Test Match
A Memory

'Tis the 13th of August, 1902;
I go, and, parting with my shilling, view
An eager crowd, discussing, *inter alia*,
The prospects of the foemen from Australia.
Here Bill announces, redolent of porter,
They can't be beat – at least they didn't orter:
But 'Arry thinks they need a little stiffenin';
'E personally would 'ave put George Giffen in.
There, in the stand, the obvious city gent,
Puffing Havanas to his heart's content,
Discourses of the latest rise in Atcheson:
But hush! all the tongues are silenced, for the match is on.
Alas! of runs the board is well-nigh barren,
When Saunders gets a beauty past McLaren.
Saunders doth next (at twisters who so skilled?) slay
('Bowl' wouldn't rhyme, unfortunately) Tyldesley.
The score's but nine, when lo! the Boy from Ballaarat
(Or somewhere thereabouts) dismisses Palairet.

The sun of hope tends rather night- than dayward
When Braund to the Pavilion follows Hayward.
Five wickets down for nine-and-forty runs!
Alas, my countrymen! – But now the fun's
Commencing: soon, I ween, the most penurious
Won't grudge their bobs, so fast 'twill be and furious.
For they shall see One-fifty-seven – no less – up
Ere the Colonials get rid of Jessop,
Or fortune recompense their fell attacks on
The Honourable Frederick Stanley Jackson,
Whose feats must glad the heart o' that proud senator,
His scarcely less illustrious progenitor.
Lo! the crowd thrills enthusiastic, rapt in
Awed admiration of the 'Gloucester Captin'.
Ye gods! the tempest, cyclone, storm and hurricane!
Up goes his bat (the handle made of Surrey cane),
Away the ball flies soaring like a comet, or
A rocket, o'er pavilion and gasometer.
Meanwhile the wary Jackson keeps his wicket up –
One-fifty runs! Hurrah! The scorers stick it up.
But Jackson falls – then Jessop. Peradventure he
Will never make a more blood-curdling century.
Sixty to win. Hirst batting. Sure no crock would
Withstand Hugh Trumble long. Ah! out goes Lockwood.
Lilley comes in. Well played! Oh, Hirst's a hero –
But Lilley's out. Buck up! *Dum spiro spero.*
Now Rhodes. Yes, he *can* bat. Did someone miss him? O-o-oh!
A tie! Well hit! We've won! Bravo! BravissimO!

Punch's Almanack, 1903

More Triangular Cricket

'Against Surrey, tomorrow, Somerset will beat Middlesex.' *Lloyd's Weekly*

4.8.1909

–|●|●|–

More Triangular Cricket

'NORFOLK V. HERTS. – This match was concluded at Chester-le-Street yesterday, Durham gaining an easy victory.' *Sportsman*

11.8.1909

–|●|●|–

That Summer and This

John Arlott reflects on Triangular Cricket

Two touring Test teams in the same season will make 1965 a rare, but not unique, year in English cricket. Australia and South Africa were both here in 1912; and S. F. Barnes, who played in those Tests, will watch these.

The autograph hunters, amateur photographers and souvenir publishers must be delighted. The members' bar oracles, however, have their doubts. Their authority may depend largely on the fact that, when they were boys, W. G. Grace allowed them to bowl him out in the nets. But they have read their set books: and, where the ordinary history book says 'Henry VIII had six wives', cricket history books as monotonously declare 'The Triangular Tournament was a failure'.

There is documentary confirmation of royal marriages: but at least no accountant could call the 'Triangular' a failure. It was Sir Abe Bailey's idea to stage a three-cornered Test series between England, Australia and South Africa for what England, in 1912, was not yet brash enough to call The World Championship of Cricket. The backwoodsmen thumped the committee tables of the shires in protest against messing up the County Championship by playing Test Matches with *two* lots of colonials in the same season. In the end, if only because he guaranteed his scheme against financial loss, Sir Abe had his way.

When the final accounts emerged, in copper-plate, from Lord's, they showed that, after all expenses were paid and Australia and South Africa had taken their cuts, even the 'second-class counties' received £24 16s 3d apiece.

It was a meagre enough profit: but it is amazing that there was not a yawning loss. The 'Triangular' was played in the wettest summer of this century. So many days of cricket were washed out that even Yorkshire, winners of the County Championship, with their affluent membership and captive crowds who had no motor cars to escape to the seaside, showed a loss of £1,000.

The great Australian 'names' of the period would have drawn spectators through blizzards – the splendid Victor Trumper, that fascinating irritant Warwick Armstrong, Vernon Ransford, spectacular at cover-point, erratically fast 'Tibby' Cotter and the virile Clem Hill. Unfortunately, the differences between the Australian cricketers and their autocratic Board of Control, which had seethed for years, boiled over a few weeks before the team sailed. Should the team manager be elected by the players or appointed by the Board? The Board won – and six of the chosen players withdrew from the trip. Five of them were Victor Trumper, Warwick Armstrong, Vernon Ransford, 'Tibby' Cotter and Clem Hill.

To complete the pattern of grotesque ill-luck, South Africa, a major cricketing power when the Tournament was mooted, were no stronger than the average county side by the time it was played. Their googly bowlers, whose novel duplicity had won two Test rubbers against England were, all at once, burnt out, and the remainder proved pathetically unsophisticated on the slow pitches of a rainy English summer.

Was the Triangular Tournament a failure? – in such circumstances that £24 16s 3d, to Monmouthshire was glorious success.

There were others, too, who found the series satisfying. C. B. Fry refused the captaincy of England before and after 1912: but on this occasion he accepted, led his side to beat two countries in one summer and stepped down as one of the few England captains who never suffered defeat or dismissal. S. F. Barnes, too, must have been satisfied with thirty-nine wickets in six matches – before he stumped back into the Leagues and never played another Test in England.

Above all, T. J. Matthews should have cherished the Triangular Tournament, for in it he won himself five ineradicable and irreducible lines in *Wisden*. A short, bony man from Williamstown, with an uncomplicatedly pioneering face, Matthews was known in Australia as 'Little Jimmy'. He was a slow right-arm bowler of whom one of the few contemporary reference books that so much as mentioned him said 'he can break both ways but cultivates the leg variety'.

Matthews played for Australia in the opening Test of the Triangular Tournament at Old Trafford in cold, gusty weather, and before a small crowd. Australia scored 448 on the first day. By four o'clock on the second, South Africa had made 265 for seven wickets, without interruption from Matthews, who then took their last three wickets with three consecutive balls. It was the eighth hat-trick in forty-four years of Test cricket. South Africa followed on, instantly lost their main batsman, Faulkner, and had come uncertainly to 70 for five when, at six o'clock, Matthews performed the ninth hat-trick in forty-four years of Test cricket. It is reported that 'very few people saw the second hat-trick. The stream out of the ground began directly Faulkner was bowled, and the place was empty when Matthews joined the cricket immortals.' T. A. Ward may have thought the Triangular Tournament was a failure. He was the third batsman in both hat-tricks.

Those six wickets were all Matthews took in the match: in his remaining five Tests of the Tournament he achieved nine more, and never played for Australia afterwards. According to the records, his career in first-class cricket barely covered fifty matches, in which he took 140 wickets.

In the 589 Test Matches since 1878, there have been sixteen hat-tricks – two of them by 'Little Jimmy' in two hours on a lonely, windy afternoon in Manchester.

English cricketers have been 'honoured' by

THE TRIANGULAR FARCE.

Scene—*A blasted pitch.*

Chorus. "WHEN SHALL WE THREE MEET AGAIN
IN THUNDER LIGHTNING OR IN RAIN?"

the presentation of an illuminated address or an engraved teaspoon for bowling their hearts out to take twice as many wickets in a season as Matthews took in his lifetime. The Australians are more realistic: they rewarded T. J. Matthews for his unique feat by making him Curator – Australian euphemism for grounds-man – of the local ground at Williamstown.

If anyone performs two hat-tricks in one Test Match this year, he should make enough in television fees, advertising contracts and serial rights to buy his local cricket ground. Nevertheless, if it rains from now until September, cricket historians of the future will say 'The double Test series season of 1965 was a failure – like the Triangular Tournament of 1912.' If the weather is fine there will be many pleasures for those who like cricket; and the usual opportunities for those who like grumbling to grumble.

More than any other touring side, the New Zealanders are always openly delighted to be here. They are less blasé about cricket tours than the Australians, less socially uncertain than some other visiting teams. Their manager, Walter Hadlee, a fifty-year-old and professionally serious accountant, was happy as a schoolboy to make the return trip he had thought impossible. At the Oval, in June, he should recall that as captain of the 1949 New Zealand team he played an innings there such as the greatest of batsmen would remember all their lives.

It was an instance, rare even in an English summer, of a frozen wicket. Two hours before the start the pitch was white with rime. The sun came out and, by the third day, the wicket was a strip of shifting soil from which the spun ball 'talked' and Alec Bedser's cutters leapt from a length to shoulder height. In these impossible conditions, and hit from ankle to eyebrow, Walter Hadlee won the match with a cool innings of 119, hitting the few loose balls that came his way for three sixes and eleven fours. The next highest score was byes – 29.

The two New Zealand batsmen, Sutcliffe, who played against England in 1947, and the captain, Reid, are now the two senior practis-ing Test cricketers. Reid, besides making more runs for New Zealand than anyone else, must be the only man to have batted, fielded,

bowled fast and slow and kept wicket in Test cricket. Young men like Cameron, Collinge, Motz, Taylor, Vivian and the miniature and much-battered Sinclair have brightness to offer. Their ambition is plain; New Zealand have never beaten England.

In the latter half of June the South Africans will arrive, bringing the newest Test celebri-ties, the much talked-of Pollock brothers and Barlow. Their chief wish will be to keep politics and cricket separate. They will remember that, thirty years ago, Wade's team became the first – and are still the only – South Africans to win a Test rubber in England.

Until its inconveniently and discourteously late withdrawal, an Indian team was to have made a tour overlapping the other two, extending the first-class fixtures to unpre-cedented length and four continents.

For a period from late June to mid-July, both New Zealanders and South Africans will be playing here. Their match lists, however, give no indication that they will meet except, perhaps, on the evening of 2nd July, when the New Zealanders travel from Birmingham to Northampton, the South Africans from Shef-field to Colchester, and both their trains pass through Rugby. The platform there is long: if the station-master has a strip of matting and a cricket enthusiast for a signalman.

12.5.1965

–|●|●|–

Triangular Cricket

'The home side were mainly indebted to S. G. Smith, Haywood, and C. N. Woolley coming together when the second wicket went down at 57.'
Daily Chronicle

27.8.1913

–|●|●|–

A New Mission

('Cricket is peculiarly a Christian game. No pagan nation has ever played it.' *Melbourne Paper*)

When wild in woods the savage ran,
Being a prehistoric man,
There is no record hinting at
His rude delight in ball and bat;
And, when, in times a shade more dressy,

People's amusements weren't so messy,
No trundler known to ancient lore
Got pagan Pharaoh leg-before;
Moses, who must have had a notion
Of heathen games as played in Goshen,
Has neither praise nor yet rebuke
Of cricket in the Pentateuch.

No Old Phoenician 'found a patch'
In any Tyre-and-Sidon match;
There is no story from Tibet
Of lamas slogging at the net;
No sporting annals tell us how,
During the dynasty of Chow,
The full-sized volley sped through space,
And took Confucius in the face.

We hear not how Achilles spent
Whole weeks inside the scorer's tent;
Nor read of Priam, stiff of joint,
Dropping a cert at silly-point;
Nor, on a nasty pitch that bumped,
Of Aristides being stumped;
Nor how, when Phoebus came out hot
At Salamis (a dampish spot),
The Attic skipper won the spin
And coolly put the Persians in.

No fable tells of Roman cricket –
How well Horatius kept the wicket,
How brother Remus took first knock,
Or Fabius played against the clock;
Or Julius Caesar showed alarm
At Brutus 'coming with his arm';
Or Cicero in palmy days
Bowled with his head and broke both ways;
Or Balbus – he that built the wall,
Played like it, blocking every ball.

Nor did our isles adopt the game
Till Christian missionaries came,
And even then the pagan sort
Failed to regard it as a sport.
No Viking, landing from his ships,
Was ever captured in the slips;
No Irish heathen learned the hat-trick,
Though freely coached by good St Patrick;
No Pict, in legends known to me,
After the interval for 'tea',
Lashing his sporran round his pad,
Appealed because the light was bad.

It was the same in our domains:
Not once on Bengal's tented plains
Did the great Nawab lift a googly
Halfway across the astonied Hooghly;

Nor yet was cricket in his thought
When the high priest of Juggernaut,
Rain having fallen after drought,
Ordered the heavy roller out.

And, if at length this art of arts
Has wooed and won exotic hearts,
To Christian Cambridge is it due
Who of her Ranji made a Blue,
Taught him – what other creeds had missed –
His speed of eye, his sleight of wrist,
Taught him – who learned it like a lamb –
To cut and push and glance and slam
And live to be a perfect Jam.

O.S.
22.5.1912

–|●|●|–

Dominion Doggedness

People who collect cricket records will already have added to their list the fact that the eighth wicket in the Test Match at Lord's last week, between England and New Zealand, put on 246 runs, but they may not have noted that it was probably the first occasion when such a partnership was interrupted and honoured by a visit from the King. That, I am sure, is an event without a parallel. The Royal Standard flying instead of the Union Jack on the pavilion flagstaff had indicated that His Majesty was expected, but no one could have foreseen the state of the game when the two elevens lined up to receive him. Such long stands are not common events even in ordinary non-Test cricket, and the feat was the more remarkable because, when the Selection Committee laid their sagacious and not too hirsute heads together and chose G. O. Allen, one of the participants in this mighty achievement, it is presumed they did so not for his fast hitting but his fast bowling – and he had not bowled too successfully. Well, cricket is like that. Is there not a phrase about glorious uncertainty?

Allen was dramatic throughout; dramatic in his failure to get length or direction; dramatic in his innings with its Royal benediction in the middle, and then in his attempt to reach his hundred before lunch. When the interval came he was 98, and who could dare not to remember 98 all through that meal, wonder-

THE LION-TAMER.

BRITISH LION (*to Mr. WARWICK ARMSTRONG*). "I KNOW A GOOD MAN WHEN I SEE ONE. SIGN, PLEASE."

ing what the first over after it had in store for him? So many a man has failed in the nineties; Woolley, the hero of this match on its first day, actually scored ninety-odd twice in a Test at Lord's against the Australians. Moreover, lunch is a great deceiver. But all was well, and Allen not only got the necessary two, from a boundary to long-off, but went on to make twenty more. And that was not all; for in the New Zealanders' second innings he bowled Mills of Auckland, who had made 34 in the first innings, first ball. Not exactly Allen's match, but Allen's display.

Until the New Zealanders in their second innings made England's bowling look so ordinary and stingless, we were calling it Woolley's match, for it was the Long Man of Kent who turned the tide in the English attack or defence on the first day and made things easier for Ames and Allen. Woolley never looked longer nor his bat a more trifling detail, while he was helped by the New Zealand captain's apparent ignorance of his favourite and most dangerous strokes. But as things turned out it was New Zealand's match, ending as it did at the close of the three days with England needing 94 to win and five of their best wickets down: a situation which no one, not even the most sapient pavilion critic, would have predicted. For what everyone was saying was that New Zealand's bowling was unequal to the task of getting us out. Well, it allowed us to make 454 in the first innings or 230 more than the enemy. But there are two sides to everything, and who, at the close of that innings on Monday afternoon, would have dreamed that before England could bat again that 230 deficit would be wiped off and 239 added? Glorious uncertainty, indeed.

One proof that the English bowling was inadequate is that that gallant warrior but most indifferent bat, R. C. Blunt of Otago, was allowed to make 96 runs. Never have I seen anything less like Test-Match form. But, sharing with C. S. Dempster of Wellington, G. L. Weir of Auckland, M. L. Page of Canterbury, and T. C. Lowry of Wellington the courage and patience which I shall evermore associate with New Zealand, he kept up his end by merely placing the bat before the ball for what seemed like an eternity. With the

exception of J. E. Mills of Auckland, a left-hander, the New Zealanders are not graceful batsmen; but they have heart-breaking qualities instead. Their crack, Dempster, is no stylist, but he is armed at every point; Page, while hitting to leg better than any Englishman, is perfectly content to block; Weir is a tower of defence. But Blunt is largely an obstacle. Yet not Allen, not Peebles, not Robins, not Voce, not Hammond could get past him until he had made four short of a hundred. Woolley, the crafty veteran of the team, might have done so, but Jardine never gave him the chance. And so our score of 454 for ten wickets was made to look foolish by New Zealand's 469 for nine, and the old proud Mother Country had to bat on a declaration! New Zealand has every right to be pleased.

There were sad disappointments before, in our first innings, Woolley, our Nestor, came to the rescue. Duleep began with address and confidence, hitting the ball where the men were not, but just as we settled down to enjoy the feast he broke this rule and was caught in the long field. Arnold, Bakewell and Hammond failed to make double figures, although they all did it in the second innings. Jardine did not stay long enough and was tamely out, making room for the Ames and Allen record. Robins's round dozen on the score sheet does not convey the ease and mastery of his strokes, and he particularly delighted me by carrying out the instructions of one of his most illustrious Middlesex predecessors. 'What,' asked a young recruit of Sir T. C. O'Brien, 'should one do with the first ball?' 'Hit it for four,' said that forceful genius. Well, that is what Robins did, and there wasn't a better stroke in the match until Hammond's second innings.

I never saw the purchasable seats at Lord's so full on the first day – the first day not only of the match but almost of the true summer – but, considering that this was a Test Match, the pavilion was ill-attended. A great game; but the next time I see the New Zealanders, I hope that the condition of affairs will enable W. G.'s maxim, 'Go for the bowling before it goes for you', to be in force. Not, however, that the bowling did go for them. It most disconcertingly did not. Coming away, I saw outside Lord's a newspaper poster which said, 'England bowling defied.' The trouble is that by the Selection Committee it had been deified.

E.V.L.
8.7.1931

-|●|●|-

Tourist Rhymes; or, a Few Australians
(With apologies)

Experts speak extremely highly
Of the bowling of O'Reilly;
O'Reilly makes 'em 'go away' –
Ball and batsmen too, they say.

We are not convinced that Bradman
Ever told a friend, 'By Gad, man,
I must keep my eye on Larwood
He is quite as fast as Gar Wood!'

There must surely be some limit
To the powers of 'Clarrie' Grimmett;
Could he, e.g., humbug Hobbs
If he merely bowled him lobs?

Hushed is every mother's babe
Before the prowess of McCabe;
Hooking boundaries off his eyebrows
Offends, however, certain highbrows.

We may rest assured that Oldfield
Is a versatile and bold field,
But he habitually picks
Himself to play behind the sticks.

Critics are agreed that Wall
Bowls a very fine fast ball;
Seldom does he stoop to folly
And deliver a half-volley.

We conclude these verses with
One remark on Fleetwood-Smith;
He, there's a reason to believe,
Has something up his left-hand sleeve.

Woon
30.5.1934

The West Indians

The arrival of our annual allocation of touring cricketers at Tilbury or Southampton is now accepted as the unofficial opening of the season. The covers are removed (from the typewriters) and the chroniclers of the summer game, reeking of embrocation, begin laboriously to get their hands in and their arms over.

First we see the tourists on board ship: the deck is wet and cold and the mackintoshes belly in the stiff April breeze. Sir Pelham Warner is there with a warm greeting and a goodly company of old England captains, just stirring from hibernation. We learn from the tourists that the party is in the pink (except for poor old Blank, the spin-bowler, who slipped on a cocktail olive in the Bay of Biscay – or was it the Channel? – and sprained an ankle) and itching to get in some practice. We read the crisp *Who's Who*-ish pen portraits of the players and file the details away for use at Lord's, the Oval or Old Trafford. ('In private life,' we shall say at some suitable moment, 'he's a builder with three children and a degree in engineering.' And the clergyman in the row behind will lean forward, cough, and say 'Excuse me, but he's thirty, actually – had his thirtieth birthday during the Nottingham match.')

Next, we follow the players on their shopping expeditions in the West End, see them on television, hear them 'In Town Tonight', and, at long last, study them at the nets. This is of course where the *real* writers peel off their overcoats. 'B. was bowling only at half-speed,' writes Mannington-Falkirk of the *Sunday Echo*, 'but it is quite obvious from his beautifully controlled run and perfect follow-through (left shoulder pointing to the tea-tent) that he will play havoc with our timid, crease-bound county batsmen. He still has an unfortunate tendency, however, to bowl full-tosses at the square-leg umpire.'

And then April runs out and the tourists and journalists travel to Worcester for the first match . . .

Well, we are already toe-deep in the new season and the writers have told us all we need to know about the West Indian cricketers.

CRICKET UNLIMITED.

FATHER TIME (*making for exit towards end of fifth day of first innings*). "I'M ONLY TIME. THIS IS A JOB FOR ETERNITY."

Nearly all, anyway: I am still doubtful about one or two points – for example, how these fellows managed to pick up their cricket. Unless we are prepared to accept the preposterous notion that cricket *evolved* in the islands, emerged from a host of indigenous pat-ball relaxations (as it did in England) to become a standard, codified national game, we must assume that it was imported.

We must assume that cricket was *planted* in the West Indies. But who were these pioneer planters? Most of them, I like to assume, were the 'difficult' sons of stiff, starchy, and therefore unbending, Victorian papas; young men lacking somewhat in moral fibre and character. They were not exactly ne'er-do-wells, and certainly not delinquents in the accepted sense, but they did, regrettably, reveal a certain inability, shall we say, to apply themselves unrelentingly to the pursuit of respectability and success in business. So they were bundled off to the Colonies where, it was thought, the great heat and poisonous insects would at last bring their manliness to the surface. They arrived, rolled up their sleeves, made clearings in the forest big enough for cricket pitches and then built their bungalows. And that, children, is roughly how the British Empire was born.

From the start the planters saw to it that the wickets were good, with plenty of unresponsive jute matting over the hard earth: the slightest flaw might have been fatal, for the bowling of the exuberant recently-emancipated coloured boys varied between very fast and fast and was intensely hostile. Day in, day out, as the bananas lengthened and the sugar cane ripened, the air of Trinidad, Barbados and Jamaica hummed and whistled with activity. The planters dug themselves in. Occasionally one of them fell under the blow of a spring-heeled, catapulting Constantine or Martindale and was buried with high honours. Such were the perils of pioneering.

From the first, too, good batsmanship of the classical Gunn-Shrewsbury school paid rich dividends on these wickets: the planters played straight with their left legs well down the wicket and their noses over the ball. And so it was when, in their turn, the coloured boys tried their luck with the bat they wasted no time on the primitive agriculture of the English village green. They were stylists from the start – which explains why the islands have been able to produce such remarkable batsmen as George Headley and Everton Weekes after only twenty-odd years of Test cricket.

The records tell us that England first took formal notice of cricket in the West Indies in 1895, when a team of amateurs toured the islands and found 'good club cricket' being played in every clearing. Two years later two strong teams captained by Lord Hawke and Arthur Priestley made the trip, and both of them were soundly beaten in their opening matches against 'All Trinidad'. The men who did the damage were two specialists in forked lightning, Woods and Cumberbatch, the first of many West Indian bowlers to hear the sweet sound of leather against prime English ribs.

Our visitors this year are once again blessed with fast-bowling talent of exceptional quality and are said to be the strongest batting side in West Indian history, yet time may prove that they have left their most valuable asset – their sub-tropical, muscle-loosening weather – at home. No amount of rum will compensate for its loss; nor will half a dozen sweaters. One way of making the West Indians feel reasonably at home, even in an inclement summer, would be for our spectators to shed their prickly reserve and wax ebullient. Batsmen such as Weekes, Worrell, Rae, Walcott and Stollmeyer are only at their best, I understand, when spectators are falling from trees with excitement, when women swoon at the possibility of a run-out and stands collapse under the tom-tom tapping of rhythmic feet. Most of our county grounds have a tree or two of sorts along the boundary, and the season is still young enough for successful transplanting. (County committees please copy.)

There is one other thing the writers have not told me – something that has given me dreadful nightmares ever since, at the age of ten, I first decided to play for England: they have not told me whether a black or dark brown hand can disguise spin more effectively than a white hand. 'Watch the bowler's hand,' they used to tell me, 'and play for the break.' Well, in my dreams I always opened my innings against

Constantine (*père* or *fils*); the arm came over, and hand and ball were merely an amorphous brown mass. I played for an off-spinner and was caught easily at first-slip off a leg-break. Some nights I played for a leg-break and was clean bowled by an off-spinner, but always I was tortured and uprooted. And I still do not know whether my fears were legitimate or not. This summer I shall be watching those brown fingers very carefully through binoculars. Williams (or Ramadhin) will puzzle Hutton, say, with a ball that nips back from outside the off-stump, and I shall be delighted that I have at last identified the off-spinner; and the next morning Mannington-Falkirk, in the *Echo*, will say '. . . Then at ninety-three Hutton almost succumbed to a superb googly from Williams (or Ramadhin)' and I shall be livid.

And that must be all for the moment. See you all at the first Test Match, then, among the branches; or falling off the gas-holder, perhaps.

Bernard Hollowood
10.5.1950

–|●|●|–

The South Africans

Few touring teams have begun a campaign in England more disastrously than Jack Cheetham's South Africans. They lost at Worcester, they had the worst of the game at Derby, their batting was dreadfully slow and timid, their bowling was all Tayfield and they muffed their catches.

According to one writer they even showed up badly on television, when at an indoor school they loosened up before the cameras and some ten million critical spectators and suffered a minor breakdown in transmission.

Then came the surprisingly easy win against the MCC at Lord's.

Cockahoop over our recent triumphs in Australia most fans interpreted the South Africans' vile start as another sign of recovery in English cricket. We licked the Aussies, the Aussies have just licked the West Indians, and if the West Indians were to play the South Africans (they don't: the colour bar restricts sunburnt South African cricket to games with 'whites'), Weekes, Walcott, Ramadhin,

Valentine and company would surely make mincemeat of them. So England is right on top, undisputed master of international cricket. Well, we shall see, and Test cricket being the eternal round it is we shall presumably go on seeing. Next summer the Australians will be here; in 1957 we take another crack at the West Indians . . .

Starting out under a cloud is nothing new to the tourists. During the early part of their highly successful tour of Australia (1952–3) the South Africans were regarded as a blight on the Antipodean summer. Pressmen urged them to go home, to send for reinforcements, to take up rounders. According to Ray Robinson, one of the wisest of Australian critics, Keith Miller sent them in to bat at Sydney with the comforting words: 'You fellas have first dig and get yourselves some runs. If you do, it will help you draw good gates.' And with the score at three for three wickets a barracker on the Hill added insult to indignity by yelling 'Bring on the West Indies. At least they lend a bit of —— colour to the game.'

What happened next is cricket history at its brightest. The despised South Africans held the invincibles to a tied rubber – two victories each – set a new standard in fighting cricket, delighted Australia by their spectacular fielding, and attracted goodly crowds wherever they appeared.

On his return from Australia Len Hutton startled the theorists of the game by suggesting that the old saw about good fielding winning matches has had its day. Fielding *is* important, he said, but Tests are now won by specialist batsmen and bowlers, by Tysons, Stathams, Mays and Cowdreys. Hutton was trying, perhaps, to say a few kind words about his notorious fumblers, about his team of non-benders and butterfingers; or he may have been dropping hints to the selectors that it is too early yet to drop such specialists as Compton, Bedser and Hutton.

Jack Cheetham and thousands of village cricketers disagree violently with England's lumbaginous captain. Village cricketers justify their very existence in the eleven by their fielding, or by their own estimation of its quality. 'I'm not much of a bat these days', says Tom Mowhook of Sodden Green, 'and I don't get much chance to bowl me leg-spinners, but what I say is fieldin' wins matches, and if I say it as shouldn't . . .' Jack Cheetham *knows* that it was fielding and fielding alone that allowed his side to halt the all-conquering heroes of Australia.

Tayfield bowled his off-spinners on bone-hard pitches to Australia's hefty drivers and tied them all down. He could be hit, but seldom accurately enough to find gaps in the ring of suicide 'sillies', Keith and Endean at silly mid-on, McGlew and Murray at silly mid-off. And if Miller, Benaud or Harvey tried the lofted drive, there was always McLean, Funston or somebody waiting in the deep with hands like mechanical grabs. Tayfield's bag was thirty Australian Test wickets, five more than the previous record held by Schwarz, the great googly merchant. And when he was congratulated on his harvest he handed on the praise to the 'suicide squad' with the remark *'They're* catching 'em.'

So far, as every commentator likes to remind us, the South Africans are *not* catching them, and Tayfield, Adcock and Heine all have worse figures than they deserve. Ingenious reasons have been advanced to explain the epidemic (all cricket writers refer to plural fielding lapses as 'epidemic' and most of them cough up the old joke: 'There was an epidemic at Lord's, but it wasn't catching'): the kindest critics have blamed our weather and cold fingers, others have expatiated upon the unfamiliar light and surroundings, and others again – less kind – have suggested that the South Africans are suffering from double vision caused by a too avid reading of *Wisden*'s paeans of praise. It is just possible, I suppose, that Cheetham's men have been trying too hard to live up to their immense reputation. Surrey have been known to drop *their* catches for much the same reason; and so – more often in recent years – have Yorkshire. When catches are floored by good fielders it is charitable to leave the explaining to the happy batsman. 'It was travelling,' he tells his colleagues. 'Got it right on the meat.' Once when Lindsay Hassett was dropped in a Test he comforted the erring fielder by describing the degree of back-spin he had imparted to the ball.

At Lord's, against the MCC, the South Africans greeted the returning sun with a display that made the blood circulate again in the frosty fingers of the critics. They were not yet the tigers described in the advance notices, they still floored difficult chances, batted without much gusto (McLean excepted) and bowled without revealing deadly powers of penetration, but by now they were hanging on to the 'sitters' and bowling 'tight'. Their victory put them in good heart for the Nottingham Test.

Lacking knowledge of the result of this match I can draw my statistics – without which no cricket article is considered satisfactory – from tales of long ago. Let me remind you then that the first Test between England and South Africa was played at Port Elizabeth in 1889, that England won handsomely and that the captain, the late Sir C. Aubrey Smith, actor, film star and round-the-corner bowler, took five Springbok wickets in the first innings for nineteen runs.

Next – we are looking for post-dated omens – to 1906 when the South Africans startled the cricket world by thrashing England 4–1, by fielding *the same eleven players throughout the series*, and by bowling googlies from both ends. The following year, in England, Sherwell's team included four exponents of the 'wrong 'un', Schwarz, White, Faulkner and Vogler, and the great Archie MacLaren complained bitterly about unfair tactics and the debased currency of cricket, and hinted at the game's early demise.

Then Barnes. The most wonderful spell of bowling in all Test cricket hit South Africa in the seasons 1912 (England) and 1913–14 (South Africa) when S. F. Barnes – in only seven matches – took 83 wickets for 818 runs. His feats included 13 for 57 at the Oval, 17 for 159 at Johannesburg, and 14 for 144 at Durham. Not bad going for a League cricketer.

Finally, a reminder that in 1935 the South Africans won at Lord's (their first Test success in England) and did so largely through the bowling – googlies again – of Xenophon Balaskas.

And now, armed with enough of fact and fiction, on to Lord's once more for the second game of the series.

Bernard Hollowood
15.6.1955

A Young Person's Guide to the Australians

Bernard Shaw explained the British Empire like this: The British, he said, spot a piece of unclaimed territory – preferably one with a hot climate – and send out a missionary to convert the natives to Christianity; the natives eat the missionary and Britain flies to arms in defence of Christianity and annexes the country as a reward from heaven.

Shaw was joking of course.

The facts are these. The English invented cricket and therefore had no ready-made international opponents. So they sent cricketers to foreign parts with instructions to create cricketing 'cells', develop the game, rouse local patriotism, and eventually prove strong enough in a playing sense to challenge the Mother Country to a series of Test Matches.

At first it proved extremely difficult to persuade decent cricketers to give up the lush life of the bone-idle aristocracy for cricketing service in primitive lands. So the Government press-ganged the proletariat into emigration. This was done by making 'transportation', or banishment for life, the penalty for such trifling offences as

forming secret societies
failing to bow deeply enough to
landowners
and stealing a penn'orth of scrag-end.

Magistrates and judges were instructed to clamp down on Luddites and Chartists, especially those capable of bowling left-arm round the wicket or of revealing orthodox perpendicularity in their forward play.

The Dorchester Labourers (*cause célèbre*) were a group of useful cricketers accused of swearing an illegal oath. A trumped-up charge. They were banished to Botany Bay. Their poor baggage consisted of a set of stumps, two cricket bats and an umpire's coat.

So Australia was colonised, and the Tests started.

Later, Australia proving extremely strong, it was found necessary to create new, more readily beatable colonies in New Zealand, the West Indies, South Africa and India. (India was later divided up into 'India' and 'Pakistan' in order to provide the MCC with an extra tour.)

Attempts to colonise the USA, Denmark, Brazil, Holland, Argentina, Hong Kong, Kenya and Canada were only partially successful, but cricket in these lands survived in some form or other, and with the formation of the United Nations (better known as the Imperial Cricket Conference) the future of the game seemed assured.

Australians wear big, baggy, green caps because

they have a surplus of Merino wool
they are ruggedly democratic and prefer to
look alike
they hate the guts of press-box commentators . . .

'I see that Simpson's moved O'Neill round to forward-short for the – '

'It's not O'Neill, I think, Jim, it's Booth.'

'Sorry, viewers, Booth it is. They all look . . . wait a minute, it's not Booth after all. Would you say that was Booth or Harvey, Alan?'

'Definitely not Harvey, I'd say. He's not touring. Could be Burge, I suppose.'

'Sorry, viewers, it's not O'Neill. How stupid of me. I can see now that it's Lawry. Amazing how they all look . . . '

In 1922 Warwick Armstrong sat down in the long-field at the Oval and read a newspaper during a noisy demonstration. He did this with a purpose – to prove that Australians *can* read. The English press was staggered: it had always supposed that the Aussies were the illiterate descendants of convicts. Armstrong made his point very effectively.

In 1956 Keith Miller wore a topper at Ascot. The thought processes of Armstrong and Miller were identical.

All Australians are supposed, by Englishmen, to be mad about cricket, to prefer it to women, racing and the bottle. And it surprises Englishmen that almost every Australian they meet in London seems pugnaciously hostile to the game. Decidedly odd.

We must face it, then, that some Australians are cricket-lovers and some aren't – which may mean that the effects of colonisation are wearing off. However, Australians always vote for cricket-loving statesmen (like Mr Menzies) in order that their representatives at Commonwealth Conferences – which are timed to coincide with Test Matches at Lord's – can hold their own, keep their end up, etc.

Australians are not taught cricket: they acquire it in infancy and boyhood through dedicated indulgence in solitary games played with such unlikely equipment as paw-paws, boomerangs, railway sleepers, garden palings, old tennis balls and kerosene cans. All promising youngsters are sent off into the outback at the age of ten to acquire cricket the hard way. And curiously this tough and lonely apprenticeship also inculcates – as a side-effect – a measure of literacy and fluency. The result is that all Australian cricketers, when they retire, can sit down immediately and write autobiographies. These begin with a long chapter on the virtues of solitary games with an old tennis ball and a kerosene can. In the outback.

The most famous Australian cricketer of all time is Victor Trumper. In Test Matches Trumper averaged 39.04 runs per innings, which compares unfavourably with Sir Don Bradman's 99.96. Trumper's fame, however, is built on something more substantial than mere statistics: to be precise, on a photograph of him that hangs in pavilions all over the world. This picture, taken at the Oval, shows Victor five or six yards up the wicket and using the long handle to an unknown bowler (if any). It is a superb study in athletic grace and aggression, and cricketers everywhere see themselves in it. This is how they would like to bat. This is how most of them *think* they *do* bat. This is how they think Trumper treated every ball.

So Trumper it is, every time. A pity for Bradman that he never posed for such a photograph.

Bradman hit too many runs to be universally popular. He made so many runs that he was always at the wicket, often when his colleagues were in the bar. So Bradman was criticised as unsociable. After a day's play cricketers love to drown their sorrows in beer or gin, but Bradman had no sorrows to drown. Cricketers also like to remind themselves, and

anyone who will listen, about their better days and better innings, but Bradman had no need for such reminiscence.

Bradman was like W. G. Grace – but without the fallibility.

Englishmen know more about Australian cricket pitches than they do about the rest of the continent. Their knowledge of Australian geology is confined to two subsoils called Bulli and Merri Creek which are used to dress certain Test wickets. They also know that Australian pitches are normally bone-hard and splintered by cracks into which press photographers can usually induce someone to insert a finger. When it rains in Australia pitches can become unplayably sticky: when it doesn't rain it is more than likely that a groundsman, or curator (or an assistant), will leave a hose on, unaccountably, overnight.

No one knows who is responsible for all the strange, sudden changes in the condition of Australian pitches. But there are various theories.

(To the tune of 'Coffee in Brazil')

A politician's daughter
Was accused of making water
And the effect upon the pitch was hardly nil:
Oh there's an awful lot of drinking on the 'Hill'.

Australians have an unfair advantage over English cricketers in that so many of them are all-rounders. The reason for this is that they do not play six-days-a-week cricket and can therefore afford to enjoy the game. They play normally only at weekends and like village cricketers in England are always desperately anxious to get into the game. So they all bat and want to bowl, wicket-keep and umpire.

English cricketers, on the other hand, have to conserve their energies for their averages.

Benaud, Simpson, Mackay, Davidson, Lindwall and Miller are typical of the Australian scene. Even Bradman tried his hand at bowling on occasion: in 1938 he broke an ankle while trying one of his celebrated slow full-tosses at the Oval. No English batsman has ever broken an ankle trying to bowl.

Cowdrey once broke a wrist while trying to bat – and he is as near as Englishmen can get to the genuine all-rounder. Figuratively, that is.

Playing only at weekends Australians are left with plenty of time to think about the game, to theorise about it, to experiment with it. The English are stupefied by cricket and off the field do their best to forget it.

So for experimenters and eccentrics we have to look to the Antipodes . . .

There was Ponsford, who decided that a personal score of anything less than four hundred was derisory.

There was Grimmett, a tiny wizened gnome of a man, who made capital of his lack of inches by bowling round-arm or lower. The ball – leg-break, googly or top-spinner – came at the batsman out of a writhing sea of spectators' boots and trousers, and was something less than easy to spot. Grimmett also had the happy knack of encouraging metaphor, and must therefore be held partly responsible for Neville Cardus.

There was Miller, who scorned the fixed bowling-mark and hair cream. He once picked a persistent barracker out of the crowd and carried him into the pavilion like a wet sweater. He once threw the ball back to Bradman when the great man had invited him to bowl. He had a habit of throwing souvenirs to the crowd at the end of a match – stumps, bats, bails and umpires.

There was Sid Barnes (not *the* Syd Barnes of Staffordshire and England), who was once reported to have been dropped from the Australian eleven 'for reasons other than cricket'. Unfairly, as it turned out. Barnes fielded very close to the bat and was once knocked out by a blow from Pollard of Lancashire. Some say the weapon was the ball, others the bat. On another occasion Barnes, out of respect for his captain, got himself out when his score reached 234. Bradman had also made 234. Barnes was something of a practical joker, a journalist and a waiter.

There was Iverson, who invented an entirely new method of bowling, with the middle finger flicking the ball from the palm – like a schoolboy projecting an ink-pellet. Iverson acquired this trick in the jungles of Malaysia during World War II – with the help of course of an old tennis ball and a kerosene can. Iverson also had an old black bat weighing as much as Sydney Harbour Bridge. Cyril

Washbrook seemed to use a similar club whenever he tried to play Iverson's bowling.

There was Carmody who invented a 'field'. This consisted of nine men arranged radially *behind* the batsman and therefore out of his sight. They were all in 'catching positions'. The effect on the batsman was often devastating: he felt lonely, ignored, insulted and fatally nervous.

An adaptation of the 'Carmody field' is often seen on village greens in England, when the local fast bowler (a plumber usually) is deemed to require a wide arc of long-stops in depth.

There was Davidson, a great bowler and a genial hypochondriac. He toured England three times on the National Health Service.

There was . . . There were scores of them . . .

Australia operates a policy of 'selective immigration' which is near neighbour to a colour bar. So Australians don't see many black men or brown men and are astonished when they *do* to find them just as respectable as white blokes. When these darkies also turn out to be fine cricketers the Australians' wonderment becomes a dazzled hero-worship.

This explains to some extent the phenomenal popularity of Frank Worrell's West Indian team 'down under'. The financial success of the tour encouraged the Aussies to import famous West Indians for use in Sheffield Shield cricket, and Messrs Sobers, Hall and Kanhai, one hopes, are the first of a few million missionaries.

A pity that Verwoerd doesn't play cricket.

Since the war Australians – like everyone else – have acquired a veneer of Americanisation. Some of them play baseball, and some of them are apt to confuse baseball and cricket. So in recent years many Australian bowlers have been pitchers, and English batsmen, quite properly, have complained.

Now the great throwing controversy is over, settled awkwardly but amicably, and the cricket writers are having to dredge elsewhere for gossip to fill their columns.

Thirty-four years ago, only two years after the signing of the Statute of Westminster, Australia and Britain were on the brink of war.

Jim Thomas, Commonwealth Secretary, had to intervene in a violent dispute between the MCC and the Australian Board of Control. There was talk, as usual, of sending gunboats.

Body-line bowling was directed primarily at Bradman. It seemed to the England captain, Jardine, that there was no other way of getting him out or containing his plethora of strokes. The body-line ball had to be directed accurately at the batsman – and bowled at top speed. And in Larwood England happened to have a bowler who was both fast and witheringly accurate.

The batsman could face this bowling in three ways. He could duck under the shorter balls. He could try a swing at them, a hook or pull. Or he could merely try to defend himself. If he tried this last course he was likely sooner or later to pop up a catch to the ring of fielders close-in on the leg side. If he swung he might be caught by the fielder stationed deep-square or deep-fine. And if he ducked he might not duck low or fast enough. Batsmen were clouted on the head. Some took enormous punishment on thighs and ribs. It was all within the laws of the game, if a trifle ungentlemanly.

Bradman was cut down to size, though he averaged more than fifty in the series. His method was to withdraw to leg and cut into the untenanted areas of the covers.

The MCC offered to end the dispute by bringing the team home. The Aussies manfully rejected the offer.

And Jardine continued to wear his loathed Harlequin cap.

Of course the rumpus is all over now – except when either country manages to find a genuinely fast and accurate bowler, when a body-line of a sort is likely to crop up two or three balls an over.

Years later Larwood went to live in Australia – probably as a permanent peace commissioner.

And the same fate awaited another demon fast bowler, the typhoon Tyson. He's out there too with the peace corps.

Trueman for High Comissioner?

And that, young person, is all you need to know about the Australians. Now go to see them: this summer our paid hacks might beat them.

Bernard Hollowood
22.4.1964

-|●|●|-

The Caribbean Flavour

The first vision, or notion, that comes to the mind as we think of West Indies cricket – I won't, on principle say 'image' – is of joyful noise, a bat flailing the air, the ball whizzing here, there, everywhere, stumps flying, shining black faces, and mouths laughing white-toothed, like melons. Such a mental picture of a West Indian cricketer is presented many times by Rohan Babulal Kanhai, who often seems to have only one object in life – to hit a cricket ball for six into the crowd at square-leg, falling on his back after performing the great swinging hit – falling on the pitch flat as a fluke. The impetus of the hit, plus sheer animal gusto, brings him down to earth, but it is a triumphant fall.

Cricket is an organism much conditioned by environment. West Indies cricket many times tells that its exponents have learned the game, played it as boys, in hot sun; and played it, moreover, intuitively, in uninhibited company, the sun going into the brain and blood. In the beginning, the West Indian temperament ran riot. The pioneer discipline of George Challenor rationalised original impulse and sin, and tabulated a few necessary first principles and commandments concerning the virtues of reasonably straight bats and of patience. Today the conception of happy-go-lucky West Indian cricketers, bashing the ball all over the field, right and left, over after over, is entirely mistaken and illusory. Any visitor to Lord's the other Saturday morning, not knowing that West Indians were anywhere near the premises, could have watched the batting of Hunte and Carew and Butcher for hours, mistaking any one of these for any average English hard-working professional: colour of face excepted. West Indies have more than once, in a Test Match, fallen behind England's rate of scoring; none the less, they have sent forth some personal glow and vitality causing the impression of livelier, more mobile combatants. The difference between the West Indies' approach to cricket, and the English on the whole is, as far as batting goes, this: when a West Indian batsman is confined to scoreless defence both he, and the rest of us watching him, are surprised at this unfruitful behaviour. We wonder what has gone wrong. Whenever the everyday English batsman plays in this negative barren way, we are not surprised, we don't need to seek reasons for his inactivity and wariness; it is his natural way of playing the game. In his case, if he should hit a six, falling on his back, we should certainly wonder what was going wrong, technically and mentally.

The first creative raptures of West Indies cricket came to personal apotheosis in the flesh and spirit of Learie Constantine, now a man of title. He was coached by his father and by his mother. He soon developed into a cricketer in whose innermost being cricket and instinct to live became one and indivisible. He was the first and fullest representative West Indian cricketer. In all his movements, swift and apparently unpremeditated, he expressed the West Indian temperament. His bowling was very fast – Jack Hobbs vowed that Constantine's freshest overs were as fast as, if not faster than, any of his experience. He used a bat as an exultant announcement of his own and his countrymen's physical abandon and disregard of all *bourgeois* decorum. Constantine's fielding also had the racial agility, he was three men in the slips, omnipresent, long armed and, surely, boneless. One day at Lord's, in the mid 1920s when West Indies cricket was still struggling to receive serious international attention, Constantine performed miracles, leading his colleagues out of a very bare wilderness. Against Middlesex, the West Indies were going down to defeat; Middlesex had amassed 352 for 6 (declared), and 5 West Indies wickets had fallen for 79. In came Constantine, and in one glorious ferocious hour he scored 86, then wrecked the Middlesex second innings by taking 7 wickets for 57, in a whirlwind of lightning bowling and flying splintered stumps. He then actually won the match by a blinding, quick-motion 103 in an hour. During all this West Indian explosion of creative cricket energy and genius, a visitor from Bar-

bados arrived at Lord's. Clearly it was his first entrance to Lord's, in those days a place of some elegance. So this visitor from Barbados had come to Lord's dressed for the occasion. He wore a light-grey frock-coat, striped trousers, white spats and a grey topper. Also he carried a tightly rolled umbrella. He watched the game from the covered stand, then a place of social exclusiveness near the pavilion. He watched the West Indies' tribulations in undisguised dolour. But at the height of Constantine's brilliant resurgence, he rose from his seat in the enclosure of the select. Far away in the free seats at the Nursery-end a group of West Indians were cheering Constantine on. The immaculately adorned West Indian rushed from the select enclosure to the field and, waving his grey topper, he ran round the boundary towards the Nursery shouting to his compatriots there: 'I'se comin' to join you, I'se coming.' He had seen, that afternoon, the prophecy of Constantine's cricket. He could hardly have foreseen, no matter how beatific his vision, that one day, which probably he would live to see, would hail a West Indies XI as World Champions.

Such eminence and renown have not come to West Indian cricket by happy-go-lucky calypso cricket. The general public in England has rather got a wrong impression of Sobers, Kanhai, Butcher, Hunte and company. Several West Indian cricketers in recent years have earned good money playing professionally in the leagues of Lancashire and other unromantic places, where no vain swashbucklings are encouraged. Consequently the first sunshine raptures of Caribbean cricket have been – dare I say? – sobered. Hunte, Carew, Butcher, even Sobers himself, could easily graduate to any Lancashire XI of the Harry Makepeace epoch, when the order of the day was 'No fours afore lunch; and not too many afore tea.' West Indian cricket, in short, has evolved from a game to an *art*, observing, mainly, the discipline that is the basis of any art. A scherzo doesn't unbalance the most classical symphony and Kanhai's gyrations don't disturb the ensemble of West Indies cricket, as it is today assembled for Test Match purposes.

Naturally enough, fast bowling is the main

weapon of the West Indies attack in the field. Every West Indian fresh from the cradle tries to bowl fast. Long before the coming of Hall and Griffith there were not Constantine but Francis and another Griffith, each of them so fast that a batsman needed to pick up his bat smartly. I remember the earlier Griffith mainly because one golden evening at Lord's he was fielding near the wicket and received a terrific crack on the skull, from some batsman's hook-stroke. The impact of ball on skull echoed around Lord's. But Griffith merely shook his head twice before picking up the ball and returning it to the bowler. And all our sympathies went out to the ball.

The present-day West Indies fast bowlers are a formidable pair to look at. Hall, I am told, sometimes goes into action wearing a crucifix on his chest, slung there from a ribbon round his neck. For my part, I should think that it's the batsman who needs the crucifix. I am reminded here of A. E. Knight, the old-time Leicestershire professional. He was religious-minded. Whenever he arrived at the wicket to bat, he would take guard then bend his head in silent prayer. One day Leicestershire were playing Lancashire, with Walter Brearley on the war-path, avid for wickets while the ball retained the shine. In came Knight, took guard then bent his head. Walter Brearley whispered to the adjacent Lancashire fieldsman: 'What's the matter with him – is he ill?' 'No,' was the *sotto voce* answer, 'no, he always does it – he's praying.' 'Praying for what?' asked Brearley. 'Why, for divine guidance to a century.' Brearley, red in the face as a lobster, exploded: 'I'll ruddy well write to the MCC about this!'

Hall and his crucifix, Griffith with his 'suspect' action – here is attraction enough to draw to all cricket grounds all sorts and conditions of men and women, many of whom, judging by what I heard at Lord's the other day, wouldn't easily distinguish a no-ball from the pavilion cat. It is to be hoped, in all good humour, that there will be no organised hunt, off the field of play, after the 'chucker'. Let's leave it to the umpires. In any case, I can't believe that any fast bowler's arm can continue throwing and not soon go muscularly out of action. The law is quite clear on this 'chuck-ing' matter. The umpire is not obliged to announce positively that a bowler throws or jerks; he can 'call' a suspect action if he is not entirely satisfied of the 'absolute' fairness of the delivery. Decades ago the famous Ernest Jones of Australia – the man who sent a cricket ball whizzing through W. G. Grace's whiskers – was thought by certain purists to throw. In a match between New South Wales and South Australia (Ernest Jones's State), a young batsman was sent in first to join in opening the NSW innings. After two NSW wickets had fallen, M. A. Noble (one of Australia's greatest cricketers) arrived at the crease. The second or third ball he received from Jones 'came back' a foot from the off, at lightning speed, just missing the leg-stump. At the end of the over, Noble walked down the pitch to talk to the young novice at the other end. 'Don't you think, son,' he asked, 'don't you think Jones is throwing one or two?' 'Yes, sir,' whispered the colt, 'yes, sir, he is – but don't say anything about it; they might take him off.' The young colt's name was Victor Trumper.

The present West Indies team is a mingling of all the cricketing talents. Every department of cricket's many skills is here on view; brilliant batsmen, dour batsmen, right-handed or left; fast bowlers, slow off spinners, again right-handed or left; slow left-handed spinners and the 'googly'. From watching these West Indians play cricket you could reconstruct the necessary elements and styles and techniques of the game if everyone of these requisites had somehow disappeared or got mislaid – as, in fact, many of them have got lost during the last years – first-class 'googly' bowling for example. It is a remarkable fact that since West Indies cricket was baptised in Test company at Lord's in 1928, it has produced players fit to form a World XI, to play in some overworld a representative company of cricket immortals headed by 'W.G.' For example, Stollmeyer (the R. H. Spooner of West Indies), Butcher, Headley, Worrell, Weekes, Walcott, Sobers, Constantine, Gibbs, Hall and Griffith. George Headley was one of the greatest batsmen of my acquaintance. On a bowler's wicket at Lord's he scored a century of such sure judgment and

"Brought their own heavy roller, apparently."

aim that if ever he edged a viciously spinning ball he did so with the edge's middle. When West Indies won a rubber against England for the first time in this country sixteen years ago, Worrell, Weekes and Walcott made history at the crease as they scored multitudinous runs. And Valentine and Ramadhin put a spell of spin on all of England's batsmen, one of the greatest of whom confessed to me that, facing Ramadhin, he hadn't a notion which direction the ball would take after pitching.

West Indies cricket has renewed the first-class game, notably in Test Matches, at a time when some rejuvenating injection was urgently wanted. Cricket, in first-class circles, was getting old, satiated with performance and records. All the known or discoverable strokes had been seen; every trick of bowling had been exploited. The West Indies brought back the first raptures, mingling the flush of adventure with the finest and most mature techniques. In captain Sobers alone, the West Indies can boast three brilliant exponents in one single ebullient personality: an accomplished batsman, a seam-bowler with the new ball, and a 'googly' spinner. He is already acclaimed as the greatest all-round cricketer of our own post-Grace period. Personally I would name Wally Hammond for this title: still, Sobers is gifted and versatile enough. But of all the delights West Indies cricket has showered on us, the galvanism of Constantine, the quiet mastery of Headley, the tripartite genius and stroke-play of Worrell, Weekes and Walcott, the enchanted improvisations of Ramadhin and Valentine, none has excited and delighted me, sent me so eagerly on the tip-toe of expectation, as Kanhai, upright or flat on his back. We can only hope that prowess in Test cricket doesn't over-rationalise natural instinct in these West Indies cricketers. For all their acquired technical sophistications let there be some echo of the calypso to the end.

Neville Cardus
1.6.1966

Grand Tours

The England cricket touring team, having played two knockabout stopover games in Fiji, settle over their bats for business this weekend with their opening three-day fixture in Auckland. They stay in New Zealand till the end of February, breaking their homeward journey with a four-week stay in Pakistan.

I admit to a twinge of jealousy when I saw them off last week at Gatwick. I have had two or three recent winters touring with them. It was fun. They are good and singular fellows. As I returned on the train from the airport to London's wintery chill I could picture them already lolling about their aircraft, changed from their blazers and regulation black shoes into track suits and loafers. Willis, the captain, would be into his new, regulation, long novel: last winter it was *Brideshead Revisited*, the year before *The Collected Wodehouse*. His vice-captain, Gower, would already have rattled off the *Telegraph* crossword and would now be looking around for somebody with a *Times* or *Guardian*. He would gobble up both sets of clues in only an hour or two.

As sure as eggs, Gatting would be engrossed in a massive tome of science fiction; Dilley and Cowans, the young fast bowlers, would be plugged into their Walkman cassette players; Bob Taylor, the veteran wicket keeper, would probably have started the first of his many letters home (he has called his house at Stoke-on-Trent, *Hambledon*, as that's where his heart is in more ways than one). Somewhere at the back of the aeroplane, the mighty Botham would be larking about with his great buddy, Lamb. That restless and lovable eccentric, Randall, would as usual be the butt of their amiably oafish jokes.

Travelling to the ends of the earth with a cricket bat is not like it used to be. Forty-eight years ago, Neville Cardus sailed Down Under with the MCC team on the *Orion*. It took five weeks, and Cardus started writing his log: 'The team went about their pleasures. Verity read *The Seven Pillars of Wisdom* from beginning to end. Hammond won at all games, from chess to quoits. Maurice Leyland smoked his pipe, and Duckworth danced each evening with a nice understanding of what, socially, he was doing. Wyatt took many photographs and developed them himself. Fry, who was covering the tour as a journalist, was armed with the most complicated of all cameras . . . and we passed little islands and all the adventure stories of our youth sprang to life, and here was Stevenson, Ballantyne, Defoe; on that little beach over there, silent and empty, there is surely Man Friday's footprint . . . '

For England's 1984 tourists, the journey will not take even a day. At 'night', say after the film show, Gatting will doubtless discard his sci-fi for an hour or two and, with Gower and Tavaré, will look to make up a four at bridge. More than anyone, Gatting misses his Middlesex colleague, Emburey – who has a year of his Test match ban to run – for the two of them are the keenest of cardsharps.

Up front, three abreast and probably in their blazers still, will sit the team's manager, Alan Smith, who likes to be known as AC, his assistant and one-time Test spinner, Norman Gifford, and England cricket's seemingly indispensable *gofer* and physiotherapist, Bernard Thomas. They will, the three of them, doubtless, already be discussing train timetables between Karachi and Faisalabad!

As the young athletes around them read and doze and dream amid the jetlagged scents of sweat and socks and private parts, the 'climate' will at least be bearable, sanitised, and fully air-conditioned. In 1936, the MCC manager was Captain Howard, of Lancashire. As the *Orion* chugged through the Red Sea one night, Cardus met him on the deck . . . 'It was just before dinner; Capt. Howard had only ten minutes ago changed into his dinner jacket. His collar was already a rag; Mr Gladstone, after four hours or so of eloquence, never more drastically reduced stiff linen to this state of shapeless wetness. From the foreheads of all of us waterfalls are descending, splashing and dashing like the cascades of a Southey poem.'

In 1936, every member of the MCC side had to dress for dinner! This lot, nearly half-a-century later, would have been in shorts and T-shirts for their first supper of the tour in Fiji. Like their stiff-collared predecessors, however, they will also have two unending sources of complaint over the next three months – the food and the accommodation.

Thus it always was and always will be.

I remember, three winters ago, on his last tour as assistant manager, the late and much loved Kenny Barrington answering a young player's moans about conditions today in the West Indies. Old Ken shook his head in exasperation and launched into a memorable sermon about the bad old days when he was a touring cricketer himself: 'I dunno, I really don't. Why, when we was in this place back in the fifties with Peter May's lot, the cockroaches was so big that even when you'd trod on them as hard as you could, you'd lift your foot but they'd still be there, and they'd look up at you as if to say "good morning" and then they'd gently amble off into the woodwork!

'You blokes don't know what good times are. Once I had 27 hours in a Pakistani train with only a bucket as a latrine, blimey! that was some tour that was. Five months when my total diet, honest to God, was eggs an' chips. Old Closey was my roommate, you ask him: once he was so ill for a whole week that all he could do was crawl from his bed to the loo on all fours every five minutes. That's all he did for a whole week. And that's a lot of crawling and a lot of crapping. I'm telling you. He never had another curry after that. He came on to my diet. Egg an' chips. 'Cos you can't muck around with eggs, and you can't muck around with chips, can you?'

So the new adventure starts here for England's latest travellers. As they flew out to the faraway fields – amid the books and the cards and the jokes and the moans, just as it ever was – I daresay that only three of the young men were actually thinking about *cricket*. Three boys are on their first expedition: Smith, the opening batsman, Foster, the fast bowler, and Cook, of the left-arm twirlers. One new boy usually makes the grade. One might come back a minor celebrity. I wonder which?

Frank Keating
4.1.1984

▄|◆|◆|▄

'ESSEX FAIL AGAINST VERITY.' – *Daily Paper*

Truth will out even the best of batsmen.

27.5.1931

To My Dormant Cricketing Ability

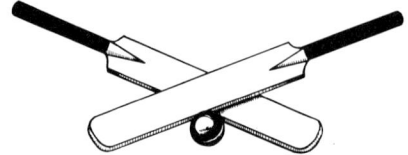

Arise, O Genius mine, arise!
  Awake, for you have slept enough;
Before the transient season dies
Appear at last to mortal eyes;
  Arise and do your stuff!

Compelled to urge with 'suasive tongue
  What should be proved by bat and ball,
Your praises I have freely sung,
But only the absurdly young
  Appear to swallow all.

For, ah! I cannot but detect,
  Even behind the indulgent air
My better-mannered friends affect,
A lurking sign that they suspect
  You are not quite all there.

Yet I have laboured heart and soul
  Nor ever shunned the nightly net
To rouse you to your glorious goal;
One year I even tried to bowl –
  But that we may forget.

Appear, then, ere I pass my prime,
  In all your dazzling glory dressed;
Like Pallas, panoplied, sublime,
Appear – and, oh, appear in time
  For the deciding Test!

23.5.1934